The HTML Web Classroom

P9-ARY-464

Paul Meyers

An Alan R. Apt Book

Prentice Hall
Upper Saddle River, New Jersey 07458

Library of Congress Cataloging-in-Publication Data

The HTML Web Classroom / Paul Meyers.
p.   cm
Includes bibliographical references and index
ISBN 0-13-796111-1 (alk. paper)
1. HTML (Document markup language)   2. Web sites—Design
I. Title
QA76.76.H94M49   1999
005.7'2—dc21   98-22465
                                                              CIP

Publisher: Alan Apt
Editor in Chief: Marcia Horton
Production Editor: Edward DeFelippis
Managing Editor: Bayani Mendoza de Leon
Art Director: Heather Scott
Designer: Judith A. Matz-Coniglio
Assistant to Art Director: John Christiana
Director of Creative Services: Paula Maylahn
Associate Creative Director: Amy Rosen
Cover Designer: John Christiana
Manufacturing Buyer: Pat Brown
Assistant Vice President of Production and Manufacturing: David W. Riccardi

© 1999 by Prentice Hall, Inc.
Simon & Schuster/A Viacom Company
Upper Saddle River, New Jersey 07458

Printed in the United States of America

10 9 8 7 6 5 4 3 2 1

ISBN 0-13-796111-1

Prentice-Hall International (UK) Limited, *London*
Prentice-Hall of Australia Pty. Limited, *Sydney*
Prentice-Hall Canada, Inc., *Toronto*
Prentice-Hall Hispanoamericana, S. A., *Mexico*
Prentice-Hall of India Private Limited, *New Delhi*
Prentice-Hall of Japan, Inc., *Tokyo*
Simon & Schuster Asia Pte. Ltd., *Singapore*
Editora Prentice-Hall do Brasil, Ltda., *Rio de Janeiro*

Preface

Using this book, ANYONE can learn HTML in order to create Web pages. No knowledge is assumed on the part of the reader. Each chapter is a step by step tutorial, walking the student through the use and understanding of HTML. Examples are carefully developed to illustrate each new idea. Written in a friendly and humorous manner, the book attempts to make what otherwise might be a tedious subject, interesting and fun. The book is quite comprehensive, covering the very basic, as well as the more sophisticated uses of HTML for the use of forms, tables and frames. An important component of this book is access to the Prentice Hall Web site, that contains an online copy of the text as well as additional resources for each chapter. As updates to HTML occur, these updates will be posted on the Website, eliminating the need for frequent revisions to this text. Additionally, the Prentice Hall Website has valuable resources for teachers who wish to offer all or part of their HTML class online.

The materials for this book originated as the content for an online class called "Developing a Web page using HTML." I was quite disappointed by my own experience while taking a class over the Internet, yet enthusiastic about the potential that I saw in online education. Developing an online class combined my background in web development gained through the initiation of the college's Web site, and my belief that an online instructional environment could be developed that in many ways would emulate the best of what happens in a traditional classroom.

The lessons that I presented online are the same materials that are presented in this book. Seventten chapters that walk the reader through a step by step understanding of HTML, while developing a Web page.

I assume no computer background on the part of the reader. I wrote the explanations in this book, as I would have liked to have them presented to me when teaching myself HTML. The intent is to present the material in a humorous, relaxing fashion, to take some of the tedium out of the technical. Web development is a form of visual communication that involves a challenging mixture of aesthetics and technology. My intent has been to present this material in such a way as to create a balance between the two.

The materials in this book can be used in a couple of different ways:

- An individual, with no other instruction, should be able proceed step by step through the lessons and gain a sound and working knowledge of HTML and Web development.

- Or, they can be used as a comprehensive text in a Web development or HTML class, where students are guided through each chapter in the development of their Web pages. It should prove equally useful in a traditional lab/classroom setting, or when used as a resource for an online class.

The most important outcome of learning HTML and developing a Web page is putting the page on the World Wide Web. Otherwise it is like singing in the shower; no matter how fulfilling the experience, it goes completely unnoticed by the rest of the world. The individual reader has the option of working with his Internet Service Provider, or contacting an online Web service such as Geocities to place his Web page online.

If the book is being used as a class text, in a college or university there are likely to be addtional options for placing the student pages on the World Wide Web. When offering these materials as an online class, my students are given FTP access to the college web server for the purpose of placing their pages online. Additionally, discussion groups, e-mail and chat groups are used as important means of class communication and facilitate a collaborative learning experience for the students. Please feel free to contact me at pmeyers@cc.cc.ca.us if you have questions regarding how to use these materials for an online class.

The Prentice Hall Web site is an important resource when used with this book. There is a Web page for each chapter that includes:

- Links to related materials on the World Wide Web
- Suggested exercises and assignments
- A quiz on the chapter's content.
- Where appropriate, additional materials that supplement the content of the chapter.

The following icon , appears at places in the content where the reader is encouraged to visit the web site for supplemental information. Additionally, the book is reproduced in its entirety online, in color and with hyperlinks to the Web site resources.

Teachers using this text for a class in Web page development, whether it is in the traditional classroom or taught online, will find other valuable tools available to them at the Prentice Hall web site.

- There is an online form enabling instructors to produce an online class syllabus for students.
- Each chapter has a separate online discussion group revolving around the content of that chapter.

- The online quizzes can be automatically marked and e-mailed to the instructor.

The above features should prove particularly valuable to teachers at institutions where the infrastructure does not exist to facilitate the development of online resources for traditional classes, or to offer courses completely online.

Acknowledgments

I have often wondered when reading the lengthy acknowledgements in a book, why so many people were required to complete that sometimes seemed like a very simple project. Now I know. When I was writing the initial online HTML lessons, it was not my intent to write a book; it just worked out that way. The transition from those lessons to a text on HTML has required a great deal of work and support. The result that you see in this book is truly a team effort involving the skills and knowledge of many people. I wish to first acknowledge the help and support of the Editors at Prentice Hall, Alan Apt, Toni Holm and Edward DeFelippis, who have been particularly patient and generous in their help for a first time author.

Shari Jackson, Adjunct Professor at the Metropolitan State College of Denver reviewed this book, and offered her insights and comments from the perspective of a college computer science instructor. Most of Professor Jackson's suggestions have been incorporated into, and have improved this text. Cori Karnos, once a student and now a colleague at Cerro Coso Community College, made significant contributions to this book in her assistance with the development of appendix materials and organization. My son Jeremy Meyers gave me time that he could not afford to give in reading and commenting on the materials, and gathering links for the website. Special appreciation to my mother in law, Barbara Auld, whose compulsive nature, and expertise as a technical editor is responsible for my correcting innumerable errors. My wife Christine has read this book more times than I, and has been generous and accurate in her suggestions. All errors that remain are my own.

To my children: Jeremy, Ann, Heather and Dave.
To my Grandchildren, Christopher and Carter.
To my parents: Jack, Mary, Howard and Barbara.
And especially to my wife Christine,
affectionately known as "Nanny."

Contents

1

Introduction to the World Wide Web   1

2

Hypertext Markup Language   13

3

The Basic Tags   27

4

Text Alignment, and Lists   38

5

The Font Tag, and Hexidecimal Color   53

6

Horizontal Rules, and More about Text   63

7

URLs: Uniform Resource Locators   74

8

Graphics Files   91

9

More Graphic Information   107

10

Editing Graphics   131

11

Imagemaps   147

12

Tables   165

13

More on Tables   184

14

Forms   203

15

More on Forms . . .   222

16

Frames   245

17

Publishing and Advertising Your Web Page   272

CHAPTER 1

Introduction to the World Wide Web

So you want to build a Web page, do you? Well, you've come to the right place!

- What Is the Internet?
- What Is the World Wide Web?
- The Internet Boom
- Going Online
- Web Browsers
- Source Code

This book is a step-by-step tutorial on using HTML (Hypertext Markup Language) for the development of Web pages for the World Wide Web (WWW). It has been written as a beginners' guide, with careful instruction and dozens of examples of how to write HTML correctly. The book also has a companion Web site provided by Prentice Hall, the publisher. Periodically you will see the following icon, which indicates that there is additional information regarding the topic on the Prentice Hall Web site.

It would be helpful to develop a little background on the Internet and the World Wide Web before we jump right into creating Web pages. It is amazing that the Internet is only 25 years old and has developed to its now global proportions. The World Wide Web is only five years old and in that period of time has revolutionized the way that its millions of users communicate every day. "Surfing" the Internet has become a common pastime, a useful resource, and in many instances an essential skill. I have concluded this chapter with some advice for those who might be new on the surfing scene.

What Is the Internet?

To answer that question, let's start with a little history lesson. During the cold war era of the 1950s and 1960s a great deal of money was spent by the government to link computers for the purpose of defense-related scientific research. Computers at that time were huge, expensive machines, and in effort to maximize their use, they were "networked," meaning they were connected together. This first network was called ARPA, standing for Advanced Research Projects Agency Network. A second purpose for the AARPnet was to maintain military communications in the event of a nuclear war. (I remember passing by the "COMPUTER ROOM" on the way to campus demonstrations when I was in college in the sixties. It had large windows and inside the room was a giant electronic box with cables going everywhere and lights blinking on and off. Several people in lab coats always seemed to be at one end catching the seemingly endless scroll of paper that was being spit out, inspecting it, and nodding their heads sagely. That room always scared me a little.)

For computers to be able to talk to one another, they must be using the same language, called *protocols.* In 1974, the TCP/IP (Transmission Control Protocol/Internet Protocol) was developed and remains the protocol backbone of the Internet infrastructure.

In the 1980s other regional networks developed, primarily on college campuses involved in research. In 1986, the National Science Foundation created the NSFNET to link the regional nets together to facilitate scientific research. Faculty and students were given access to these networks, and use increased dramatically. In 1991 a new national network was created called the National Research and Education Network. Its purpose was to give grades K–12 and community colleges access to computer networks, since the NSFNET was primarily focused on university education and research.

Today's Internet is a huge computer network made up of regional networks, colleges, universities, and businesses. It doesn't have an owner, as the costs for it are distributed throughout its structure. There are no boundaries to the Internet; it is a global information system.

What Is the World Wide Web?

The terms *the Internet* and *the World Wide Web* are often used interchangeably, but they have different meanings. As was pointed out above, the Internet refers to the huge network of computers that are linked to one another. Until the early 1990s for one to be able to use the computer to communicate with another computer via the Internet required a good deal of knowledge and the ability to understand and use some fairly esoteric commands, such as are used in UNIX. There was really no easy way to get around. Rather than surfing, it was more like trudging through the mud.

The World Wide Web was created in 1992, and refers to the means of organizing, presenting, and accessing information over the Internet. Developed by CERN (the European Council for Nuclear Research), the driving force in the consolidation of the European Internet, the World Wide Web applied three very important new technologies.

1. HTML (Hypertext Markup Language): The language that is used to write Web pages and the focus of this book.
2. http (Hypertext Transfer Protocol): The protocol for the transmission of Web pages.
3. A Web browser: The software that receives the information over the Internet, interprets the HTML, and displays the results.

Central to the World Wide Web is the use of *hypertext*—text that is linked to other information. Hypertext is very similar to the table of contents in a book. For example, when I find the chapter and the page that has the information I want, I jump directly to the appropriate page in the book. On a Web page, you might be presented with a list of contents, and by "clicking" on one of the items in the list be instantly taken to that information. Hyperlinks allow information to be explored in a nonlinear or lateral direction. I can't tell you how many times I have started to look for one thing on the Internet and have been drawn in many unexpected but relevant directions.

There are links to additional information about the Internet and the World Wide Web on the Prentice Hall Web site.

The Internet Boom

The development of the Internet and the World Wide Web represent a revolution in technology, providing us with almost unlimited and instantaneous access to information and communication. The commercialization of the Internet is changing the way that many of us do business. Teaching and learning are being altered dramatically by access to the resources on the Internet.

And on a lighter side, the popularity of the Internet has resulted in some people living their entire lives on the Internet: meeting, dating, marrying, having sex, having virtual children, going on virtual vacations, and ultimately divorcing—all without the inconvenience of having to meet face to face.

Many factors have influenced this rapid growth in popularity.

- The development of the World Wide Web and the graphical user interface (GUI) has made the Internet easier to use and more interesting. In addition to text, *hypermedia,* including graphics, sound, and movies, can be integrated onto a Web page and delivered over the Internet.
- It is now easier and cheaper to get access to the Internet. No longer does one have to be affiliated with the government or a university to get access. Commercial ISPs (Internet Service Providers) exist in almost every town. I live in a town of 30,000 people, and we have three commercial ISPs. This competition has of course lowered the cost of getting Internet access. Additionally, there are international commercial ISPs such as AOL (America Online), which use proprietary systems in addition to providing access to the World Wide Web. (As of this writing, AOL had just bought CompuServe.)
- With the development of faster modems and improved compression technologies, transfer speeds are improving, making the Internet a more efficient medium of communication.
- Because of improvements in technology, the costs of computer hardware continue to go down, making computers more affordable to a larger percentage of the population.

Going Online

We have previously established that the Internet is basically thousands of computers linked together and talking via TCP/IP. In the case of the World Wide Web, they are communicating using http or Hypertext Transfer Protocol. Let's take a look at how this actually works and how one gets hooked into the network.

The World Wide Web is a *client-server* network. When you go to the bank to withdraw money, you are the client, and the teller behind the window is the server. When you are behind your computer on the World Wide Web, your computer is the client computer and is getting information from another computer, called the server. A server is a computer that stores information

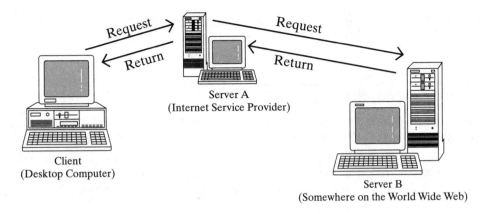

Figure 1.1

and supplies that information to the client computer when requested. The server also tells the client program how the information should be displayed.

In Figure 1.1, your computer is the client computer. Server A is your ISP. Your service could be provided through work, through school, or through a commercial service that you are paying to connect you to the Internet. To communicate with your ISP you must have a TCP/IP connection so that the two computers understand one another. This could be accomplished in several ways:

- Your computer could be wired directly into the same network as the server.
- You could use a modem to connect via your phone line.

Once you are connected to the server, you can use your *Web browser* to go onto the World Wide Web. A Web browser is software that uses http to transfer information to and from a server that is running http software, the protocol for transferring Web pages over the World Wide Web.

Let's say that I want to obtain some information from Server B, which is located somewhere on the World Wide Web. Using my Web browser, I send a request to my server (Server A) along with Server B's Web address—that is, its location on the Internet. Server A forwards the request for information to Server B. If I have entered the address correctly and Server B has the information that I am requesting, the information will be sent back through my server and to my desktop computer. It doesn't matter where the servers are physically located; as long as we can establish the TCP/IP connection, we can do business. Web addresses or URLs (Uniform Resource Locators) will be covered more completely in a later chapter.

Web Browsers

To effectively design and create Web pages, one needs to spend a good deal of time surfing the World Wide Web to see what the possibilities are. It is important that you know how to use your browser, how to navigate the World Wide Web, how to perform searches, and how to create bookmarks. If someone comments on how much time you're spending on the World Wide Web, just tell them to buzz off; you're studying!

A Web browser is the software that is used on the client computer and to travel the World Wide Web, hence it is called *client* software. There are a number of Web browsers that can be used on the World Wide Web, the most popular being Netscape and Internet Explorer. There are browsers for virtually any platform, such as IBM or Macintosh, and for any operating system. Most browsers use a graphical user interface, allowing full access to Hypermedia on the World Wide Web. A few, such as Lynx, are "text only" for dial-up UNIX connections. One of the difficulties in designing Web pages is to design them so that they work on as many browsers as possible.

When information is received using a Web browser, it is normally received as a Web page. When it is seen on the screen, it looks somewhat like a page out of a book or magazine. It may have pictures, sounds, and even movies as part of the page. It is the task of this book to teach you the basic information to put together a Web page. Web pages are created through the use of HTML. HTML is basically a set of text instructions that tell a Web browser how to display information on the client software. It is HTML that allows us to communicate over the World Wide Web, and it is important to learn. We will get into the nuts and bolts of HTML in the next chapter.

But first, let's take a look at several Web browsers and talk about some of their most important features. In the interest of fairness, I have included examples of both Internet Explorer and Netscape below (Figure 1.2). They are both excellent browsers with many exciting features. You should notice immediately that they have very similar features, making it very easy to move from one browser to the other. In other words, if you start out with one, you don't have to be concerned about being stuck with it for life.

I have minimized both screens to show both on the same page. In the window of each browser is the home page of each of the respective companies, Netscape—the maker of Netscape—and Microsoft—the maker of Internet Explorer. These are the browser giants who are battling it out to gain

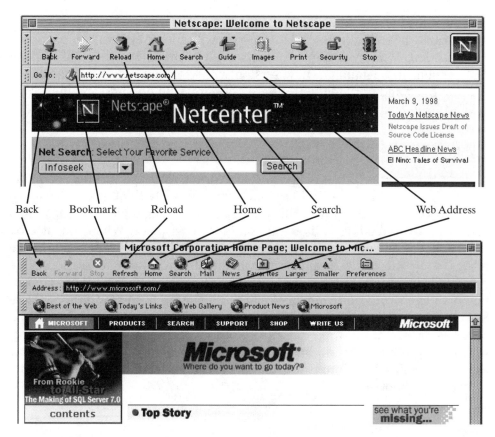

Figure 1.2

dominance over the Internet browser market. I had a heck of a time getting both pictures on the same page; they kept trying to push one another off.

It is important to understand the features of each browser.

The Back Button

This button is a navigation tool. Oftentimes you will land on a page that doesn't have the information that you want and doesn't allow you to go back to the previous page. You can go backwards using the Back button. If you think about it, it's interesting how important going backwards is in a medium that is supposed to be so futuristic. Related to the Back button is the Go button (unmarked). This button also enables you to go backwards. Both browsers keep a record of where you've been. When you hit the Go button, it gives you a list of all of the pages that you have visited during your current session, allowing you to go back to any of them. If you hit the Forward button, located next to the Back button, you will go forward to the page you have just left. When you quit the browser, all of the information is lost from that session. In beginning a new session with your browser, you will notice that the Back and Forward buttons are both gray and don't do anything. You haven't been anywhere yet!

Bookmark

Called "Bookmarks" in Netscape and "Favorites" in Explorer, they're really the same thing. When you get to a site that you really think is cool, you can add it to your Bookmark list. This is similar to sticking a piece of bacon in a book you're are reading so that you don't lose your place. When you click on the Bookmark in your browser, you return to the chosen site. Bookmarks are recorded by the browser and are available from session to session. One caveat: If you are sharing a computer with others, such as in a school lab setting, you can't count on your bookmarks remaining from session to session. Since bookmarks can be deleted as well as added by any user, someone could come along and easily wipe out all of your carefully researched bookmarks with a click of a mouse. Additionally, some schools erase such files regularly as part of their lab maintenance. In such a case, it would be wise to keep a copy of your bookmarks.

Reload

Called "Reload" in Netscape and "Refresh" in Explorer, both buttons are used for the purpose of reloading the current screen. Occasionally something will happen when you are loading a screen and it won't load completely. The Reload button tells the browser to go back to the site and get the page again. Another important reason to reload a page is that pages are held in cache, or memory, by the browser. If changes are made to the page, you won't notice them until the page is reloaded.

Home

Has a nice sound to it, doesn't it! Your home page is where your Web browser first goes when you open it. Your preferred or default home page can be changed in Netscape by going to the File menu and selecting Preferences. In Internet Explorer, go to View then Options. This is important, because once you have authored your first Web page, you will want to make it the home page on your browser.

Search

The Search button in each browser connects to sites where you find very powerful tools for searching the Internet. The Internet is so vast and amorphous that without search tools one could stumble around indefinitely without finding what is desired. Imagine what it might be like if all of the books in the Library of Congress were stored on shelves in no particular order, with no cataloging system. For you to find a book on any topic you would have to wander up and down the aisles, hopelessly trying to find something. Fortunely, there are many companies on the Internet in the business of gathering information and storing it in databases that can be searched. There is no cost for searching; these companies make money by selling advertising. Search sites provide an essential service, without which getting information on the Internet would be difficult if not impossible.

Search tools are so efficient that you often get far more information than you expected. I just did a search for the word "cockroach," and I received a response listing 8,960 pages. My favorite was the "Society for the Preservation of the Cockroach and Adoption as a Household Pet Home Page." I'm not listing the address; I don't think that you want to go there.

Web Address

Called "Netsite" in Netscape and "Address" in Internet Explorer, it refers to the same thing. Every document that is available over the World Wide Web has a distinct address called a URL (Uniform Resource Locator). When you visit a site using your browser, the URL appears in the Address box. One way to go to another site is to enter the address of the site you want to go to into the Address box and hit return on your keyboard. More specific information regarding URLs will be covered in a later chapter.

Visit the Prentice Hall Web site for links to learn more about Web
browsers.

Source Code

Now that you are familiar with the Web browser, it's time to do something productive with it. Remember, our goal is learn HTML in order to create Web pages. Let's look at a Web page first. I suggest we go to The White House home page because it is a very interesting page, and because I know that it's still going to be available when this book is finally printed.

The Web address is: http://www.whitehouse.gov/WH/Welcome.html

Please enter: http://www.whitehouse.gov/WH/Welcome.html in the Address box of your browser.

The image below is what I get in my browser (Figure 1.3).

It's a very nice page, tasteful and well designed—appropriate for the highest office in the country. If you went online, you have noticed that the flags are actually waving. (Those are animated gifs, which we will talk about later in this book.)

Now let's try something different. I stated above that a Web page is made from HTML or Hypertext Markup Language, which is a set of text instructions that tells your browser how to display a Web page. We can look at the HTML, which is called the *source code.* In both Internet Explorer and in Netscape, we go to the View menu. Select Page Source if you are using Netscape, or simply Source if you are using Internet Explorer. We will get a window that looks like the window shown in Figure 1.4.

It is very hard to resolve this very odd-looking conglomeration of text with the very tasteful Web page we saw in Figure 1.3. But, in fact, the HTML is what is telling your browser to display the White House as we saw it in the

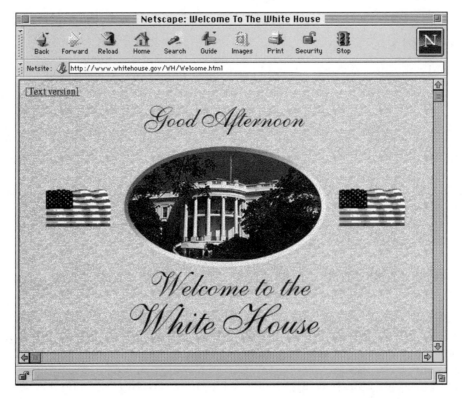

Figure 1.3

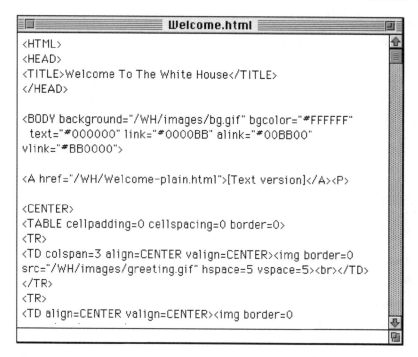

Figure. 1.4

first picture. As we proceed through the book, you will begin to understand how the text, like that used above, creates a Web page.

An important fact to understand about creating with HTML is that it is a *cross platform*. Since HTML consists entirely of generic text, it doesn't matter if it is written on a Macintosh or a PC. Creating HTML doesn't require any special software—it can be written on the simplest word processor or text editor.

So much for the background information. It's time to get started with the fun part, developing Web pages. As we work through the chapters in this book, please spend a good deal of time looking at Web pages. This will rapidly improve your understanding. Look for pages that you like and then look at the source code. Attempt to "deconstruct them" and learn what makes them appear or function the way that they do. Be sure to bookmark the ones that interest you.

Important Points of This Chapter

- A brief summary of the history regarding the Internet and the World Wide Web.

- A description of the Internet as a client-server network.
- A description of the most popular Web browsers.
- A description of the most important features of a Web browser.
- Information about the HTML or the source code of a document.

The Prentice Hall Web site is an important component of this book. Each chapter has a separate Web page that contains numerous resources that expand upon the topics covered in the book.

Visit the Prentice Hall Web site

- There is a list of recommended activities and assignments for this as well as all other chapters.
- There is a short quiz to test your knowledge of the information in this chapter.
- There are important links to additional information regarding the topics covered in this chapter.

CHAPTER 2

Hypertext Markup Language

- Why Learn HTML?
- What Is HTML?
- HTML Standards
- Compatibility
- Tools Required
- What Does HTML Look Like?
- How to Revise a Web Page

Why Learn HTML?

There are currently many good tools available for creating Web pages that don't require any knowledge of HTML. My first experience in Web page development involved using such a Web authoring program. I swore that I would never bother to learn HTML, but I found out very quickly that the program that I was using was limited and would not allow me to do everything that I wanted to do. So, I made the decision to learn to create pages from scratch and learned to use HTML. At the same time I learned that HTML is actually pretty easy.

Web editors have been improved and are great time-saving devices for writing HTML. However, I still find that it is important to know HTML, for a number of reasons:

- Standards for HTML are expanding rapidly, creating new possibilities for Web page creation. Web editing programs can't keep up with the advancements rapidly enough to stay up to date.
- Web editing programs seem to have their own way of doing things. Being able to edit, design, correct problems, and have complete control over your page requires an understanding of HTML.
- Many of the really dynamic features of the Web page development that facilitate interactivity such as CGIs, Java, Active X Controls, and so on, require a knowledge of HTML to integrate them and implement them on Web pages.

As tempting as it might be, I would hesitate to become too dependent upon Web authoring programs without developing a good foundation in HTML. The best way to learn to use HTML is to practice using it. You will find that if you slug it out with the HTML in this book, your ability to use Web authoring tools in the future will be greatly enhanced.

 Web authoring programs are getting better everyday. Links are included on the Prentice Hall Web site to evaluations of various products.

What Is HTML?

Basically, HTML is not nearly as complicated as a programming language. It is really made up of a series of structure "tags" that allow you to organize information on a Web page. For example, I want to post the following announcement on a Web page

Help, I'm being eaten by *slime people!*

The text above has a number of different qualities that I want to retain when seen through the browser:

- The sentence is made up of different sizes of text.
- Some words are bold and some are plain.
- Some words are italicized and another is underlined.
- The words would be seen in different colors.

For the sentence to be displayed exactly as above, I must send instructions along with the sentence to the browser. The instructions, called HTML, are in the form of tags that surround each word that requires special instructions. For example the word "Help" will have instructions that indicate that it will be displayed as bold, larger text. The words "slime people" will have instructions that they are to be displayed as purple and italicized. (Appropriate for slime people, don't you think?)

Your Web browser software is programmed to recognize the meaning of the HTML tags and displays the Web page appropriately. Since the options in your browser might be set differently than the options in mine, we might end up seeing something different.

HTML describes a document's structure rather than its appearance. The browser on your computer makes the decision about how the document should appear. For example, the default text on my browser might be Times, and the default text on yours might be set to Chicago. I will see my announcement displayed in Times text, and you will see the announcement in Chicago text. However, we will see the sentence structured the same as shown above.

This book will systematically introduce all of the important HTML tags so that you will be able to structure the information in your Web page. To assist in this, I have constructed a style sheet that shows all of the essential HTML tags and illustrates how they are used. The style sheet is located in the appendix of this book. You will find that this style sheet will be a valuable resource to which you will need to refer often.

There are dozens of such style sheets available on the World Wide Web, and many of them are listed and linked to on the Prentice Hall Web site.

HTML Standards

HTML must be a common language to be applied effectively. Let's say that the HTML tags that I use to turn text red are interpreted on your browser as making the text smaller. You would not be able to see my Web page as I designed it. The HTML that we use must have a common meaning, and this is what as known as *HTML standards.*

Standards have been established that make viewing a document through one browser somewhat consistent with viewing it through another. There is actually a group of people who meet and decide what will be acceptable tags in HTML and create the list of standards. The group is called the World Wide Web Consortium and is made up of representatives of large companies and organizations who have a vested interest in promoting stable development on the World Wide Web. (These people are so dedicated that they had a meeting on Superbowl Sunday to discuss punctuation and nobody missed the meeting. Probably because they were giving away free pocket protectors!)

The Web site for the World Wide Web Consortium is located at: http://www.w3.org/pub/WWW.

This site contains a wealth of information about the development of the World Wide Web and you can discover more than you will ever want to know about HTML standards.

The Prentice Hall Web site contains links to the World Wide Web Consortium.

Compatibility

Sometimes progress in developing HTML features by browser companies has been ahead of the accepted standards. Some of this progress has been driven by the competition between Netscape and Internet Explorer and others, each trying to make its browser software the most appealing and the most full featured. The result is that one browser will introduce a feature that is not supported by the others. If that feature is included in your Web page, viewers using browsers that don't support the feature will not be able to see it.

The problem is compounded by the fact that older versions of a browser do not support current HTML standards. For example, Netscape 2.0 does not support many of the features supported by Netscape 3.0. We need to keep this in mind in order to design Web pages that can be viewed the same by the most people, being careful to not include features that are not widely supported. Some of these features will be discussed more in later chapters, and in some cases there are ways of designing alternatives into your Web page to accommodate the shortcomings of a "challenged" browser. The information that we cover in this book will not exceed the HTML 3.2 standards, which are the most current as of this writing.

The Prentice Hall Web site contains updates regarding the most recent HTML standards.

Before we can actually get to work creating Web pages we need to make sure that we have the right tools.

Tools Required

You will soon learn how to create Web pages on your computer and be able to view them using a Web browser. The drawback to this arrangement is that no one else will be able to see them; it's like singing in the bathtub. For your pages to be visible to the outside world they must reside on a Web server that is connected to the World Wide Web. The following basic tools are required to create Web pages and to transfer them to a server on the World Wide Web. Let's briefly review what's needed.

Hardware

Computer

Web authoring using HTML is truly cross platform. Your Web page will work equally well on the World Wide Web whether it is produced on a Macintosh or on a PC. You don't really need a new souped-up computer either. But, if you've been looking for an excuse to buy one, here's your chance. My computer is a two-year old Macintosh, slow by today's standards but it works fine.

Since some readers will be working on the Macintosh platform and others on the PC, I will offer two sets of instructions where appropriate. I have to admit to being a dedicated Macintosh person, but now also own a PC. Hopefully my instructions will be accurate on either platform.

Modem

If you are a student or work for a large company, it is possible that you have access to a computer lab that is connected directly to the Internet. Connections such as this are usually supported by T1 lines and are extremely fast. Consider yourself very lucky.

If you are connecting from home to an Internet Service Provider (ISP), like most of the world, you will need a modem. A modem is a device that allows your computer to connect to another computer over a phone line using TCP/IP.

Modem speed can be important. The faster your modem, the faster you will download Web pages and be able to upload your files. A 14,400 baud modem is marginal, but if it's all you have it will work. (Plan on spending lots of time staring at your screen.) If possible, try to shoot for a 33,600, or a 56,000. If you've got some money to burn, you might look into ISDN, which is now supported by many local phone companies. Keep in mind that your Internet service provider must support your modem speed for you to get the maximum effectiveness from your modem.

The Prentice Hall Web site contains information on modems and transfer speeds.

Software

Web Browser

In order to view your Web page, whether it is on your hard drive or on the World Wide Web, you will need a Web browser. I have already talked about Netscape and Internet Explorer in Chapter 1. Another popular browser software is Cyberdog, developed by Apple. My recommendation would be to try all of them them and see which you like the best. At the time of this writing they were all available free for education.

One word of warning: All of the browsers listed are big applications, and all require a lot of memory. New versions come out regularly, and I would say run the newest browser available, with the exception of "betas," or test versions. If you are working on an older computer system and are limited in hard drive space or RAM, make sure that your computer will run the latest version. Memory is an important consideration, and anything less than 16 megs of RAM is very limiting. In my opinion, run the newest version that your computer can handle.

To download the software, go to the Web site for each browser.

Netscape: http://www.netscape.com

Internet explorer: http://www.microsoft.com

Cyberdog: http://cyberdog.apple.com/overview index.html

You will notice that most of the examples in this book use Netscape. Where the instructions are quite different for another browser, I have tried to point out the differences.

We will try to avoid the HTML tags that are unique only to Internet Explorer or to Netscape.

Text Editor

You will need a text editor, which is just a very simple word processing program that deals with text. Macintosh comes with SimpleText, Windows comes with NotePad or Word Pad. You can use a word processing program such as Microsoft Word or Word Perfect as long as you remember to save your documents as text only. While using a word processing program for writing HTML is almost overkill, like using roller blades to chase a snail, it's nice to have spell check. When saving your pages, however, word processing programs have a hard time accepting the fact that you want to save your document as text. You will be prompted not to save as text, and you might begin to feel a little insecure about your decision. Hang in there. If your document is not saved as text, it will not function as a Web page. The beauty of HTML is that it is text and the tools are very basic.

Graphics Software

Several chapters in this book deal with the use of graphics on a Web page. Graphics include, for example, photographic images, clip art, scanned images, or original art. The best tool you can have for Web graphics is Adobe PhotoShop, but there are other shareware programs that will serve the purpose for considerably less money. (Shareware is software that can used for free on a trial basis, but requires payment to the distributor for continued use.) Later in the book I will introduce two such programs that can be downloaded from the World Wide Web. The program for the Macintosh is called Graphic Converter, and the program for the PC is called Paint Shop Pro.

FTP

Once you have created a Web page, you will need to transfer it from your computer to the server where it will reside. The process of developing a Web page and placing it on the server is called Publishing the document to the World Wide Web. As much care should be given to the content and the appearance of a document that is published to the Web as is given to documents that are published in traditional print form. Take pride in your work!

The most common way to publish Web pages to the server is to *FTP* the file. FTP means File Transfer Protocol. Just as http is the protocol for the transfer of hypertext, FTP is the protocol for the transfer of files. Basic instructions will be offered in a later chapter on transferring files using FTP.

FTP software is available on the World Wide Web and can be obtained in both shareware and freeware versions. The Macintosh software of choice is called Fetch. There are several popular types of software on the PC side. Ws_ftp has a freeware version for education purposes. Chapter 17 deals more with FTP.

E-Mail

In order to use e-mail (electronic mail), you must have an e-mail account, provided by your ISP, through school, business, or a commercial ISP. E-mail access is important to have if you are to be effective on the Internet. If you are taking this as a college class, an e-mail account is probably required to communicate with your instructor. When you are on the World Wide Web, there will be many occasions when you will want to contact someone for more information, or you may be required to provide your e-mail address to download shareware or freeware. Overall, an e-mail account is essential.

Netscape and Cyberdog have e-mail programs integrated into them. Internet Explorer can be configured to automatically launch your e-mail software of choice. A very popular and full feature e-mail program is called Eudora.

Now that everything is together and ready to go, let's get to work!

What Does HTML Look Like?

It was pointed out at the end of Chapter 1 that the HTML that structures a Web page is called the source code. There is a very easy way to view, save, and edit the the HTML source code for any document that you view through your browser on the World Wide Web.

Please go through this exercise step by step. These instructions may not be exactly the same for you, depending upon what version of browser you are using, and what platform you are working on.

- Using your Web Browser, connect to the World Wide Web and go to the White House home page. The Web address is: http://www.whitehouse.gov/WH/Welcome.html
- Go to the menu at the top of your screen and select View. Scroll down the menu until you find View Document Source, Source Code, Page Source, or Source. Selection will vary, depending upon the browser or platform that you are using. Your browser will now give you a separate window showing the source code for the White House Web page that we looked at in Chapter 1.
- **If you are on a Macintosh:** Your browser should automatically launch SimpleText, the text editor that comes with the operating system. If all goes well, the source code, meaning the HTML tags and the information in the document for this page, will be displayed. You should be looking at something that appears like the image in Figure 2.1. Since you are in a text editing program, you can edit and/or save the source code as a text document. You can also move easily back and forth between Netscape and your text editor.

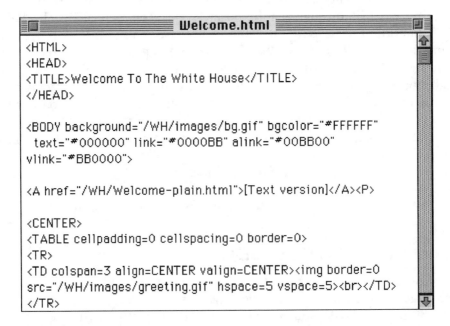

Figure 2.1

- **If you are on a PC and using Netscape:** When you select View Document Source, you will get a separate window that shows you the source code. The source code cannot be edited in this window. The easiest way to save the source code is to select the entire document (Ctrl-A), copy the document (Ctrl-C), open your text editor, and paste it onto a new page (Ctrl-V). The document can then be edited and saved.

- **If you are on a PC and using Internet Explorer:** When you select View Document Source, Notepad, a simple text editor, will open and show your source code. You can use Notepad to edit and save the source code. Your source code will look very much like the one in Figure 2.1.

The important part of this exercise: You are looking at the HTML that structures the White House page. (Figure 2.1) (Confusing?) You can look at the source code for any page on the World Wide Web and see how it is put together. It is an excellent way to learn, to get ideas, to troubleshoot your own page, and to expand your abilities using HTML. I use this technique constantly; you will learn how to make good use of this technique very soon.

How to Revise a Web Page

Let's Start to Work!

I have already started a basic Web page for you. It is located on the Prentice Hall Web site. Your mission during this lesson (should you decide to accept it; music, drum rolls, dramatic lighting, shortness of breath, slight sweat on the mouse hand, etc.) is to

1. **View** your Web page over the Internet.
2. **View** the source code for your Web page.
3. **Alter** the content by placing your name on your Web page.
4. **Save** the source code for your Web page as an HTML document into a folder on your hard drive.
5. **View and Proof** the change through your Web Browser
[1]6. **FTP** the completed Web page to your Web site on your ISP if you have one.
[2]7. **View** your revised Web page over the Internet, if it has been loaded on your ISP.

---

[1]Providing that you have established an Internet account that will carry your home page.

[2]If you take the first letter of the red highlighted keywords in each sentence you get the acronym "VVASVPFV." Coincidentally, I am told that is also the Australian aborigine name for "buttered onion bagel." Keeping that acronym in mind should help you to remember the steps.

The above set of steps are basically those that will be followed throughout this book as you make revisions to your home page. In future revisions to your page, you will be viewing your page on your hard drive or over the Internet from your own ISP, rather than from the Prentice Hall Web site.

If you do not have an Internet account that provides space for carrying your Web page, you can still make changes to your Web page, but you will be limited to viewing them from your hard drive rather than over the Internet.

It is important that you understand and feel comfortable with these steps at the conclusion of this chapter . For that reason, I will carefully walk you through the steps the first time. For future revisions to your page, please refer back to the steps that we are following for this exercise.

1. **View your page over the Internet.**

   I have created a generic Web page on the Prentice Hall Web site for you to view. It is located at:

   http://www.prenhall.com/meyers

Let's take a look

The first thing that you notice about your page is that it is boring, lacks content and artistic merit, and is nothing like what you imagined your arrival on the World Wide Web to be. It doesn't even contain your name! I get emotional just thinking about it.

It looks like Figure 2.2. Sad, isn't it? All of that will change as you work through this book.

2. **View the source code for your Web page.**

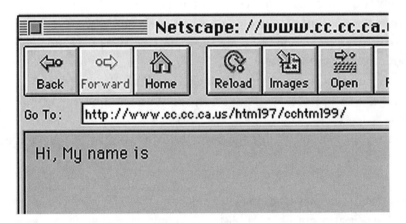

Figure 2.2

No amount of desperate typing will change it while it is in the browser state. Let's view the document source for your page. Go to the View menu and select Document Source. You should now be looking at the nuts and bolts of your document, something like this:

```
<HTML>

<HEAD>

<TITLE>

</TITLE>

</HEAD>

<BODY>

Hi, My name is

</BODY>

</HTML>
```

3. Alter the content by placing your name on your Web page.

Let's not worry about anything other than getting your name in here.

Mac Users: When you view the source code, you are now in your text editor. Put your name in after "Hi, My name is" by typing in your real, authentic name. (People on Witness Protection programs should consider the ramifications of this!)

PC Users: As I described above, you may have to go through that extra step to edit your document. Copy and paste it into your text editor. Put your name in after "Hi, My name is" by typing in your real, authentic name.

4. Save the source code for your Web page as an HTML document.

Now would be a good time to make a folder on your computer where you will save all of your work. You should give it a name that you won't easily forget and can type easily such as: "h_t/zy_r*". Just kidding . . . It is a good idea to get into the habit of giving it the same name as your directory on your ISP's server.

Now we want to save the source code to that folder. You may want to give it some flamboyant name to match your current exhilaration as a new Web author, but please call it "index.htm." I will explain the importance of using the name index later, but for now please trust me: "**index.htm.**"

Web pages always have either .html or .htm as a suffix to the file name. This suffix tells the browser that it is an HTML document and that it should display it. Either suffix will work, but for consistency we will use ".htm." PCs will not allow four letters in a files' suffix, Macs don't care one way or the other, so let's hang with ".htm." *A browser must see the suffix .htm or .html to see your document as a Web page.*

Now you are ready to save the source code to the folder that you created to your hard drive. But first, make sure that you are saving it as "text." If you are using Notepad on the PC or Teach Text on the Mac, there is no problem. They can only save as text. If you are using your word processing program, such as Microsoft Word, you must tell it to "save as text." *This is essential, because all Web pages are text documents.*

Remember to name your file "index.htm." Since file names are case sensitive in HTML, get into the habit of naming all files using lowercase only. This way you will have an easier time remembering them.

After you are sure that you have done the above correctly, save the file to your folder on your hard drive.

We're smokin' now!

5. View and proof the change through your Web browser.

Before you submit your page to the Web server, you must view it through your Web browser to see that you haven't made any mistakes. With Netscape, go to File and then to Open File in Browser. If you are using Internet Explore, go to File and then to Open. This feature allows you to browse for and open files that are on your computer in your browser. Find and open your file. It should look like this now, with your name included (Figure 2.3).

It's not much, but it's mine!!

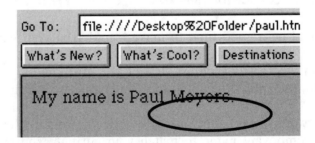

Figure 2.3

Sometimes you won't see the changes after you reopen the file. Browsers hold information about previously viewed pages in memory, called cache. Try hitting the Reload button; if that fails, go to Options then Network Preferences and click on Clear Disk Cache Now. This will clean out Netscape's memory. If you still don't see the changes, then you might have saved your file to another location and are reopening the original unchanged file. Try resaving the file, making sure that you overwrite your original. I have made all of the above possible mistakes, and more. . . . If none of the above works, you might try moving to another neighborhood, changing your name, and wearing a disguise. The original version of the file will never find you.

6. FTP the completed Web page to your Web site on your ISP if you have one.

Transferring your Web page to your ISP will vary, depending upon what type of account you have and what kind of arrangements have been made for updating pages. The most common means of uploading Web pages to a server is accomplished through the use of FTP. FTP software is described above. It is used to connect to your account on the Web server, and to transfer your revised Web page to your Web directory, in most cases overwriting your previous page. New pages, graphics, and other media files are uploaded to the Web server in the same way.

I have developed a step-by-step FTP tutorial for both Macintosh and PC client software. It is located on the Prentice Hall Web site for this book.

7. View your revised Web page over the Internet, if it has been loaded on your ISP.

This is what it's all about, finally seeing your Web page on the Internet! I would invite some friends over, have some refreshments, and let them watch in awe as your name appears for the first time on the World Wide Web. (Even if you don't have a Web account with an ISP, you can show it off your hard drive and tell them it's on the Internet.)

Congratulations. You have just completed the first step in becoming a Webmaster. The rest of this book now deals with introducing new HTML features created through the use of tags. You are encouraged to add all of the new features to your home page, as exercises, so that you become familiar with HTML. At the conclusion of the book you can eliminate the exercises from your home page and fine tune it so that it says exactly what you want it to say in the way that you want to say it.

Be sure to visit the Prentice Hall Web site to learn how to FTP.

Important points of this chapter

- A few reasons why it is important to learn HTML.
- Definitions: What is HTML? What are HTML standards?
- A description of the tools required to create Web pages using HTML.
- What is the source code?
- Step-by-step instructions for revising a Web page.

Visit the Prentice Hall Web site

- There is a list of recommended activities and assignments for Chapter 2 related to the topics that were covered.
- There is a short quiz to test your knowledge of the information in this chapter.

CHAPTER 3

The Basic Tags

Basic HTML Tags

Break Tags

Headings

Basic HTML Tags

Okay, let's jump into it. Now we're really going to get some text on our hands. In your text editor, please open the text file "index.htm" that you saved on your hard drive in the last chapter with your text editing program. It should look something like this

```
<HTML>

<HEAD>

<TITLE></TITLE>
```

```
</HEAD>

<BODY>

<Hi, My name is Paul Meyers>

</BODY>

</HTML>
```

What you are looking at is actually quite profound. You are seeing the basic HTML tags that are necessary for an HTML document.

If you look at the top and the bottom of the above text, you will see that it starts with **<HTML>** and concludes with **</HTML>.** All Web pages begin and end in the same way. This is also quite characteristic of HTML tags: Most of them have an opening tag **<HTML>** and a closing tag, which is indicated by a forward slash **</HTML>.** Everything that is included between these two tags will be affected by whatever structuring the tags define. In this case these tags state the beginning and ending of an HTML or Hypertext Markup Language document; a Web page.

The easiest thing to forget when doing HTML is the closing tag or the forward slash in the closing tag. You will probably do this often for a while and you will be amazed by the crazy kinds of results you will get.

An HTML document is like a person. It can be divided into two major parts, the **Head,** represented by the **<H></H>** tags, and the **Body,** defined by the **<body></body>** tags. Like a person, the document requires both to function, and the head is always on top. You will notice that I deliberately typed the **<H></H>** tags in uppercase and the **<body></body>** tags in lowercase. It doesn't really matter, they can be either. For clarity and organization, it is probably best to do it one way or the other. Making them all uppercase will assist you in quickly finding your tags in a complex document amid an army of text. This option is definitely preferred. (I have to admit I'm pretty sloppy; I can't type and it is usually joy enough to hit the right key, let alone the right case.)

In this text, all HTML tags will be presented as uppercase and in bold, to make them stand out as much as possible.

What Goes into the Head?

Title

For now, the most important element that goes into the head of the page is the title of the page, defined by the **<TITLE></TITLE>** tags. The title is different from the file name that you gave your Web page document. The information enclosed within in the title tags will be displayed by your browser at the top of your Web page in the Title bar. Let's verify that by doing another follow-along exercise.

Open your page in your text editor and give your page a title by typing the title of your page between the title tags. There should be no space between the tags and the text.

Example

<HTML>

<HEAD>

<TITLE>Paul's Effort to Overcome Homepagelessness</TITLE>

</HEAD>

<BODY>

Hi, My name is Paul Meyers

</BODY>

</HTML>

Now, save the changes to your hard drive by overwriting your previous file.

Using your Web browser, open the Web page that is located on your hard drive by going to File—>Open File in the browser. You can then locate and open your file. Once it is opened, look at the top of the page in the Title bar and you should see your new title (Figure 3.1). If your title doesn't show up, remember that sometimes it is necessary to reload your page to be able to see the changes.

Your title should be descriptive of the information contained on your page. Search engines—Internet tools for locating information—will find your page through the keywords in your title.

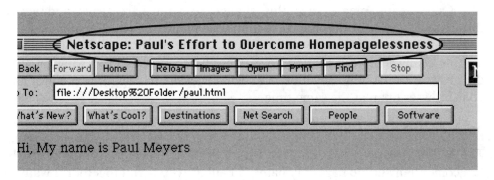

Figure 3.1

What Else Goes into the Head?

A small set of tags called META tags are used for including information about the document. This can be valuable if we want to list the contents of the page in a series of keywords that can be targeted by search engines. Since we don't have any content yet, it would be difficult to add keywords. We will discuss entering keywords in Chapter 17. If we wanted to add a Java Script to the page, we would also add this to the head portion of the document.

What Goes into the Body?

Everything Else!

Everything that you see on your page is contained in the body of your HTML. Let's get busy and begin to improve it. How about adding a greeting? The usual "Hi, Welcome to my home page" always works.

Right now my page says," Hi, My name is Paul Meyers." Using your text editor, open your page. Change the text to "Hi, Welcome to my home page," followed by your name.

The HTML will look like this:

```
<HTML>

<HEAD>

<TITLE>Paul's Effort to Overcome Homepagelessness</TITLE>

</HEAD>

<BODY>

Hi, Welcome to my home page. My name is Paul Meyers

</BODY>

</HTML>
```

Once again, please save this change to your hard drive and verify through your browser that the correction was made.

Developing a Web page using HTML is done pretty much in this fashion: making changes in your text editor, saving the changes, and viewing them in the browser to see how they look. You will generally have your text editor and your browser open at the same time.

Please Try This Experiment

The HTML for my page is below. I hate the way those two sentences, "Hi, Welcome to my home page. My name is Paul Meyers," run together. I want to have them on separate lines. Please view your page in the text editor; you should have something similar.

```
<HTML>

<HEAD>

<TITLE>Paul's Effort to Overcome Homepagelessness</TITLE>

</HEAD>

<BODY>

Hi, Welcome to my home page. My name is Paul Meyers

</BODY>

</HTML>
```

In your editor, hit your return key after the word "page" to put the second sentence on another line.

Your HTML should look like this

```
<HTML>

<HEAD>

<TITLE>Paul's Effort to Overcome Homepagelessness</TITLE>

</HEAD>

<BODY>

Welcome to my home page.

My name is Paul Meyers

</BODY>

</HTML>
```

Save your document and view it through your browser.

Nothing happened! No matter how many times you refresh your screen, the two sentences will remain on the same line.

Let's examine what is going on here; it is very important to understand. What happens when we create text on a text editor or word processor to be printed and what happens when we create text to be viewed on a Web page are quite different.

Text Created on a Word Processor

In a word processing program, if I type a line of text that is longer than the page is wide, it will automatically "wrap" the text to the next line. It puts in a "soft return" without my having to hit the return key. If I get to the end of a line before I reach the right margin of the page, and I want the following text to start on the next line, I have to hit the return key, which creates a "hard return." Text page widths in a word processing program are normally 8.5 inches to correspond to the standard size of computer paper. Consequently, the printed page will appear the same as it does on the computer screen.

Text to Be Viewed on a Web Page

As we have seen above, when we enter our text for our Web page, the soft breaks and the hard breaks from the word processor or text editor do not affect the final document; they will be ignored by our Web browser. We must enter HTML tags, instructions, to tell the browser where we want the breaks to occur. We are not going to print our document, we are going to view it on a computer monitor. A Web page can be seen in a variety of widths, depending upon the size of the monitor. If we put long lines of text onto a Web page and do not indicate any breaks, the text will span the screen and automatically wrap where the screen ends.

Please try this:

I have made a copy of this paragraph and placed it in the Prentice Hall Web site. Using your browser, please go to the page and try the following: Choose a sentence to watch in the paragraph. Grab the lower right corner of your screen, and stretch it out so that it is as wide as you can make it. As you get wider, the soft returns or breaks in the line appear at different places. Now grab the corners of your screen and make the screen image narrow. Again, the soft return appears in a different place. The text is being adjusted to the width of your screen. You should have noticed that the hard breaks, created through HTML, remain constant. Each paragraph begins and ends at the same place. The next section describes how to create page or line breaks using HTML.

Break Tags

The HTML equivalent to hitting the return key in a word processing program is the use of the paragraph **<P></P>** tags or the break tag **
. The paragraph tag **<P></P> is like hitting the return key twice; it creates a blank line as well as a break. The break tag **
** is like hitting the return key once.

Paragraph Tag

The **<P></P>** tags are used to create paragraphs. Text enclosed by paragraph tags will start on a new line, separated from previous text with a blank line. Let's go back to your text editor and enclose the sentence that we want on a second line in the paragraph tags.

It should look like this:

<HTML>

<HEAD>

<TITLE>Paul's Effort to Overcome Homepagelessness</TITLE>

</HEAD>

<BODY>

Hi, Welcome to my home page.

<P>My name is Paul Meyers</P>

</BODY>

</HTML>

Save your page and view it through your browser. It should look like the text below.

Hi,Welcome to my home page.

My name is Paul Meyers

Remember

- **If it doesn't look any different:** Don't forget to reload the page. You might be seeing the previous version that Netscape has saved to cache.
- **If it still does not work:** Double check your tags for errors.
- **If it still does not work:** Sometimes you have to clear the cache on your browser. Depending upon the browser that you are using, go to Options on the Preferences menu, then to Network Preferences. You should look for a button that says, "Clear Disk Cache Now." You'll get a warning message. Ignore it, click okay, and try to reload your page.

One of those possibilities has to work.

Note: Browsers can be extremely tenacious about retaining Web pages in cache. Sometimes they are as stubborn as a pitbull that has a hold of your pant leg. On rare occasions I have had to close and restart the browser in order to convince it to forget the old version of the page on which I was working.

Line Break Tag

The line break tag **
** is used for creating a break in a line of text. It is the HTML equivalent of a hard return on the word processor. It would force text that follows it to the next line.

I have written the address for the college where I teach below. (Please feel free to write.)

Cerro Coso Community College, 3000 College Heights Blvd., Ridgecrest, California, 93555

It is not a very useful way to read an address—it's all strung out into one line. If I use paragraph tags, **<P></P>,** to break the line, I will also end up with a blank line between each line like below.

Cerro Coso Community College,

3000 College Heights Blvd.,

Ridgecrest, California 93555

I would prefer not to show each line as a paragraph, but to be able to insert a hard return where the line should break. To accomplish this I use the **
**, or line break, tag. The **
** tag is one of several tags that are called "singlets." They do not require a closing tag. The HTML will look like this:

<HTML>

<HEAD>

<TITLE></TITLE>

</HEAD>

<BODY>

Cerro Coso Community College,

3000 College Heights Blvd.,

Ridgecrest, California 93555

</BODY>

</HTML>

and the text will appear

Cerro Coso Community College,

3000 College Heights Blvd.,

Ridgecrest, California, 93555

Organize your HTML so that it is easy to read and edit.

I have repeated the above HTML in a different organization below. It does not really matter if your HTML looks like it does below; it will still work if the correct tags are there, and you have not put in any unwanted spaces.

However, I do not recommend trying to write Web pages in this manner; you will drive yourself nuts trying to find errors or make changes. It is far wiser to get into the habit of organizing your HTML as in the example above, with each of the elements arranged on separate lines.

```
<HTML><HEAD><TITLE></TITLE></HEAD><BODY>Cerro Coso Community College,<BR>
3000 College Hts. Blvd.,<BR>Ridgecrest, California, 93555</BODY></HTML>
```

The importance of clear organization will become more apparent to you as you begin to work on larger documents or view the source code of more complex pages.

Headings (Text Size)

So far we have been working with "default" text. The word default refers to the way an element, in this case text, will appear without any HTML instruction. Standard text in a browser will usually appear as 12 point text. The font that will appear depends upon which font is the default font for the browser. If we were to make all of our documents using only one type of text, then our Web pages would be boring and difficult to read. We need to be able to change our text to add interest.

The heading tags **<H></H>** are very useful in adding interest and helping to make text more easily read. Text can be organized under headings to give it a more logical order. The tags always include a number, 1 through 6, which identifies the size of the text. **<H1></H1>** is the largest, **<H6></H6>** the smallest.

The following illustrates how the use of the <H></H>tags changes text size

```
<H1>Gummy Bears are Good</H1>
```

Gummy Bears are Good

```
<H2>Gummy Bears are Good</H2>
```

Gummy Bears are Good

```
<H3>Gummy Bears are Good</H3>
```

Gummy Bears are Good

```
<H4>Gummy Bears are Good</H4>
```

Gummy Bears are Good

```
<H5>Gummy Bears are Good</H5>
```

Gummy Bears are Good

```
<H6>Gummy Bears are Good</H6>
```

Gummy Bears are Good

Four additional important points about headings

- Heading tags will create a blank line after the heading, much the way a paragraph tag does.
- If you forget to close the **<H>** tag with the **</H>** tag, all of your text will be resized.
- Heading tags will make the text they enclose bold, as well as defining the text size.
- <H3></H3> is just about the default size for standard text.

Example

I would like to add the following information to my Web page. With all the text being the same size and emphasis, it will be difficult to read.

Hi, Welcome to my home page

My name is Paul Meyers

A little bit about myself

I live in Ridgecrest, California, where I teach at Cerro Coso Community College. I am normally an art instructor, teaching ceramics, sculpture, and three-dimensional design. This year I have embarked on something very different: teaching an online course on creating home pages using HTML.

For more information contact me at

Cerro Coso Community College

3000 College Heights Blvd.

Ridgecrest, California

93555

Example after adding headings

Hi, Welcome to my home page

My name is Paul Meyers

A little bit about myself

I live in Ridgecrest, California, where I teach at Cerro Coso Community College. I am normally an art instructor, teaching ceramics, sculpture, and three-dimensional design. This semester I have embarked on something very different, teaching an online course on creating home pages using HTML.

For more information contact me at

Cerro Coso Community College

3000 College Heights Blvd.

Ridgecrest, California

93555

While not very interesting, it definitely reads better.

Important Points of This Chapter

- The basic HTML tags:

`<HTML>`

`<HEAD>`

`<TITLE></TITLE>`

`</HEAD>`

`<BODY>`

`</BODY>`

`</HTML>`

- Break tag

`<BR>`

- The paragraph tags

`<P></P>`

- Headings

`<H1-6></H1-6>`

Visit the Prentice Hall Web site

- There is a list of recommended activities and assignments for Chapter 3 to enhance your understanding of the above HTML tags.
- There is a short quiz to test your knowledge of the HTML tags covered in this chapter.

CHAPTER 4

Text Alignment, and Lists

Text Alignment
Options

Default Alignment

Center

Nesting Tags

Lists

<BLOCKQUOTE>

Text Alignment Options

If you have been putting the information from the previous chapters into practice, your Web page should be well into the growing stages and full of text. You are probably getting a little bored with everything being neatly lined up on the left margin. We will now cover some options for alignment of text.

Let's work with the following paragraph

> Harry Peabrain, a Very Odd, but Special Person. Harry Peabrain is an itinerant soldier of fortune in the nasty war against outdated dairy products

remaining on grocery store shelves. Scarred at an early age by a particularly fetid container of sour chocolate milk, he has vowed to protect others from being exposed to similar atrocities. Harry lists the following products as being the most likely to be spoiled and out of date: Chocolate milk, Ostrich eggs, Moose cow milk. Harry insists that the problem varies from one region of the country to another, with the following regions and grocery store chains being cited as the worst offenders. Midwest: Groovin Groceries, Inc., Buy Low, Sell High, Corp. In a recent interview Harry stated: "If I let moss grow under my feet, then mildew will be growing in every cooler in America."

If you were to run across the above paragraph on the World Wide Web, you probably wouldn't bother to read it, in spite of its great literary value. It is not very visually inviting. Materials on the World Wide Web need to be presented in such a way that information can be read quickly. Using the tools you have already have learned, some quick restructuring can be accomplished to improve its readability. (By the time we're through working with this paragraph, your going to be as sick of Harry as Harry is of bad dairy products.)

Please do this as a quick review exercise before looking ahead in the chapter.

The complete Harry Peabrain paragraph is located on the Prentice Hall Web site.

After connecting to the Prentice Hall Web site and opening the page that includes the Harry Peabrain paragraph, please follow these directions.

Copy the Harry Peabrain text directly off your browser screen by selecting the text with your mouse and pasting it into your text editor:

- On the Mac: Click just in front of the text you want to copy and drag to the right until it is all highlighted. Use the keyboard (Command-C) to copy, then open your text editor and paste it (Command-V) into a text document.
- On the PC: Everything is done the same except use the (CTRL-C) and the (CTRL-V) keys.

This is a very useful trick for quickly copying information that you want to use from the World Wide Web.

Using the paragraph, break, and heading tags, try quickly restructuring the above Harry Peabrain text so that it is more logically ordered and easier to read.

No peeking now!!

This how I did it. How does it compare to what you did?

```
<HTML>

<HEAD>

<TITLE>Inspirational Sagas</TITLE>

</HEAD>

<BODY>

<H3>Harry Peabrain:<BR>

A Very Odd but Special Person.</H3>

<P>Harry Peabrain is an itinerant soldier of fortune in the nasty war against outdated dairy products remaining on grocery store shelves. Scarred at an early age by a particularly fetid container of sour chocolate milk he has vowed to protect others from being exposed to similar atrocities. Harry lists the following products as being the most likely to be spoiled and out of date:<BR>

Chocolate milk<BR>

Ostrich eggs<BR>

Moose cow milk<BR>

Harry insists that the problem varies from one region of the country to another, with the following region and grocery store chains being cited as the worst offenders.<BR>

Midwest: <BR>

Groovin Groceries, Inc.,<BR>

Buy Low, Sell High, Corp.<BR>

In a recent interview Harry stated: <BR>

"If I were to let moss grow under my feet, then mildew would be growing in every grocery cooler in America."</P>

</BODY>

</HTML>
```

Look at the above source code and look at the results below. Please keep me honest—make sure that I did it correctly.

Harry Peabrain

A Very Odd but Special Person.

Harry Peabrain is an itinerant soldier of fortune in the nasty war against outdated dairy products remaining on grocery store shelves. Scarred at an early age by a particularly fetid container of sour chocolate milk, he has vowed to protect others from being exposed to similar atrocities. Harry lists the following products as being the most likely to be spoiled and out of date

Chocolate milk

Ostrich eggs

Moose cow milk

Harry insists that the problem varies from one region of the country to another, with the following region and grocery store chains being cited as the worst offenders.

Midwest

Groovin Groceries, Inc.,

Buy Low, Sell High, Corp.

In a recent interview Harry stated: "If I were to let moss grow under my feet, then mildew would be growing in every grocery cooler in America."

The statement is much easier to read, but I think we can improve on it even more. How did you do?

Default Alignment

The "default" alignment for everything on a Web page is to the left margin of the page. Remember, default is how your elements on your page will appear if you don't provide instructions for them to appear otherwise. Notice how obediently everything lines up to the left.

Steps to Cover

Figure 4.1 illustrates the areas of the above text that we will reformat by changing the text alignment.

1. Center the title.
2. Indent the entire text block.
3. Create a bulleted list from the dairy products list (unordered list).
4. Create a numbered list from the grocery companys list (ordered list).
5. Create a **<BLOCKQUOTE>** of Harry's statement.

Center

One alternative to a left alignment would be to reformat the page so that everything is centered on the page. To center elements on a Web page we can use the center tag **<CENTER></CENTER>**. Let's try something wild and

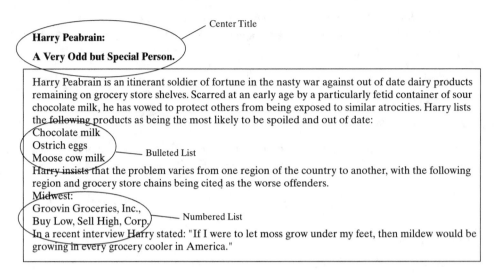

Figure 4.1

crazy and place a center tag **<CENTER>** at the beginning of the page and a closed center tag **</CENTER>** at the end. Remember, everything must be inside the **<BODY></BODY>** tags. I'll abbreviate the source to simplify.

The HTML

    <BODY>

    <CENTER>

    <H3>Harry Peabrain:

    A Very Odd but Special Person.</H3>

    *

    *

    *

    If I were to let moss grow under my feet, then mildew would be growing in every grocery cooler in America.</P>

    </CENTER> </BODY>

    </HTML>

This is the result:

Harry Peabrain

A Very Odd but Special Person.

Harry Peabrain is an itinerant soldier of fortune in the nasty war against outdated dairy products remaining on grocery store shelves. Scarred at an early age by a particularly fetid container of sour chocolate milk, he has vowed to protect others from being exposed to similar atrocities. Harry lists the following products as being the most likely to be spoiled and out of date

Chocolate milk

Ostrich eggs

Moose cow milk

Harry insists that the problem varies from one region of the country to another, with the following region and grocery store chains being cited as the worse offenders.

Midwest

Groovin Groceries, Inc.,

Buy Low, Sell High, Corp.

In a recent interview Harry stated: "If I were to let moss grow under my feet, then mildew would be growing in every grocery cooler in America."

Yikes! What a change!

I think that we could all agree that centering doesn't really work effectively for displaying this information. As you surf the Web you will see many pages where a centered format works well. Most often your page will be a mixture of various alignments, and later we will explore other alignment possibilities. But let's not drop the center idea completely; the title actually looks pretty good there. Let's align only the title to the center by using the center tag.

I will leave the opening center tag **\<CENTER\>** at the beginning of the title and move the closing center tag **\</CENTER\>** from the end of the text to the end of the title. I have abbreviated the HTML.

```
<BODY>

<CENTER>

<H3>Harry Peabrain:<BR>

A Very Odd, but Special Person.</H3> </CENTER>
```

    *

    *

    *

"If I were to let moss grow under my feet, then mildew would be growing in every grocery cooler in America."

</BODY>

</HTML>

Let's see what that looks like

Harry Peabrain

A Very Odd, but Special Person.

Harry Peabrain is an itinerant soldier of fortune in the nasty war against outdated dairy products remaining on grocery store shelves. Scarred at an early age by a particularly fetid container of sour chocolate milk, he has vowed to protect others from being exposed to similar atrocities. Harry lists the following products as being the most likely to be spoiled and out of date

Chocolate milk

Ostrich eggs

Moose cow milk

Harry insists that the problem varies from one region of the country to another, with the following region and grocery store chains being cited as the worse offenders.

Midwest

Groovin Groceries, Inc.,

Buy Low, Sell High, Corp.

In a recent interview Harry stated: "If I were to let moss grow under my feet, then mildew would be growing in every grocery cooler in America."

Nesting Tags

Before we continue to develop the Harry Peabrain statement, there is an important concept that we need to understand: nesting tags.

An HTML document is made up of a set of "nesting tags." Nesting tags are HTML tags that are included within other HTML tags. An entire HTML document is nested within the **<HTML></HTML>** tags. The information in the body of the document is nested within the **<BODY></BODY>** tags, which are in turn nested in the **<HTML></HTML>** tags, and so on.

If I want to change the size of some text to **<H3>,** as well as make the text into a paragraph, the HTML would look like the following.

<P><H3> Harry Peabrain is an itinerant soldier of fortune</H3></P>

The result

Harry Peabrain is an itinerant soldier of fortune

The **<H3></H3>** tags are nested within the **<P></P>** tags. In the above example I have given two commands to the browser about this sentence: Make it an H3 size and make it a paragraph. These commands will not affect the rest of the page since they are both closed at the end of the sentence.

Hopefully, understanding the concept of nesting will make it easier to understand the following section.

Lists

One excellent way to organize materials on a Web page is through the use of lists. There are two types of lists: ordered lists and unordered lists. **Ordered lists** are are usually numbered and often used when items are listed in some kind of sequence. For example:

Important things to do today:

1. Eat breakfast
2. Take a nap
3. Eat dinner

<OL></OL> are the tags used to create an ordered list.

Unordered lists (which sounds like an oxymoron) are lists that don't require any special order and are usually bulleted. For example:

Things in the refrigerator
- Road Kill Wiggle
- Sewer Soup
- Rancid Relish

<UL></UL> are the tags used to create an unordered list.

When either of these sets of tags is used, the text that they enclose will be indented to the right. In the following examples I have use the **<UL></UL>** tags, but I could have just as easily used the **<OL></OL>** tags to indent the text.

Example 1

I have isolated the following sentence from our statement.

> Harry Peabrain is an itinerant soldier of fortune

If I do not enclose it with any tags, it will by default align itself to the left as below.

> Harry Peabrain is an itinerant soldier of fortune

Example 2

> <UL>Harry Peabrain is an itinerant soldier of fortune</UL>

If I enclose the same sentence with **<UL></UL>** tags, notice how the sentence below is now indented from the left to the right.

> Harry Peabrain is an itinerant soldier of fortune

Example 3

> <UL><UL>Harry Peabrain is an itinerant soldier of fortune</UL></UL>

If I nest the **<UL></UL>** tags, I can indent the sentence to the right even more.

> Harry Peabrain is an itinerant soldier of fortune

And so on. . .

Now let's go back to our the entire Harry Peabrain statement. I want to indent all of the text so that there is a larger margin on the left and the lines are shorter and easier to read. To accomplish this I will use the unordered list tag **<UL></UL>,** which actually tells the browser that the text is a "list" and to indent it (I could have used the **<OL></OL>** tags instead.)

I will place the tag after the title, since the title is already being instructed to be centered, and at the end of the text, just before the closing body tag. I have abbreviated the document to make it easier to understand.

<BODY>

<CENTER>

<H3>Harry Peabrain:

A Very Odd, but Special Person.</H3></CENTER>

<UL>

  *

  *

  *

"If I were to let moss grow under my feet, then mildew would be growing in every grocery cooler in America."

</UL>

</BODY>

</HTML>

The result? The whole document has moved to the right, with a larger margin on the left. Please look at the result below.

Harry Peabrain
A Very Odd, but Special Person.

Harry Peabrain is an itinerant soldier of fortune in the nasty war against outdated dairy products remaining on grocery store shelves. Scarred at an early age by a particularly fetid container of sour chocolate milk, he has vowed to protect others from being exposed to similar atrocities. Harry lists the following products as being the most likely to be spoiled and out of date

Chocolate milk

Ostrich eggs

Moose cow milk

Harry insists that the problem varies from one region of the country to another, with the following region and grocery store chains being cited as the worse offenders.

Midwest

Groovin Groceries, Inc.,

Buy Low, Sell High, Corp.

In a recent interview Harry stated: "If I were to let moss grow under my feet, then mildew would be growing in every grocery cooler in America."

Unordered Lists: The Bulleted List

Our next step will be to make a bulleted list from the list of dairy products. We will once again use the **<UL></UL>** tag and place it at the beginning and the end of the list that we want to modify such as below:

<UL>

Chocolate milk

Ostrich eggs

Moose cow milk

</UL>

The result will be to indent the list of words. To make the list into a bulleted list, we need to add the list tag, **<LI>** in front of each item on the list.

The **<LI>** tag does not require a closing tag, but you can use one if you so choose. Since it it will automatically create a break after each item, notice that I have removed the **
** tags.

The HTML looks like this:

<UL>

<LI>Chocolate milk

<LI>Ostrich eggs

<LI>Moose cow milk

</UL>

The result will look like this:

- Chocolate milk
- Ostrich eggs
- Moose cow milk

Ordered Lists: The Numbered List

Our next step is to make a numbered list out of the companies that Harry doesn't like, shown below:

Midwest

Groovin Groceries, Inc.,

Buy Low, Sell High, Corp.

I want the word "Midwest" to be indented from the paragraph above it, and I want the list of stores to be numbered.

For this purpose we will use the ordered list tag **<OL></OL>.** Either the **<UL></UL>** or the **<OL></OL>** will indent text when used independently.

When the **<LI>** tag is used in combination with the **<OL></OL>** tags, the result will be a numbered list rather than a bulleted list as we have already created with the **<UL>** tag. Let's give it a try:

<OL>

<LI>Midwest

<OL>

<LI>Groovin Groceries, Inc.,

<LI>Buy Low, Sell High, Corp.

</OL></OL>

The result will look like this:

1. Midwest
    1. Groovin Groceries, Inc.,
    2. Buy Low, Sell High, Corp.

<BLOCKQUOTE>

Now let's tackle the last task for this exercise. Let's set off the following quote by Harry so that his words of wisdom get proper attention.

In a recent interview Harry stated: "If I were to let moss grow under my feet, then mildew would be growing in every grocery cooler in America."

A **<BLOCKQUOTE>** is usually used when you want to set off a quotation or any paragraph by indenting on the **left** and the **right.** The **<BLOCK-QUOTE>** tags are **<BLOCKQUOTE></BLOCKQUOTE>**, which is why it is usually avoided by people like me who cannot type.

The HTML

In a recent interview Harry stated:

<BLOCKQUOTE>"If I were to let moss grow under my feet, then mildew would be growing in every grocery cooler in America."</BLOCKQUOTE>

The Result

In a recent interview Harry stated:

> "If I were to let moss grow under my feet, then mildew would be growing in every grocery cooler in America."

Notice how the the quote is now indented from the right and the left margin. We could have used a **<BLOCKQUOTE>** to Harry's entire page instead of the **<UL></UL>** to narrow and center the text and still maintain a left alignment..

Now let's put the page back together and see how it turned out.

After readjusting a few tags, here is the final HTML:

<HTML>

<HEAD>

<TITLE>Inspirational Sagas</TITLE>

</HEAD

<BODY>

```
<UL>
<CENTER>
<H3>Harry Peabrain:<BR>
A Very Odd, but Special Person</H3>
</CENTER>
<P>Harry Peabrain is an itinerant soldier of
fortune in the nasty war against outdated
dairy products remaining on grocery store
shelves. Scarred at an early age by a
particularly fetid container of sour
chocolate milk, he has vowed to protect
others from being exposed to similar atrocities.
Harry lists the following products as being the
most likely to be spoiled and out of date:</P>
<UL>
<LI>Chocolate milk
<LI>Ostrich eggs
<LI>Moose cow milk
</UL><BR>
<P>Harry insists that the problem varies from one region
of the country to another, with the following region
and grocery store chains being
cited as the worse offenders.</P>
<OL>
<LI>Midwest:
<OL>
<LI>Groovin Groceries, Inc.,
<LI>Buy Low, Sell High, Corp.
</OL></OL><BR>
```

In a recent interview Harry stated:

<BLOCKQUOTE>"If I were to let moss grow under my feet,

then mildew would be growing in every grocery cooler

in America."

</BLOCKQUOTE>

</UL>

</BODY>

</HTML>

The Result

Harry Peabrain

A Very Odd, but Special Person

Harry Peabrain is an itinerant soldier of fortune in the nasty war against outdated dairy products remaining on grocery store shelves. Scarred at an early age by a particularly fetid container of sour chocolate milk, he has vowed to protect others from being exposed to similar atrocities. Harry lists the following products as being the most likely to be spoiled and out of date

- Chocolate milk
- Ostrich eggs
- Moose cow milk

Harry insists that the problem varies from one region of the country to another, with the following region and grocery store chains being cited as the worse offenders.

1. Midwest
    1. Groovin Groceries, Inc.,
    2. Buy Low, Sell High, Corp

In a recent interview Harry stated:

> "If I were to let moss grow under my feet, then mildew would be growing in every grocery cooler in America."

Now, I'm willing to admit that this is hardly a work of art, but it should hopefully illustrate how to take greater control of the organization of your information through alignment and the use of lists.

Important points of this chapter

- Default or left alignment.

- Text alignment using the **<CENTER></CENTER>** tags
- An applied review of the **<P>** and **
** tags.
- Introduction to the concept of nesting tags.
- The use of lists:
- Ordered lists: **<UL></UL>**
- Unordered lists: **<OL></OL>**
- The use of the **<BLOCKQUOTE>** for indenting: **<BLOCKQUOTE></BLOCKQUOTE>**

Visit the Prentice Hall Web site

- Learn more about the trials and tribulations of poor old Harry Peabrain.
- There is a list of recommended activities and assignments to improve your skills in working with the alignment and organization of text.
- There is a short quiz to test your knowledge of the information in this chapter.

CHAPTER 5

The Font Tag, and Hexidecimal Color

Blinking Text
_____

Font Tags
_____

Tᴴ̇is chapter deals with changing the appearance of text to add interest and variety to your Web page. But first, no book on HTML would be complete without introducing the often hated and sometimes reviled blinking text.

Blinking Text

I'm just throwing this one in so we can start with something kind of fun, and dangerous at the same time.

Try to imagine that you are looking at your computer screen, and your name at the top of your Web page is flashing on and off, on and off . . .

First of All: How Do You Do It?

Easy! Use the blink tag **<BLINK></BLINK>**. Any text enclosed by these tags will go off and on like the emergency flashers on your car. I'll wait here while you try this real fast; you probably think that I'm kidding.

Second: Why Do It?

The blink tag is the most maligned tag in HTML. I think that it came out when people were hungry for any form of animation or movement on a Web page, and it got overused. It really does get annoying and makes things hard to read. Also, it is not supported by all browsers.

I used to have this tag on our college Web page for important telephone numbers, such as for registration. I took it off after getting threatening e-mails and crank phone calls at three in the morning. I was sure that I was being followed by someone who kept flashing lights on and off in my rear view mirror. (Some people take all of this Web stuff very seriously and play for keeps.) At any rate, all of the above problems stopped as soon I took off the blinking text. Use at your own risk!! (The blink tag is no longer supported by Internet Explorer.)

Font Tags

Netscape initially came out with the font tags **<FONT></FONT>**, and these are now widely supported. Like the **<H></H>** tags, the font tags can be used to change the size of text. Font tags can be used to change the color of text and even specify a particular font. Unlike the **<H></H>** tag, the font tag does not force a break after the text that it encloses. We can use the font tag in the middle of a sentence. I will give examples of this shortly.

The font tag changes only the text that it encloses. For example:

<FONT>Dogs eat cats</FONT>

By itself the tag doesn't do anything; it must be given **"Attributes"** for size, color, or face (type face). An attribute is an option that can be used within the tag. An attribute is usually followed by a "**Value**," indicating a specific choice within the range of choices for that attribute. All of the font attributes can be nested within a single font tag.

Size Attributes

To change the size of text, enclose it with the font tags. After the word **FONT** in the opening tag, leave a space and include **SIZE=N** where "N" is any number between 1 and 7. The number 1 is the smallest size text size and 7 is the largest text size. (Default text size is about 3 on the font scale.)

Examples

<FONT SIZE=1>Cheese Brain</FONT>

Cheese Brain

<FONT SIZE=2>Cheese Brain</FONT>

Cheese Brain

<FONT SIZE=3>Cheese Brain</FONT>

Cheese Brain

<FONT SIZE=4>Cheese Brain</FONT>

Cheese Brain

<FONT SIZE=5>Cheese Brain</FONT>

Cheese Brain

<FONT SIZE=6>Cheese Brain</FONT>

Cheese Brain

<FONT SIZE=7>Cheese Brain</FONT>

Cheese Brain

Face Attribute

The face, or typeface, attribute can be used to tell the browser in which font to display designated text.

Normally, the font typeface that you see when you are looking at your Web browser is a default font. This is designated in the options for your browser. These options can be changed, and you can choose to surf using any font that you have on your machine.

However, if I want you to see something in a particular font typeface, such as Helvetica, I can enclose the text with the following font tags and attributes

<FONT FACE="HELVETICA"> Dog Breath</FONT>

Face is the attribute and Helvetica is the value.

Notice the use of quotations around the value of what is being specified, "HELVETICA." They are essential.

If everything works, you should be seeing the words "Dog Breath" displayed in Helvetica. This of course depends on one important requirement: **You must have Helvetica on your computer.** This is the drawback to using designated typefaces. If you don't have the designated typeface, your browser will display the text using your default typeface.

You might be asking the question, "Why not design my page for the people who have the right fonts, and let the rest of the world see it however they see it?"

The problem is that they may see your page in a way that may not only appear poorly designed, but may not even be readable. When designing Web pages, we should be designing them so that the maximum number of people see that same information in the same way. In fact, this is one of the biggest challenges in Web design. I never use the face attribute, and I probably will not until standard fonts are more widely supported. I also have developed a burning desire to increase my control over what others see.

One area where designating the typeface is probably more predictable and useful is Web pages that will be used primarily on an Intranet. The Internet is a global entity; computers connected all over the world. There is no way to maintain precise standards, such as a common standard set of fonts. An Intranet is a network more focused and often closed to the outside world. For example, a large company might have an internal network with which they communicate and do business using a Web server. In this instance, it is easier to maintain standards, and know what kinds of fonts are available to users.

Color Attribute

I saved color for last because color is a little more complicated. The principle of including an attribute and value within the font tag is basically the same. The color of text can be changed by enclosing the text in font tags. The word FONT is followed by a space and the attribute "COLOR" followed by an equal sign (=) followed by the value of the color desired expressed as *Hexadecimal numbers,"* enclosed in quotations (""). Did I say all of that?

This is what it looks like

```
<FONT COLOR="#hexadecimal color number">Colored Word</FONT>
```

The hexadecimal number must be preceded by a number sign (#)

What the Heck is a Hexadecimal Number?

I found a very comprehensive explanation of the reasons for using a hexadecimal numbering system in a book that was about 900 pages long and decided that for our purposes we do not really need to know. It has something to do with nybbles. . . .

Well, here is my version to at least get us started.

We have ten fingers and ten toes. It only makes sense that our numbering system should be based on ten. I don't want to offend anyone, but I have found that computer people are a little odd in the way that they do things sometimes. Hexadecimal values for color are based on a 16-number numbering system, 0-15.The only thing that I can figure out is the guy that came up with this must have had eight fingers on each hand.

In writing out hexadecimal numbers, everything works fine for 0–9. However, when we get to 10-15, we have double-digit numbers, and for some reason this does not work in the computer scheme of things. At this point, letters are introduced A=10, B=11, C=12, D=13, E=14, F=15.

Together it looks like this

0 1 2 3 4 5 6 7 8 9 A B C D E F

What Does This Have to Do with Color?

We're getting there, be patient!

The color that we see on the computer screen is made from red, green, and blue, called *RGB color*. When we want to specify a color, we must do so by telling the computer how much red, green, and blue to mix to achieve the desired color. We can have up 255 values for each color.

For example, the RBG color values for the following colors are

Red:	255,0,0
Green:	0,255,0
Blue:	0,0,255
Black:	0,0,0
White:	255,255,255

The difficulty is that computers do not understand RGB values until they have been converted into hexadecimal numbers.

As you can see from Figure 5.1, hexadecimal values for describing color consist of three pairs of numbers, for a total of six numbers. The first two numbers are the value for red, then green, then blue. Each number in each pair has a value range from 0–15. Remember 10 or above are double-digit numbers and are replaced by A–F.

00 is the absence of a color, and FF indicates an RGB value of 255.

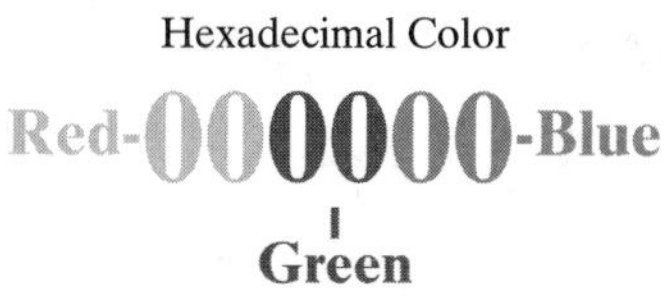

Hexadecimal Color

Red-**000000**-Blue

Green

Figure 5.1 The first two numbers are red values, the second two are green, and the third two are for blue.

Color	Hexadecimal Value	RGB Value
Red:	#FF0000	255,0,
Green:	#00FF00	0,255,0,
Blue:	#0000FF	0,0,255
Black:	#0000000	000
White:	#FFFFFF	255,255,255

Figure 5.2

For comparison, shown in Figure 5.2 are the hexadecimal color values and their corresponding RGB values for some basic colors.

About now, you might be thinking, "How much of this stuff do I really need to know to be able to use color on my Web page?"

Fortunately, not very much. The Internet is loaded with generous people who share information, and as a result there are any number of color charts that show hexadecimal numbers.

 On the Prentice Hall Web site, you will find a chart that enables you to select hexadecimal colors or make conversions between RGB color and hexadecimal colors. There are additional links to other color-related resources and a discussion and example of "Browser Safe Colors."

Using Color

After all of the explanation of hexadecimal color and RGB color above, using it is really quite simple. To change the color of text using the font tag, we would first go to the color chart and copy the correct hexadecimal value for the color we want to use.

We enclose the text whose color we want to change within the font tags. Leave a space after the word FONT, and add the COLOR attribute followed by an equal sign (=) followed by the hexadecimal color value in quotations (""). Remember, the hexadecimal color value must be preceded by a number (#) sign.

Example

<FONT COLOR="#99FFFF">Powder Blue</FONT>

We should see:

Powder Blue

Many colors can be indicated by entering the name of the color rather than its hexadecimal number value.

Example

<FONT COLOR="BLUE">BLUE</FONT>

We should see:

BLUE

The color names listed in Figure 5.3 are recognized by HTML Standard 3.2 and can be safely used instead of the hexadecimal number.

In searching the Internet you will undoubtedly be able to find many lists of additional colors that can be entered by name. Remember, the color names may not be as widely supported as those listed above.

Nesting Attributes

One of the really useful qualities of the font tag is that more than one attribute can be defined within the same tag. For example, if I want to change the size, color, and typeface of text, I can do it this way

```
<FONT COLOR="#FF0000" SIZE=5

FACE="IMPACT">HELP!</FONT>
```

The Result (if you have Impact font on your computer)

Help!

Remember to put a space between **FONT** and the attributes that you are adding.

Try to recreate the following word and the color effect as an exercise.

FONT

Make the "F" red.
Make the "O" blue
Make the "N" green.
Make the "T" turquoise blue.

The HTML and a colored example are included on the Prentice Hall Web site.

Black	Navy	Silver	Blue
Maroon	Purple	Red	Fuchsia
Green	Teal	Lime	Aqua
Olive	Gray	Yellow	White

Figure 5.3

Other Applications of Color

Until now, you have been looking at the default colors for your page. For example, the background of your page is gray, and the text is black. It's time to change some of that. The colors of all of the page elements that I have listed below can be changed, and the changes are made in the **<BODY></BODY>** tag. You might think of the body tag as the color "control panel" for the page.

- Background color
- Text color for the whole page
- Link colors
- Visited link colors
- Active link colors

To Change the Background Color of the Page

You will probably get very tired of the drab gray default page background. There is something about that color that makes a page look unfinished. Before you change the color of your page, you should give it some thought. What are the colors of the text and graphics on the page? If you have dark text and change to a dark-colored background, you will lose contrast and make it hard to read your text. It is very easy to run across examples of this mistake on the World Wide Web. In my opinion, you should strive for clarity and simplicity, at least in the beginning. Changing the background color of your page is quite easy.

Inside the **<BODY>** tag add the attribute "BGCOLOR," followed by the hexadecimal color that you want the background to be.

For example, to achieve a black page background.

```
<BODY BGCOLOR=" #000000 "></BODY>
```

To Change the Text Color

The default text color for a Web page is black. Let us say that you really like the way a black body background looks. If you do not change your text color, you will not be able to see anything. Rather than having to place font tags around everything, to change the color, we can simply change the default color in the body tag to white.

Inside of the **<BODY>** tag add the attribute "TEXT," followed by the hexadecimal color that you want the background to be.

For example, to achieve a white page background.

```
<BODY TEXT="#FFFFFF"></BODY>
```

To Change the Link Color

You will find that once you start making changes, things snowball; you have to change everything. The link color is the color that hypertext links appear on your page. The default color is a dark blue, which probably won't show up very well on our black background. Let us change the link color to red.

Inside the **<BODY>** tag add the attribute "LINK," followed by the hexadecimal color that you want the link to be.

```
<BODY LINK="#FF0000"></BODY>
```

To change the Visited Link Color

Once you have gone to a site, the next time the hypertext link to that site appears on a Web page, it will appear a different color than the regular link color. This is your browser's helpful way of reminding you that you've "been there, done that." On my browser the visited link color is purple. Since we have a red link above, let us change the visited link to orange.

Inside the **<BODY>** tag add the attribute "VLINK," followed by the hexadecimal color that you want the visited link to be.

```
<BODY VLINK="#FF6600"></BODY>
```

To Change the Active Link Color

When you click on a hypertext link, there is a momentary change of color, just to let the user know that something is happening. That is the active link color. We will make our active link color yellow.

Inside the <BODY> tag add the attribute **"ALINK,"** followed by the hexadecimal color that you want the active link to be.

```
<BODY ALINK="#FFFFOO"></BODY>
```

To Change All the Colors in the Body Tag

For the purpose of illustration I have changed the various color attributes of the body tag individually. In practice, all the changes would be made at once by nesting all of the attributes within the body tag, as in the final example

```
<BODY BGCOLOR="#000000" TEXT="#FFFFFF"

LINK="#FF0000" VLINK="#FF6600"

ALINK="#FFFF00"></BODY>
```

The above will be the defaults for the entire Web page.

We have made some important decisions with the changes that I have just introduced. It is imperative that you test everything you do. Developing a good Web page is a process of constant tweaking, until everything comes together just right.

Important points of this chapter:

- Blinking text**<BLINK></BLINK>** Perhaps most important to use sparingly.
- The use of the font tag **<FONT></FONT>** and how it differs from the **<H></H>** tags.
- The use of hexadecimal colors and how they are determined from RGB.
- How to use color in the font tags **<FONT></FONT>.**
- How to use color in the body tags**<BODY BGCOLOR TEXT LINK VLINK ALINK></BODY>**

Visit the Prentice Hall Web site:

- There is a great deal of information on color and the conversion of color from RGB to hexidecimal color values. There is a discussion of "browser safe" colors and six color charts of browser safe colors accompanied by their RGB and Hexidecimal values.
- There is a list of recommended activities and assignments to improve your skills working with the font tags and the use of color.
- There is a short quiz to test your knowledge on the information in this chapter.

CHAPTER 6

Horizontal Rules, and More about Text

Horizontal Rules

Paragraph and Heading Alignment

Preformatted Text

Text Styles

Previous chapters have primarily dealt with how to format and structure text. There are a few additional points that need to be covered before we move on. This chapter will cover horizontal rules, additional means of aligning text, and some important means of changing text style.

Horizontal Rules

The shadowed line directly above this heading is a horizontal rule. It is commonly used on Web pages to break the page into sections for better organization. The method for achieving the horizontal rule is the **<HR>** tag, which is another "singlet," meaning it does not have a closing tag.

The HTML

    <HR>

The Result

NOSHADE Attribute

Notice that the default horizontal rule appears with a slight shadow to make it appear three-dimensional. On a page design that already has a linear pattern, the default shadowed horizontal rule doesn't display very well. The shadow can be eliminated by including the "NOSHADE" attribute in the **<HR>** tag.

The HTML

    <HR NOSHADE>

The Result

A solid line.

Width Attribute

Notice that the default horizontal rule is almost as wide as the page, maybe about 90 percent. If you make the page wider, the rule will stretch and maintain the same proportion to the width of the screen.

You can control the width of the horizontal rule in one of two ways

1. Give the horizontal rule a fixed width in pixels. If for some reason I want the horizontal rule to have a specific width that doesn't change as I stretch the screen, I can give it a fixed width by defining how wide it will be in pixels.

How do I know how many pixels wide to make it? I don't even know how big a pixel is!

The average 13-inch monitor will open a Netscape page about 490 pixels wide. (This is something that we have to keep reminding ourselves so that we design for the "masses.") Let's say that my life won't be complete until I have a horizontal rule 50 pixels wide.

The HTML

    <HR WIDTH=50>

The Result

Do your worst; stretch your screen, compress your screen, that horizontal rule is going to remain 50 pixels wide

2. Give the horizontal rule a percentage width. As I have already pointed out, the default width for the horizontal rule is almost 90 percent of the page. You can control the width proportionally by defining the width as a percentage.

The HTML

```
<HR WIDTH=50%>
```

The Result

When you stretch the screen, you will see that the horizontal rule stretches so that it will always be 50 percent of the original default horizontal rule size.

Size Attribute

You can also control the thickness of the horizontal tag. The default is approximately 2 pixels. To increase the thickness, increase the number of pixels in the size attribute.

The HTML

```
<HR SIZE=10>
```

The Result

Combining Attributes

The horizontal rule attributes can be combined as in the following example.

The HTML

```
<HR NOSHADE WIDTH=50% SIZE=10 >
```

The Result

You can also control the alignment of the horizontal rule. Remember, the default alignment on a Web page is left and rarely has to be defined. The other options are center and right. I have specified the width in the following example, added "NOSHADE," and increased the size so the results are more obvious.

The HTML

```
<HR SIZE=5 WIDTH=200 ALIGN=LEFT

NOSHADE>
```

The Result

The HTML

<HR SIZE=5 WIDTH=200 ALIGN=CENTER NOSHADE>

The Result

The HTML

<HR SIZE=5 WIDTH=200 ALIGN=RIGHT NOSHADE>

The Result

Paragraph and Heading Alignment

We have already used the paragraph tags **<P></P>** and the heading tags **<H></H>**. In the section above, I demonstrated how the horizontal rule **<HR>** could be aligned left, center, or right by including the align attribute in the **<HR>** tag.

In a similar fashion, alignment of paragraphs and headings can also be controlled by including the align attribute into the **<P></P>** or **<H></H>** tag. Examples are shown below.

Left Alignment

The HTML

<P ALIGN=LEFT> Peter Pan Loves Tinkerbell**</P>**

The Result

Peter Pan Loves Tinkerbell

Remember that the default alignment is to the left and rarely has to be entered.

Center Alignment

The HTML

<P ALIGN=CENTER> Peter Pan Loves Tinkerbell**</P>**

The Result

Peter Pan Loves Tinkerbell

Right Alignment

The HTML

<P ALIGN=RIGHT> Peter Pan Loves Tinkerbell**</P>**

The Result

Peter Pan Loves Tinkerbell

The results will be similar using the **<H>** tags.

Left Alignment

The HTML

<H2 ALIGN=LEFT> Peter Pan Loves Tinkerbell</H2>

The Result

Peter Pan Loves Tinkerbell

Center Alignment

The HTML

<H2 ALIGN=CENTER> Peter Pan Loves Tinkerbell</H2>

The Result

Peter Pan Loves Tinkerbell

Right Alignment

The HTML

<H2 ALIGN=RIGHT> Peter Pan Loves Tinkerbell</H2>

The Result

Peter Pan Loves Tinkerbell

Preformatted Text

Sometimes you will want to incorporate text into your Web page that has a specific formatting, and you want to preserve that formatting. Perhaps it has been created in a word processing program and the formatting is important.

Let's use poetry as an example. Poets don't write like the rest of us—they want to have their writing broken up into a lot of odd length lines, and often these lines have all sorts of odd spacing. It's kind of a code to be able to distinguish the real poets from the normal people.

The preformatted text tag **<PRE></PRE>** will enable you to display text while maintaining its original formatting. On the rare occasions when I have used **<PRE>** , it seems to work best if you copy and paste your original formatted text into your HTML document and then enclose it with the **<PRE>** tag. Occasionally, I have had some difficulty getting the final text displayed on screen to behave precisely the same as my original formatted text. This might vary depending upon the browser. In other words, I don't think that the **<PRE>** is always playing with a full deck.

Many word processing programs promise to convert your text documents "magically" to HTML documents. For the most part, what they're doing is putting the **<PRE>** tags around everything.

To illustrate the use of the **<PRE>** tag I have included short example, from an original poem. Before viewing the poem, please read and agree to the following.

(Any attempts to copy or reuse this poem, or parts of this poem, in any form other than that for which it was originally intended, or to profit financially by its publication without my written consent, will result in legal action, and potentially severe penalties under the law. This of course does not apply to anyone who is considering this poem for a Pulitzer Prize.)

```
A Cosmic Revelation
The
   silence bore
down on
        HIM like
a piano
    d
    r
    o
    p
    p
    e
    d
(Splat!)
from a
                three
                story
             building.
```

As you can see, the full universal meaning of this poem demands that it is in its correct physical format. If I simply copy and paste the text into my Web page, it will look like the following:

```
A Cosmic Revelation The silence bore down on HIM like a
piano dropped (Splat!)from a three story building.
```

I am sure that you will agree that to read my poem like this would be like viewing the Mona Lisa with sunglasses on.

To make sure that my poem is viewed as I had intended, all I have to do is enclose the poem with the preformatted text tags as below:

The HTML
<PRE>

A Cosmic Revelation

The
   silence bore
down on
         HIM like
a piano

         d
         r
         o
         p
         p
         e
         d

(Splat!)

from a
             three
             story
             building.

<PRE>

The Result

A Cosmic Revelation

The
   silence bore
down on
         HIM like
a piano

    d

    r

    o

    p

    p

    e

    d

(Splat!)

from a

              three
              story
              building.

My poem will appear just as it appears in my first example since it is enclosed in the **<PRE></PRE>**.

Text Styles

The following section lists some of the tags that are used to change text styles. Many others are listed in the Style Sheet in the appendix.

 See the Style Sheet in the appendix for examples of the different text styles and visit the Prentice Hall Web site for more information relating to this topic.

There are two categories of style tags:

1. **Logical** style tags are those whose appearance is controlled by the preferences in the viewer's Web browser.

2. **Explicit** style tags are those where the author specifies the text appearance.

You will notice a good deal of similarity between some of them. Logical style tags are considered to be more standard, with more predictable results.

Logical Style Tags

Emphasis

The HTML

But Tinkerbell loves <EM>Captain Hook.</EM>

The Result

But Tinkerbell loves *Captain Hook.*

(Usually displayed as italic)

Strong Emphasis

The HTML

But Tinkerbell loves <STRONG>Captain Hook.</STRONG>

The Result

But, Tinker bell loves **Captain Hook .**

(Usually displayed as bold)

Citation

The HTML

But Tinkerbell loves <CITE>Captain Hook.</CITE>

The Result

But Tinkerbell loves *Captain Hook.*

(Usually displayed as italic)

Explicit Style Tags

Bold

The HTML

But Tinkerbell loves <B>Captain Hook.</B>

The Result

But Tinkerbell loves **Captain Hook .**

(Usually displayed as bold)

Italic

The HTML

But Tinkerbell loves <I>Captain Hook.</I>

The Result

But Tinkerbell loves *Captain Hook.*

(Usually displayed as Italic)

Typewriter

The HTML

But Tinkerbell loves **<TT>**Captain Hook.**</TT>**

The Result

```
But Tinkerbell loves Captain Hook.
```

(Usually displayed as mono-spaced font)

The above tags can be used together. Try using emphasis and strong emphasis together to achieve a bold/italic, such as the example below

This is emphasis and strong emphasis combined.

I have listed the most commonly used style tags; there are many other style possibilities listed in the Style Sheet in the appendix. Please take some time to look them over; try them and see how they work.

Important points of this chapter

- Horizontal rules, created by using the singlet **<HR>**, are commonly used for page organization and design.
- Some attributes of the horizontal rule that can be used with the **<HR>** tag are WIDTH, SIZE, and NOSHADE.
- The three alignment options for paragraphs and headings are LEFT, RIGHT, and CENTER. These attributes are included within the **<P> </P>** or **<H></H>** tags, as in the following example: **<P ALIGN= CENTER></P>.** Remember that LEFT alignment is the default alignment and rarely needs to be specified.
- The preformatted text tag **<PRE></PRE>**, allows you to display text, while preserving the original formatting.

- There are two categories of text style tags: logical, where text appearance is controlled by the browser's preferences, and explicit, where the author specifies the appearance of the text.

Visit the Prentice Hall Web site:

- For more information on text styles and related subjects.
- There is a list of recommended activities and assignments to improve your skills in working with horizontal rules, alignment, and text styles.
- There is a short quiz to test your knowledge on the information in this chapter.

CHAPTER **7**

URLs: Uniform Resource Locators

Hypertext

Anchor Tags

Uniform Resource
Locator (URL)

Name Attribute

Mailto: Link

It's time for you to become part of the growth of the WWW.

> In the last few years, Internet growth has been explosive. Thousands of
> new users are connecting to it every day. Hundreds of new Internet service
> providers have come into business, offering the public low-cost connec-
> tions. A design that permitted no centers of authority has become the
> largest functioning anarchy in the world. Now, the World Wide Web is
> here; it's the ideal way to organize the Internet's diverse resources.
>
> *Larry Aronson,* HTML3 Manual of Style, *Ziff-Davis Press, 1995*

Mr. Aronson's comments, written in 1995, sound almost like understate-
ment only two years later. The world map in Figure 7.1 illustrates how truly

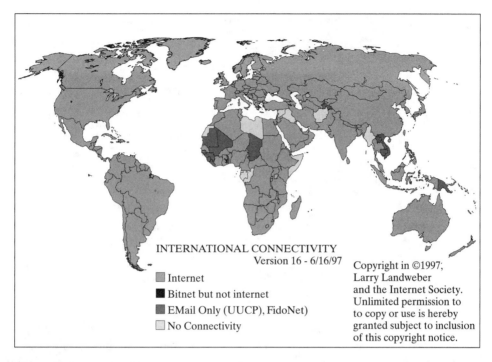

INTERNATIONAL CONNECTIVITY
Version 16 - 6/16/97

Copyright in ©1997;
Larry Landweber
and the Internet Society.
Unlimited permission to
to copy or use is hereby
granted subject to inclusion
of this copyright notice.

☐ Internet
■ Bitnet but not internet
■ EMail Only (UUCP), FidoNet)
☐ No Connectivity

Figure 7.1

global the Internet has become. Only a few countries in the entire world cannot be accessed through the Internet.

The growth of the World Wide Web has been equally explosive, as is illustrated by the chart in Figure 7.2. In June 1995, the year that Mr. Aronson wrote the above statement, there were 23,500 World Wide Web sites. In August 1997, approximately the time that I am writing this chapter, there are 1,269,800 sites, representing a growth of 5400% since 1996. From January 1997 through June 1997, only a six-month period, the number of sites almost doubled.

The Internet and the World Wide Web are expected to grow until all 5 billion people on this planet have access to them. The ability to link computers and information globally will theoretically result in our ability to communicate with every other human being on this planet.

To find out more about the history of the Internet and the World Wide Web visit the Prentice Hall Web site.

You might ask, "What do those statistics have to do with me?" Well, you're about to become an important part of the growth of the Internet.

We often hear the Internet called the "Information Superhighway." We can get on it and travel to any place in the world. In that context we might

WWW Growth:

Date	Sites	Date	Sites	Date	Sites
06/93	130	07/96	299,403	2/97	739,688
12/93	623	08/96	342,081	03/97	883,149
06/94	2,738	09/96	397,281	04/97	1,002,612
12/94	10,022	10/96	462,047	05/97	1,044,16
06/95	23,500	11/96	525.906	06/97	1,117,255
01/96	100,000	12/96	603,367	07/97	1,203.096
06/96	252,000	01/97	646,162	08/97	1,269,800

Hobbe's Internet Timeline Copyright (c) 1993-7 by Robert H Zakon
Available at: http://info.isoc.org:80/zakon/Internet/History/HIT.html

Figure 7.2

consider the Web pages that we have been constructing as "cul de sacs" on that highway. We can pull into them and out of them, but they don't take us anywhere else. We are about to change that by adding hyperlinks to your pages—linking your pages to the fast lane and to the rest of this global community.

Hypertext

Links on a Web page are most often achieved through the use of *hypertext*. Hypertext is text that is connected or "hyperlinked" to other information on the World Wide Web. When clicked upon, you will be taken to the information that the link is anchored to.

    Hypertext is colored and underlined to set it off from the rest of the text. The default color for hypertext is blue, but it can be changed as you learned in the last chapter by changing the link's color.

Anchor Tags

Essential to creating hypertext links is the anchor tag**<A></A>.** The anchor tags enclose text that will become the hypertext link. For example, if I want to create a hypertext link from this page to the White House's home page, I start by enclosing the text with the anchor tags

```
<A>White House</A>
```

By themselves, the anchor tags don't do anything; they must contain information that indicates where the White House home page is located. We need to add an attribute to the tag that has the address. This attribute is called the **Hy**pertext **REF**erence, or **HREF.**

HREF Attribute

The **HREF** is included in the anchor tag, preceded by a space and followed by an equal sign, followed by the address, or URL in quotations. Be sure that the link is concluded by the close anchor **</A>** tag.

For Example

    <A HREF="address">White House</A>

The address or location of information on the Internet is called its *URL*.[1]

Uniform Resource Locator (URL)

URL is an acronym for *Uniform Resource Locator,* which is the computer name for "Web address." I don't know why they just didn't just call it Web address to start with. There are two types of URLs: absolute and relative.

Absolute URLs

An absolute URL gives the precise location of a resource on the World Wide Web. It includes the following information in this order

1. The protocol or method to be used to access the information.
2. The name of the computer (server) that contains the resource.
3. If required, the port number to be used on the server.
4. The directory path within which the resource is contained.
5. The resource file name.
6. Specific named element in the HTML document.

An Example of an Absolute URL

Let's look at an example of an absolute URL and analyze it a little. Once again we'll pick on the White House. Below is the URL or Web address for the White House:

---

[1]Important Tip: Trying to be cool and appearing to know what you're talking about is extremely important in this computer stuff. URL is pronounced *U.R.L.* It is not pronounced *YERL,* as I once did and was guffawed out of the room.

http://www.whitehouse.gov/WH/Welcome.html

http

The URL begins with "**http,**" which describes the protocol or method that the browser is to use to create the link. **HTTP** is another acronym—it stands for *Hypertext Transfer Protocol,* which is the protocol used by Web servers and browsers that allows them to communicate.

The "http" is always followed by a colon and two slashes and the address of the computer (server) to which you are connecting, in this case the White House.

http://whitehouse.gov

The word "gov" in the address indicates that this is a government agency (not to be messed with). "edu" indicates an education address, "org" indicates an organization such as March of Dimes, and "com" indicates a commercial Web site.

The above address will take us to the White House. But we actually want to go to a specific resource within the White House Web site, so we add the *directory path* to the address. In this case, the visitor page is located in a directory called "WH." and the filename of the visitor page is called "Welcome.html."

http://www.whitehouse.gov/WH/

The final addition is the name of the file that we want to see, which in this case is called, "Welcome.html." The complete URL is as follows:

http://www.whitehouse.gov/WH/Welcome.html

This process is summarized in Figure 7.3.
Now, let's back up a little and complete the link to the White House. It should look like the following:

The HTML

<A HREF="http://www.whitehouse.gov/WH/Welcome.html" >The White House</A>

Figure 7.3

The Result

The White House

When the link is created, it will show up on your Web page as hypertext, or the underlined text as above. If you were on your computer and clicked on the link, you would be transported to the White House. Pretty simple, huh?

Relative URLs

When links are made between files that reside on the same server and in the same directory, only a partial address or URL is required. For example, the directory on the server where my home page resides is called "paul." Inside of the directory I have two files, my home page, with the file name "index.htm," and another page called "my life.htm" (guaranteed to be exciting reading). I have an additional folder for my images. It is always a good idea to create an image folder rather than dump your images and Web pages into the same folder.

When we look at my open directory, what we see is shown in Figure 7.4.

I would like to create a link between the "index.htm" file and the "mylife.htm" file. Since they are both in the same root directory on the same server, I do not have to include the complete address including the server name. This is called *relative URL addressing*. All of the other information is taken from the open document. The link to "my life.htm" from index.htm would look like the following

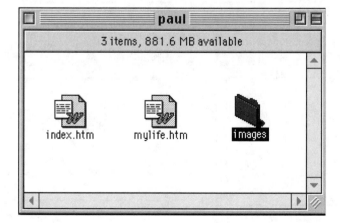

Figure 7.4

The Text

Click here to read about my life.

Create the link

Click here to read about <A HREF="mylife.htm"> my life.</A>

The Result

Click here to read about my life.

To use relative URLs requires some knowledge of the directory structure in the server. For example, I have a friend named Joe, who also has a Web page on our server. I would like to link to his page. His page is not located in the same directory as mine, but in a directory called "joe." Both of our directories are located in the main directory, called "web." When we open the Web directory, this is what we see (Figure 7.5):

For me to link to Joe's page, I must tell the browser to go from my directory, up to the Web directory, and down into Joe's directory to get his page. Figure 7.6 shows the process.

We have to create a map for the browser to follow, much like I have mapped the path above. To make this map we must go up in the directory structure. Two periods and a forward slash are used (../) in the relative URL. This tells the browser to first go up to the Web directory. Next we need to indicate the directory where the file is located, which is called "joe," (../joe). Finally, we need to indicate the file name, "index.htm" (../joe/index.htm).

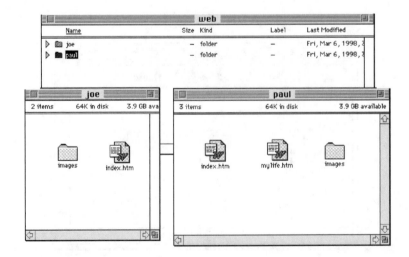

Figure 7.5

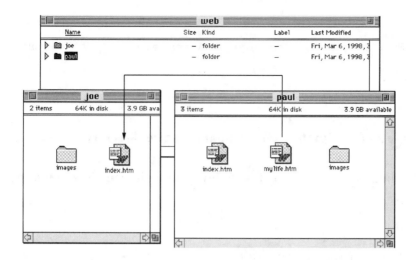

Figure 7.6

The relative URL to Joe's "index.htm" page from my "index.htm" page is:

../joe/index.htm

The link would look like the following:

The Text

Please take some time to visit my friend Joe's page.

The HTML

Please take some time to visit my friend<A HREF="../joe/index.htm"> Joe's page.</A>

The Result

Please take some time to visit my friend Joe's page.

If you were viewing this online, you would immediately jump to my friend Joe's page where you would have to listen to his Midi rendition of "She'll be comin' round the mountain when she comes."

To Review

A quick summary of the mechanics:

To create a link to another Web site, the complete Absolute URL must be included.

To link to the White House

The HTML

<A HREF="http://www.whitehouse.gov/WH/Welcome.html"> The White House</A>

The Result

The White House

To create a link to another page within the same directory, a Relative URL is used.

To link "index.htm" to "mylife.htm," the following link would be placed on "index.htm".

The HTML

Click here to read about <A HREF="mylife.htm"> my life.</A>

The Result

Click here to read about my life.

A Few Words of Advice Regarding File Names.

When you connect to a server using a Web browser and ask for a directory, the server will look inside of that directory to see if there is a default file that it should automatically open. The name of the default file varies from server to server. The default file on my college server is called "index.htm" or "index.html." If you have named the home page of your website "index.htm" or "index.html," it will automatically be opened without the filename being specifically named in the URL. Since default file names vary, you will need to check with the system administrator to find out the default file name for your home page.

For example: my home page is located at

http://www.cc.cc.ca.us/web/paul

Notice that the URL ends with a directory name, not the file name of my page. The server knows to open, by default, my page called "index.htm."

If I were to change the file name of my home page, I would have to add the file name to the URL.

For Example

If I were to call my home page "filename.htm," I would have to include the name of my home page in the URL.

http://www.cc.cc.ca.us/web/paul/filename.htm

You will find it helpful if the folder and files that contain our HTML pages on your hard drive have the same names and directory structure as the folders on your Web server. For one, it is simply one less thing to remember. Additionally, when you transfer pages or even whole folders to your Web site, the directory and file names will be the same, ensuring that your links work. It also makes it easier to update your pages, because you can simply overwrite your previous pages with the same file names.

Some Important Things to Remember

The following image (Figure 7.7) is the most overused and unpopular statement on the World Wide Web.

When you get this page it indicates that you have encountered a broken link, meaning a link that is not connected to any information. There are three primary reasons why a link may be broken:

1. The author of the page entered the URL incorrectly.
2. The user entered the incorrect URL into the browser.
3. The information no longer resides in the same location on the World Wide Web.

When copying a URL, copy it exactly. I never try to type long involved URLs. I always highlight them, and copy and paste. It's the best way to copy them accurately. Even a slight error will give you the message above.

As a Web author, it is very embarrassing when someone sends you an e-mail indicating that one of your links is bad. I speak from personal experience. *Be sure to test all of your links before you submit your page.*

Testing is accomplished in the same manner as previewing your page, with the exception that you must be online with your ISP to test links to other Web sites. Open your Web page in your Web browser and simply try each link to make sure that it connects correctly.

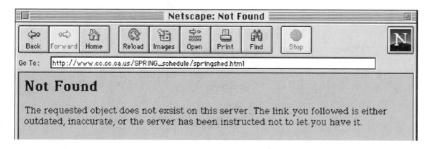

Figure 7.7

URLs do not have any spaces in them. Name all of your directories and files without any spaces in their names.

File names are case specific. For example, if I name a file "Page.html," and I try to link to it as "page.html," I will get an error message. For this reason, it is a good idea to get into the habit of always naming files the same way, such as all lowercase, first letter always a capital, or the like. In this way you will have an easier time remembering file names. By convention I try to maintain all lowercase files on my Web site.

Name Attribute

Linking to the Same Page

You will occasionally find the need to link from one place on a Web page to another location on the same page. For example, suppose that we have a page that has so much information that it makes it impractical to scroll through the page to locate a particular topic. It would be helpful to have a hypertext index at the top of the page, so that when we click on a topic we will jump to the related information on the page. It might look like the diagram in Figure 7.8 of a page called "topics.htm."

Our goal is to make the index at the top of the page into hypertext links to the topic headings further down on the page. The first step is to give the topic headings "names" to link to from the index. Topic headings have been made all caps to make the example clearer. The topic heading is first enclosed by the anchor tags **<A></A>.**

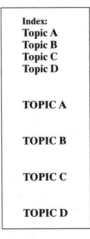

Figure 7.8

For Example

    <A>TOPIC A</A>

Next the name attribute is included into the anchor tags.

For Example

    <A NAME>TOPIC A</A>

Next the topic heading is given a name, enclosed in quotation marks.

For Example

    <A NAME="A">TOPIC A</A>

These steps are repeated until all of the topic headings are named.

It will look something like the following:

    <A NAME="A">TOPIC A</A>

    <A NAME="B">TOPIC B</A>

    <A NAME="C">TOPIC C</A>

    <A NAME="D">TOPIC D</A>

Linking the Index

The next step is to create links from the index to the topic headings. The index item is enclosed with anchor tags **<A></A>** and the **HREF** attribute:

For Example

    <A HREF>Topic A</A>

The name of the topic heading to be linked to is included in the anchor tag, preceded by a number (#) sign.

For Example

    <A HREF="#A>Topic A</A>

When all of the links are created from the index, the HTML will look like the following:

    <A HREF="#A">Topic A</A>

    <A HREF="#B">Topic B</A>

    <A HREF="#C">Topic C</A>

<A HREF="#D">Topic D</A>

When we put all of this together, we will have a document whose HTML looks like the following:

Index

<A HREF="#A">Topic A</A>

<A HREF="#B">Topic B</A>

<A HREF="#C">Topic C</A>

<A HREF="#D">Topic D</A>

<A NAME="A">TOPIC A</A>

<A NAME="B">TOPIC B</A>

<A NAME="C">TOPIC C</A>

<A NAME="D">TOPIC D</A>

The page will look and function somewhat like the diagram in Figure 7.9.

Index

When Topic A is clicked in the index, we will jump to TOPIC A on the page, and so on.

Notice that the topics in the index have changed color and are now hypertext links. However, the topic headings on the page do not look any different even though they now have names attached to them.

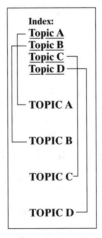

Figure 7.9

Linking to a Location on Another Page

It can be quite useful to jump from one page to a specific location on another page. Let us assume that I want to create a link from my "index.htm" page to the page that is called "topics.htm." Rather than connecting to the top of the topics page, I want to link directly to TOPIC C. In other words, I want something that looks like the diagram in Figure 7.10.

The first step is to name the part of the "topics.htm" page to which I want to link. I have already named TOPIC C on the "topics.htm" page, but to review: Enclose the text with anchor tags **<A></A>.** Include the name attribute followed by a name in quotations.

The HTML

    <A NAME="C">TOPIC C</A>

Now I want to create the link from the text on the "index.htm" page. I will make the entire sentence, "Visit TOPIC C on the topics page," the hypertext link. First, I will create the link from "index.htm" to "topics.htm." Since they are in the same directory, the relative URL will be quite simple.

The HTML

    <A HREF="topics.htm">Visit TOPIC C on the Topics Page</A>

If I leave the link as above, when I click on the sentence, it will take me to "page.htm," but to the top of the page, rather than to TOPIC C. I need to add the anchor name to the file name preceded by a number sign (#).

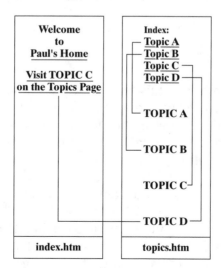

Figure 7.10

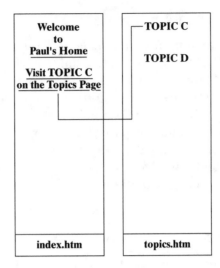

Figure 7.11

The HTML

```
<A HREF="topics.htm#C">Visit TOPIC C on the topics page</A>
```

The result will be similar to the diagram in Figure 7.11. My text has now become a hyperlink as indicated by the blue color and underline. When I click on it, I now jump directly to TOPIC C, which as you can see on the "topics.htm" page, has loaded to the top of the screen.

Mailto: Link

With Web authorship comes this bizarre desire for self-affirmation, the approval of others, and a need to know what surfers *really* think about your Web page, no matter how destructive that might be to your self-esteem.

We have the perfect tool to facilitate our noble search for **feedback!**

It is called the "mailto:" link. (It is more accurate to define "mailto" as a protocol.)

E-mail is a great way to make contact with people who have similar interests as yours. You should always include someplace on your page for visitors to make contact with the author of the page, in other words, you. I'm sure that you have all seen the messages at the bottom of Web pages telling you to send your comments to the "Webmaster." Clicking on that text launches a mail window, with the address filled in, and all you have to do is enter your comments and hit send.

Here is how you set it up:

On your page use your name for the text that is to be linked; in my case Paul Meyers. The name is enclosed with an anchor tag **<A></A>** with an HREF= in the opening tag, followed by mailto: and the e-mail address where you want the message sent, all enclosed in quotations. This is what it should look like

The HTML

For comments on my page, please contact

<A HREF="MAILTO:pmeyers@cc.cc.ca.us"> Paul Meyers</A>

The Result

For comments on my page, please contact Paul Meyers.

Try it, it works!

Important Points of This Chapter

- Hypertext is text that is connected or "hyperlinked" to other information on the World Wide Web.
- The anchor **<A></A>** tags are used to create hyperlinks.
- The two attributes used with the anchor tags are the **NAME** and **HREF** attributes. **NAME** is used to link to specific points in a document and **HREF** is used to link to a new document.
- A URL, Uniform Resource Locator, is the virtual address of a Web site.
- Absolute URLs give an exact location of a Web site, whereas Relative URLs give the location of a document within the current directory.
- When copying a URL, be sure to copy it exactly and remember that URLs do not have any spaces in them.
- File names are case specific.
- The mailto: protocol is a simple, but not universally supported, method of receiving feedback on your Web site.
- An important thing to remember in HTML authoring is to always check your links *before* you FTP your Web page.

Visit the Prentice Hall Web site:

- To learn more about the history of the Internet and the World Wide Web.
- There is a list of recommended activities and assignments to improve your skills working with URLs, anchors, and mailto:.
- There is a short quiz to test your knowledge on the information in this chapter.

CHAPTER **8**

Graphics Files

Image Tags

Graphic File
Formats

File Sizes

Respect Copyrights!

Well, we've gotten through a series of chapters that have primarily had to do with text and links. Now it is time to learn how to add graphics to your Web page. (I'm sure that you're saying, "It's about time!") I'm also sure that it's not necessary for me to describe the advantages of including graphics to dress up your page and to visually enhance what you are trying to communicate.

By graphics, I mean any type of still, pictorial imagery. It can be a picture or a design that you have created in a drawing or paint program. It can be a piece of clip art that you've gotten from the Web or from another source. The graphic may be a photographic image of you, your family, your business, or products that you are selling. Graphics may be used as links to other sites, as backgrounds, as bullets, and as horizontal rules. We will cover these possibilities and more in the following chapters.

While the HTML to add graphics is quite simple, there are many peripheral issues that we will need to cover. Topics such as file types, sizes, color, editing, uploading, linking to files, and others will also be considered in these chapters. While it is beyond the scope of this book to do more than briefly touch on the most important and immediate graphics needs, learning how to edit graphics is important in designing pages for the World Wide Web.

Preparing or editing graphics for use on a Web page often requires the use of special graphics software. The premiere software for image editing is Adobe PhotoShop. It is an expensive program and includes many very sophisticated features required by graphic artists in order to produce commercial artwork. While PhotoShop is a fantastic program, PhotoShop is not required to accomplish most of the fundamental editing required for Web page graphics.

I recommend two graphics programs for getting started, one for the Macintosh and one for the PC. They are both inexpensive and easy to learn to use; they are both shareware,[1] and are available for download on the World Wide Web. Both programs are quite powerful and will perform most of the functions that you need for editing graphics intended for use on the Web. As you spend time on your own working with these programs, you will become more comfortable and adept at editing your images. The examples on graphics in this book include screen shot examples using both programs.

 Visit the Prentice Hall Web site for links to the recommended graphic programs.

- The program for the Macintosh is called *Graphic Converter.* It can be found on the World Wide Web by doing a Netsearch, or you can go to the Prentice Hall Web site for the current location for downloading.
- The Program for Windows on the PC side is called *PaintShop Pro.* It can also be found on the World Wide Web through a Netsearch, or the current location can be found at the Prentice Hall Web site.

Image Tags

Let's jump right into this and give away the most important part first: the HTML for including graphics on your Web page.

---

[1]Shareware is a unique form of marketing that allows you to try software before actually having to buy it. Usually available over the Internet, the software can be downloaded, tested, and if you decide not to keep it, there is no cost involved. However, if you decide to keep the software, you are obligated to pay for it. It is one of the last remnants of doing business on the "honor system," and it is important that we are all responsible in the use of shareware. Otherwise we might see the end of the independent and creative software developers who have made such an important contribution.

I have a picture that I want to include in this part of the document. It has the filename "cow.gif." To include the picture on this page I use the **<IMG>** tag, which is another singlet (not requiring a closing tag), in the location where I want the picture to appear. Inside of the **<IMG>** tag, preceded by a space, I include the attribute SRC, referring to the source or location of the image. The SRC attribute is followed by an equal sign (=) and the URL, in quotations, for the location of the graphic file. It looks like this

```
<IMG SRC="location of graphic file">
```

The HTML

```
<IMG SRC="cow.gif">
```

The Result (Figure 8.1)

Figure 8.1   A brief interjection: You might remember the eccentric Harry Peabrain. This picture was to be used as a kind of "poster child" on hamburger packages, in one of Harry's campaign's to locate "missing cows." Somehow it just never caught on.

Important Points

As you can see, linking to images is quite simple—or is it? The above example illustrates some very important points that must be understood.

- An image is not actually included within the Web page; it is linked to from the page's HTML. The actual location of the image must be accurately included in the image tag.
- Most of your Web development will probably take place on your desktop computer and your files will be transferred to a Web server. For your links to continue to work on the server, the files must be in the same relative location as they were on your desktop, including your graphics.
- Not only must you upload your Web pages to the server, you must also upload your graphics files to the server.
- The above image has the suffix "gif." Image files must be of the proper file format; either GIF, or JPEG.

Directory Structure and URLs

Let's do a brief review from Chapter 7. The diagram below is how my Web pages are stored on both the server and my desktop. Notice (Figure 8.2) that I have a folder called "images." It is really a good idea to put all of your graphics files into a separate images directory for good organization.

The example that I gave above to link to the graphic, "cow.gif" is repeated below.

    <IMG SRC="cow.gif">

Let's assume that I want to link to the graphic from my home page, or "index.htm." The graphic link <IMG SRC="cow.gif"> would only work if the cow image and the "index.htm" page were located in the same directory.

As I pointed out above, we want to store our graphics in a separate folder called "images."

To link from "index.htm" to the "cow.gif" located in the directory "images," the HTML would be:

    <IMG SRC="images/cow.gif">

As illustrated in Figure 8.3, when the browser opens the "index.htm" page, it reads the image link to the "cow.gif" image, goes to the image folder, and loads the image onto the Web page.

In many school situations, students are not allowed to save files on the hard drive; files are usually saved onto a floppy disk. It is still important to maintain the organization of files that is described above.

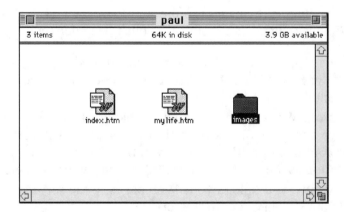

Figure 8.2

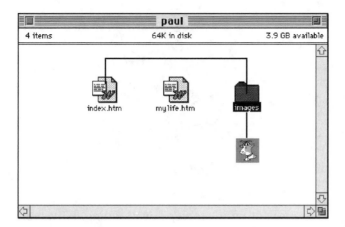

Figure 8.3

Graphic File Formats

Henry Ford was quoted as saying, "You can have any color car you want, as long as it's black." In Web design you can have any picture you want as long as it's in a GIF or a JPEG format.

What Does That Mean?

Graphic files contain a lot of information and tend to be quite large. Using large files really slows down how fast your page will load for viewing. To make the transfer of graphic files practical, compression is used to make the file smaller. The GIF format, or Graphic Interchange Format, was the first form of compression developed for viewing files over the Internet on CompuServe, which is why it is oftentimes called the CompuServe GIF. It is pronounced as both "jif" or as "gift" without the "t." Since it was the first form of compression, it is the most widely supported file format.

JPEG, or Joint Photographic Experts' Group, is the other form of compression that is widely supported. (Wouldn't you like to have been a fly on the wall in one of the meetings where these names are chosen?)

The only graphic files that are widely supported on the Internet are either in the GIF or JPEG format. Files that are in other graphic formats can be converted to GIF or JPEG, using graphic software such as that recommended above.

Which of the two formats is best? Each format has its advantages and disadvantages: Since GIF was the first compression format, it is the most widely supported. GIF compression usually does not compress files as small as

Figure 8.4

JPEG compression, resulting in slower downloading. However, GIFs decompress faster, resulting in the files opening faster. The newest form of the GIF format, GIF89a, supports interlacing. Interlaced GIFs appear gradually on the screen in increasingly sharper layers, holding the attention of the viewer.

Transparent GIFs

The GIF89a format also supports transparency, meaning one color in the image can be made transparent, so that it appears the same color as the background. Let's call back our cow image, but in its original form with its gray background (Figure 8.4).

The GIF89a format allows one color in an image to be selected and made transparent. The image is opened in a graphics program, the color intended to be transparent is selected, and the image is saved in the GIF89a format.

The Result (Figure 8.5)

Figure 8.5

You can see that this is quite useful for integrating odd-shaped graphics on to a page without the awkward-looking background box around the image. Such graphics can also be very useful as buttons.

One of the big disadvantages of the GIF format is that it only supports 256 colors. Images converted to the GIF format must first be converted to 8-

bit color. This makes the GIF format less suitable for photographic images, which normally have a much wider color range.

GIF Animations

Visit the Prentice Hall Web site for examples of and links to GIF animations.
Another fun and exciting feature of the GIF89a format is the possibility of creating GIF animations. GIF animations are created in a way similar to that of movie animations. A series of images are created, each representing a frame in the animation. To create a sense of movement, each frame is slightly different from the previous frame. For example, if we wanted to show a ball bouncing, the ball would be in a slightly different position in each frame, with enough frames to show the full motion of the ball. When viewed rapidly in sequence, it appears that the ball is moving. Next, the frames are loaded into a small program that compresses them to a single GIF file that when viewed through a Web browser appears to be animated.

Programs for Creating GIF Animations

For the PC: *Animagic Gif Animator,* available on the World Wide Web[1] as shareware.
For the Macintosh: *GiffBuilder,* available on the World Wide Web[1] as shareware.

JPEGs

The JPEG format supports millions of colors and generally creates smaller file sizes than GIFs; however, JPEGs decompress more slowly. JPEGs are usually more suitable for photographic images, since photos tend to be larger files initially and require more than 256 colors. JPEG is a "lossy" compression, meaning that some information is lost during compression. This is generally a disadvantage for many simple graphic images, but does not necessarily negatively affect photographic images. Most graphics conversion software allows you to set a JPEG's compression.

- The greater the compression, the smaller the file size, but the greater potential loss of image quality.
- The less the compression, the less image quality will be lost, but the larger the file size. (The significance of file size will be dealt with shortly.)

---

[1]Both of these programs can be located by doing a Web search, or by visiting the Prentice Hall Web site where current locations are listed.

The JPEG format does not support interlacing or transparency; however, there is a new format called Progressive JPEG that does support interlacing. Progressive JPEGs are not as universally supported by all browsers as are GIFs or JPEGs.

OKAY, OKAY!!! What do I use?

Probably the best the guideline to follow when deciding which format is most appropriate is:

- If you are using a photograph or other graphic image requiring more than 256 colors, use the JPEG format.
- Otherwise choose GIF.

File Sizes

I recently conducted an informal poll asking people what they thought were the five most important qualities of a good Web site. Without exception, everyone included that the page should "load quickly." By "load" I mean how quickly the information is transferred from the server to your screen. Many factors affect load time:

- The efficiency of the server, which could include bandwidth and how busy the server is.
- The type of connection that you are making, either over a network or via a modem, and the speed of the modem.
- The processor speed of the computer on which you are working and many other factors.

The factors that I listed above are not really under our control as Web authors. One important factor related to load time that is our direct responsibility is the size of the files that are being transferred. How quickly a page loads is a direct result of the types of information and the sizes of the files that are included on the page.

- Pages containing only text load very quickly, but can be dull, not holding the attention of the reader.
- The opposite can also be true. Pages can be rich in graphics, but load so slowly that no one waits around to see them.

You will want to be very careful about the size and number of graphic images that you include on your page.

The following elements of graphic files all affect file sizes and need to be considered carefully when including graphics on a Web page.

Resolution: Since your images are intended to be viewed on the computer screen, they should not have greater than 72 dpi resolution, which is also screen resolution. A higher resolution will not improve the appearance of the image; it only makes the file size larger.

Color: The larger the number of colors that you are using in your graphic, the larger the quantity of information needed to display it—thus, the larger the file size. Your graphics program will allow you to modify the color depth. Keep in mind that a large number of viewers can only see 256 colors on their monitors, and your images that contain millions of colors will be lost to them.

Size: Carefully consider the physical size of the image. Scale it down as small as you can but still have it be effective. Consider the use of "thumbnails" for large images so that you give the viewer the choice whether to load a big picture, based on a smaller preview image. We will cover how to do this later.

Careful Cropping: Use your graphics program to crop your images, in order to eliminate any unneeded information. Get right down to the "meat and potatoes" of what you're trying to show. This will help considerably in reducing the file size and probably improve your images, particularly if they are photographs.

Number: Having too many images can be as bad or worse than having large images. The file sizes add up and cause the page to load more slowly. Try to keep the number of images down to what is really important to communicate your idea. If you don't, you run the risk of losing your audience and communicating nothing.

I will briefly readdress these issues later when we discuss editing graphics.

Sources of Images

By now you're ready to start slapping some pictures onto your Web page, but you wonder, "How am I going to get my favorite picture of my 97-year-old aunt Harriet bungee jumping topless, from the Coit Tower in San Francisco on President's day onto my Web page?" You've tried gluing it to the screen, and that doesn't work. You even tried folding it up and sticking it in through the floppy drive slot. In other words how can you get your images into a digital format, so that they can be used on the computer?

Scanning: A process that electronically records text or images in a digital form. Desktop scanners have gotten very inexpensive, and if you plan to do much Web development, you might consider buying one. Make sure that you get one that includes an OCR program that converts text to a digital editable form and an imaging program like PhotoShop. Many copying businesses now do scanning as well as printing digital materials but it is somewhat expensive.

Digital Cameras: Digital photography is a rapidly growing technology. Relatively inexpensive cameras, capable of good quality pictures for Web work, are now available. The pictures can be transferred directly to your computer.

Photo CDs: The next time you take your film in for developing, you might ask about photo CDs. For a price, you can have your pictures digitized and put onto a CD-ROM, in addition to getting prints. I've never done it, but I understand that the price is reasonable and the quality is good.

Commercial Clip art and Photographic CDs: If you go to any computer outlet, in the software departments you will find commercial clip art and photographic CDs for sale. They are usually royalty-free, although you should read the fine print carefully if you intend to use the images for commercial purposes. It's a competitive market and the prices can be quite low. I saw a package of 65,000 clip art images on eight CDs for only $35.00. Be careful when buying clip art to be sure that it is in a file format that you can use on your computer.

Other Graphic Resources

The possibilities that I have listed above pertain to getting external sources for graphics onto your computer. There are also many sources for graphics that already reside on your computer or on the Web.

Create Images

Using your graphics program you can create your own artwork. These can be buttons, banners, drawings, scenes, and so on. A very simple but effective use of graphics is to create a heading for your page using a special font. For example, you can get away from the monotony of your browser font just by typing a heading into your graphic program and saving it as a GIF image such as the one shown in Figure 8.6.

Web Resources

Clip Art and Image Archives

There are literally hundreds of clip art and image archives on the Web where you can download buttons, bars, and images related to almost any topic.

Buffo's Bird Brainded Page

Figure 8.6

Figure 8.7

I have developed a fairly comprehensive list of links to online graphics resources. This list is available at the Prentice Hall Web site.

"Appropriating" Images

It is a simple matter to copy any graphic that you see on the Internet. Let's pretend that you saw the cow image that I have been using for this chapter on a Web page. Suddenly you become compulsive about having the image and putting it on your page. You literally become obsessed with it; you have to have that cow image but you don't know how to get it.

You have two choices:

- Seek counseling for "obsessive cow image desire disorder."
- Or simply hold your cursor over the image of the cow (Figure 8.7), click, and hold your mouse button down. (Right click your mouse if you are on a PC.

If you are on a Macintosh you will get a window that looks like Figure 8.8.

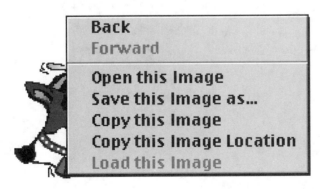

Figure 8.8

By Selecting

Open this Image: You will get a Netscape window with only the image.

Save this Image as . . .: Gives you a dialog box where you can rename and designate where on the hard drive you want to save the image file.

Copy this Image: Copies the image onto your clipboard, from where you can paste it into another location.

Copy this Image Location: Copies the URL for the image to your clipboard. This can be useful if you want to include images on your page that actually reside on the computer at another site.

If you are on a PC, you will get a window that looks like Figure 8.9 with similar options for saving the image to your computer.

Linking to an Image at a Remote Location

The image that you want to use does not necessarily have to be on your server for you to able to include it on your home page. For example, it is possible to link to the picture of the White House on the White House home page and

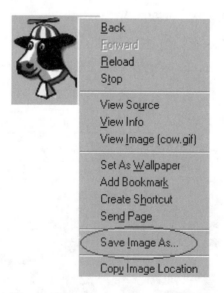

Figure 8.9

have the image show up on my home page (Figure 8.10) To accomplish this, I first visit the Web page on which the image is displayed. The White House's URL is: http://www.whitehouse.gov/WH/Welcome.html.

I then click on the image that I want to show up on my page (right click on the PC) to bring up one of the dialog boxes shown in Figures 8.8 and 8.9. After selecting "Copy Image Location," I paste the URL into my HTML as shown below:

```
<IMG SRC="http://www.whitehouse.gov/WH/images/bevel.gif">
```

The result will be the image showing up on my home page.
There are only two advantages to linking to remote images

- Your disk space is saved.
- The image may reside on a faster server.

The disadvantages far outweigh the advantages, however.

- You have no control over changes to the image.
- You are at the mercy of the remote server.
- You are adding a future unknown to your page.
- Depending on another site adds a second point of failure to your page.

Figure 8.10

Respect Copyrights!

While it is quite easy to appropriate images from the Web and from else-where, remember that someone usually owns those images and may not want them reproduced without permission or even some payment. This is particu-larly true if you are using them for commercial purposes. Please be careful and respectful of copyright laws!

The following statement was provided for this book through the generos-ity of Archie K. Lytle IV, an attorney and Web author. It defines one's re-sponsibilties regarding copyrights and offers excellent advice regarding how to protect your own original materials.

Intellectual Property and the Internet

Software, files, programs, graphics, audio, and video resources placed on the Internet instantly become accessible to the public. Many individuals on the Internet don't mind giving these resources away, others place a higher value on them. If a resource creator values these resources, intellectual property laws help to protect against wrongful use from unauthorized indi-viduals. Intellectual property is a body of law, which includes patents, copyrights, trademarks, and trade secrets.

Extremely valuable resources placed on the net may require the assistance of an intellectual property lawyer to ensure the owner's rights are pro-tected, but there are some very simple ways to protect one's rights without an attorney. (Wow, do-it-yourself legal advice—$175 per hour back in the pocket.) A discussion of intellectual property could be a volume of books, but this discussion will be limited to simple tasks to protect intellectual property on the Internet.

A fairly simple, no cost or low cost, yet powerful, method of protecting the rights of the owner of resources on the Internet is by the use of the copy-right. In the United States, copyright protection can be used on any origi-nal work of authorship that can be fixed in any tangible medium of expres-sion. These include, literary works, musical works, pictorial, graphic, audio, and visual works. Copyright cannot be used to protect ideas, procedures, process, system, concept, principle, or discovery. Patents typically are is-sued to protect any novel, nonobvious, and useful machine, article of man-ufacture (or its unique appearance or design), or composition of matter or process. On the Internet, a copyright is commonly used to protect text, graphics images, video, and audio files, whereas a patent is more likely to protect software and hardware.

The copyright is simply adding the name of the copyright creator or owner, the year in which it was copywritten, and the word "COPYRIGHT" or © in a prominent location. For example, it is not necessary to place anything other than "© 1997 Archie Lytle" on a web page or digitized photograph to protect the copyright for Archie Lytle. Anyone copying that page or photo must request permission from Archie.

The copyright protects the authorship for the life of the author plus fifty years. Substantial similarity to copyrighted material plus access to the material is sufficient to show a copyright infringement. There is also legal significance on failure to recognize the copyright—in a law suit, the wrongful user of the copywritten material may owe the creator damages.

A more substantial way of protecting information is the use of a statutory copyright, which includes filling out a simple form and sending a $20 filing fee into the Register of Copyrights, United States Copyright Office, The Library of Congress. Penalties for violation of a copyright can include recovery of damages or even conviction, if the violation is willful and for purposes of commercial gain.

Copyrights are internationally recognized. Some countries require the reservation of rights to the copyrighter. Thus, adding "All rights reserved" to the "© date copyright creator" will ensure protection of the copyright in foreign countries as well. After reserving all rights, one may wish to grant certain rights to the user. In one website, the following text was placed to reserve most and grant some rights

© 1995–1997 Archie Lytle. All Rights Reserved. No portion of this electronic file or other electronic files within this site/server location may be reproduced in whole or in part in any form without the express permission of the author. Rights are granted for the limited purposes to 1. fair use, 2. viewing from the author's server location, or 3. a limited (30 day) caching of the file in a personal browser program

Copyrights are a great way to protect work the author considers valuable from unfair use.

Visit the Prentice Hall Web site for further information on copyright laws and other ways to protect your creations.

Important points of this chapter

- Shareware allows a user to try out a piece of software before having to purchase it.
- Be conscious of your directory structure in order to help keep your Web pages organized.
- The image tag **<IMG></IMG>** is used to insert graphics into your Web page.
- The two most common graphic file formats used on the Internet are GIF and JPEG.

- Transparent GIFs allow for one color in an image to be transparent.
- Animated GIFs can add movement and interest to your Web page.
- Remember to take into consideration the file size of your image and make an effort to reduce the size if possible by changing or altering the resolution, color, size (by cropping), and keeping the number of images to a minimum.
- There are numerous sources of images, some of which are scanning, digital photography, photo CDs, and clip art. You can also create your own, or find graphics through the numerous sources on the Internet itself.
- Linking to a remote image can save disk space on your Web site, but it also adds an element of possible failure and a future unknown that may be better to avoid altogether.
- Respect the copyrights of others as you would want them to repect yours.

Visit the Prentice Hall Web site:

- For links to the recommended graphic programs.
- For links and examples of GIF animations.
- To learn more about copyrights and other means of protecting your creations.
- There is a list of recommended activities and assignments to improve your skills working with images, graphic file formats, file sizes, and finding resources for images.
- There is a short quiz to test your knowledge on the information in this chapter.

More Graphic Information

This chapter is a "nuts and bolts," "no holds barred," "rough and tumble" lesson on using graphics. Background images, alignments, image size, linked images, and thumbnails will be covered.

Background Patterns

For this chapter we'll start by backing up a little. In the section on color, I described how to make a colored background by including the attribute BG-COLOR in the **<BODY>** tag. To achieve a yellow background, the HTML would look like this:

```
<BODY BGCOLOR="#FFFF00">
```

The result would be a Web page whose overall background color is yellow.

Many Web pages use a background texture rather than a color. Background images or textures are achieved by using a small graphic image that is "tiled" over the page to give the appearance of a uniform background. By using a small image, the file size remains small, and the page will load faster than if a single large background image was used.

Here's how it is done. Let's start with the following small GIF file of a texture. It's 100x100 pixels, and its file name is "texback.gif" (Figure 9.1)

Figure 9.1

I want my whole page to have this background, so I include the BACK-GROUND attribute in the **<BODY>** tag followed by the location of the graphic that I want to use as the background. (*Remember:* There is never more than one background tag for an HTML document. The attributes: BG-COLOR, BACKGROUND, TEXT, etc., are all included within the one **<BODY>** tag.)

The HTML

```
<BODY BACKGROUND="texback.gif">
```

The Result (Figure 9.2)

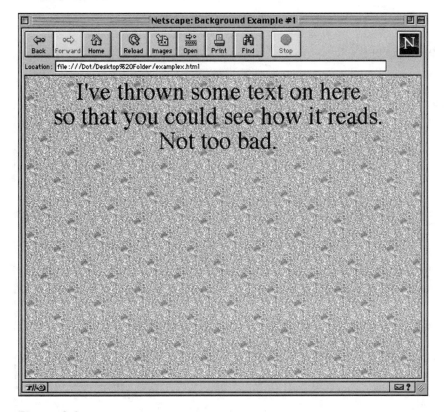

Figure 9.2

Let's do that all over again with a slightly different background image.

In this case I have put a border around the image in order to demonstrate what is really happening. The revised background image, "text-back2.gif," is shown in Figure 9.3.

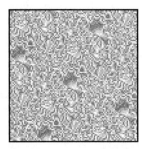

Figure 9.3

Using the Same HTML

<BODY BACKGROUND="texback2.gif">

The Result (Figure 9.4)

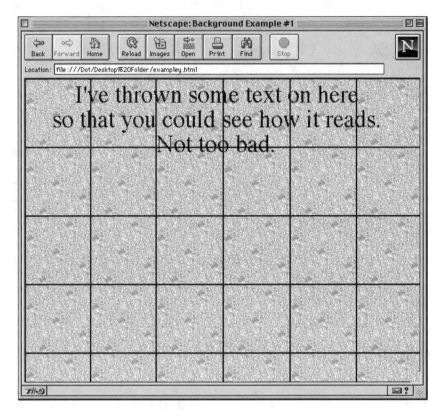

Figure 9.4

The above Web page nicely illustrates what is happening when a background image is used to create a textured background. The same texture image is being repeated or tiled over the page. The image really only downloads once, and since it is a small graphic file, the impact on the load speed of the page is very small.

One of the really big dangers in using background images is that if the background is too busy, it will make your pages more difficult to read. In my opinion this is one of the most commonly made mistakes on the World Wide Web. Take a look at the following example—which isn't even close to the worst that I have seen—and see how difficult it is to read the text on this page (Figure 9.5)

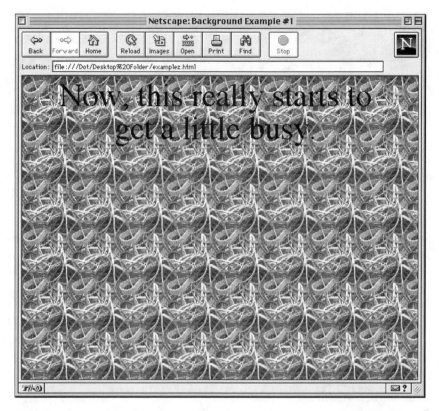

Figure 9.5

If you are not sure what to do regarding backgrounds, you can almost never go wrong if you just make the background white (unless, of course, you make your text white as well).

Any **GIF** or **JPEG** image file can be used as a tiled background. The size of the tiling is determined by the original dimensions of the graphic.

Visit the Prentice Hall Web site for links to sources for background images.

A Little Trick

A very popular page design on the World Wide Web today is the use of a colored vertical band on the left side of the page, which often contains a list of menu items. This effect is also created by tiling a background image.

In the example below, using a graphics program, I have created a very long and thin background image (Figure 9.6). The height is only 20 pixels, and the length is 1000 pixels.

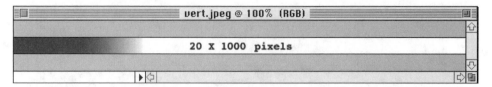

Figure 9.6

The file name is called vert.jpeg and the HTML is:

<BODY BACKGROUND="vert.jpeg">

Since the image is so long, it is only tiled vertically, creating a background similar to the one shown in Figure 9.7.

Figure 9.7

The Alternative Attribute

Text only browsers, such as Lynx, do not support images. Additionally, some people set their browsers so that images do not load in order to load pages more quickly. It is recommended that you include the ALT attribute within your image tag to accommodate these folks. The ALT attribute is followed by a name that describes your graphic. For example here's a face you might recognize, Rush Limbaugh (Figure 9.8).

Figure 9.8

The following illustrates how to create an alternative for text only users.

The HTML

```
<IMG="rush2.gif" ALT="Rush Limbaugh">
```

The result for text-only browsers will be to see the alternative text displayed as below

[Rush Limbaugh]

If the page is being viewed through a browser that has disabled the viewing of images, the following box and text will be displayed (Figure 9.9).

Alternative text should be short and to the point; a short descriptive title, no more.

Figure 9.9

Alignment

When an image is placed on a Web page, the image aligns itself with the text on the page and is subject to the same formatting rules. You have probably noticed that all of the graphics that I have used so far have been aligned to the left, the default alignment. Let's take Rush's picture and follow it with some text.

Example 1

The HTML

    <IMG SRC="rush2.gif">Rush Limbaugh, a controversial radio personality.

The Result (Figure 9.10)

Rush Limbaugh, a controversial radio personality.

Figure 9.10

Notice that the text follows right after the image of Rush, the same as it would have if the image had been text. The image is treated like just another word.

Example 2

This time let's put the picture in the middle of a sentence.

The HTML

Rush Limbaugh, <IMG SRC="rush2.gif"> a controversial radio personality.

The Result (Figure 9.11)

Rush Limbaugh,   a controversial radio personality.

Figure 9.11

The picture is inserted in the same way as if we had inserted a word.

Example 3

This time we place the picture to the right of the sentence.

The HTML

Rush Limbaugh, a controversial radio personality.<IMG SRC="rush2.gif">

The Result (Figure 9.12)

Rush Limbaugh, a controversial radio personality.

Figure 9.12

Vertical Alignment

In the previous examples, you have probably noticed that all of the above text has aligned itself at the bottom of the picture; that is the default alignment. If we want to change the vertical alignment of the text, we can use the ALIGN attribute within the image tag and designate TOP, BOTTOM, or MIDDLE for the test alignment.

Example 1

The HTML

Rush Limbaugh, <IMG ALIGN=TOP SRC="rush2.gif"> a controversial radio personality.

The Result (Figure 9.13)

Rush Limbaugh,   a controversial radio personality

Figure 9.13

Example 2

The HTML

Rush Limbaugh, <IMG ALIGN=MIDDLE SRC="rush2.gif"> a controversial radio personality.

The Result (Figure 9.14)

Rush Limbaugh,  a controversial radio personality.

Figure 9.14

Example 3

The HTML

Rush Limbaugh, <IMG ALIGN=BOTTOM SRC="rush2.gif"> a controversial radio personality.

The Result (Figure 9.15)

Rush Limbaugh,  a controversial radio personality.

Figure 9.15

Remember that the BOTTOM alignment is the default and doesn't require definition.

Text Wrap

The ALIGN attribute also allows text to wrap around an image. By defining LEFT or RIGHT, we can determine whether the image will be to the left or to the right of the wrapping text. For the following examples, and to achieve political balance, I have gone to the White House home page and downloaded a picture of President Clinton and an official, nonpartisan description of the President (Figure 9.16).

Figure 9.16

"Faster than a speeding bullet, more powerful than a locomotive, able to leap tall buildings in a single bound. And who, disguised as Bill Clinton, mild-mannered President of the United States of America, fights a never-ending battle for Truth, Justice, and the American Way."

(Gee, why does that sound familiar?)

This type of alignment really wastes space. It would improve the appearance of the page if we wrapped the text around the Clinton picture.

Example 1, Align Left

The HTML

<IMG ALIGN=LEFT SRC="Clinton.jpeg">"Faster than a speeding bullet, more powerful than a locomotive, able to leap tall buildings in a single bound. And who, disguised as Bill Clinton, mild-mannered President of the United States of America, fights a never-ending battle for Truth, Justice, and the American Way."

The Result (Figure 9.17)

Faster than a speeding bullet, more powerful than a locomotive, able to leap tall buildings in a single bound.

And who, disguised as Bill Clinton, mild-mannered President of the United States of America, fights a never-ending battle for Truth, Justice, and the American Way."

Figure 9.17

In the example above we have really put the squeeze on Old Bill with our text; the Secret Service is threatened by the encroaching text, and the text is more difficult to read. We can create space between the text and the wrapping text by using the VSPACE and HSPACE attributes. In Example 2, I will create a space to the right of the image by using the HSPACE attribute and give it a value of 30 pixels.

Example 2, Align Left Plus Space

The HTML

```
<IMG HSPACE=30 ALIGN=LEFT SRC="Clinton.jpeg">"Faster than a speeding bullet,
more powerful than a locomotive, able to leap tall buildings in a single bound. And who,
disguised as Bill Clinton, mild-mannered President of the United States of America, fights
a never-ending battle for Truth, Justice, and the American Way."
```

The Result (Figure 9.18)

"Faster than a speeding bullet, more powerful than a locomotive, able to leap tall buildings in a single bound. And who, disguised as Bill Clinton, mild-mannered President of the United States of America, fights a never-ending battle for Truth, Justice, and the American Way."

Figure 9.18

Looks better, doesn't it?

Example 3, Align Right

If we want the image on the right (which is where some people say Clinton has already gone), we do the following

The HTML

<IMG ALIGN=RIGHT SRC="Clinton.gif">"Faster than a speeding bullet, more powerful than a locomotive, able to leap tall buildings in a single bound. And who, disguised as Bill Clinton, mild-mannered President of the United States of America, fights a never-ending battle for Truth, Justice, and the American Way."

The Result (Figure 9.19)

"Faster than a speeding bullet, more powerful than a locomotive, able to leap tall buildings in a single bound. And who, disguised as Bill Clinton, mild-mannered President of the United States of America, fights a never-ending battle for Truth, Justice, and the American Way."

Figure 9.19

Additional Alignment

The ALIGN attribute in the image tag allows you to align your image to the text on the page. What if you want your image to be by itself without the text wrapping around it? Suppose that we want a short caption to appear directly below the image. We can use the **
** or the **<P>** tags to force the text to an area below the image.

Example 1

The HTML

<IMG SRC="Clinton.gif"><P>Bill Clinton,
President of the United States. </P>

The Result (Figure 9.20)

Bill Clinton,
President of the United States

Figure 9.20

Example 2

To center the image along with the caption, enclose the image tag, **<IMG>** and the text in a tag that allows alignment, such as the heading tag, **<H>**.

The HTML

```
<H3 ALIGN=CENTER><IMG SRC="Clinton.gif"><BR> Bill Clinton, President of the
United States.</H3>
```

The Result (Figure 9.21)

Bill Clinton, President of the United States

Figure 9.21

Image Size

The image tag also has HEIGHT and WIDTH attributes by which the display dimensions of the image can be designated. In keeping with our political theme, let's work with a picture of Newt Gingrich (Figure 9.22).

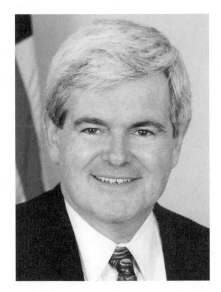

Figure 9.22

The above picture is 150 pixels by 200 pixels.

I can change the size that the image will appear on the Web page by changing the HEIGHT and WIDTH attributes of the image tag. For example to show the image one-fourth its original size:

Example 1

The HTML

```
<IMG WIDTH=75 HEIGHT=100 SRC="newt.jpg">
```

The Result (Figure 9.23)

Figure 9.23

What happens if we want the size of picture to be larger?

The HTML

<IMG WIDTH=450 HEIGHT=600 SRC="newt.jpg">

The Result (Figure 9.24)

Figure 9.24

Keep in mind that all we have done is resize the original 150 pixel by 200 pixel graphic. The good news is that we get a larger picture, and we are still only downloading a relatively small file. That's the good news. The bad news is, look at how badly the image is breaking up as we increase the size. We are attempting to cover a much larger area with the same amount of information.

Another way that we could use the HEIGHT and WIDTH attributes would be to start out with a larger image than we want to use on our page and display it as a smaller image. This might be a small advantage if we can't or don't want to convert the image's size in a graphics program. It is important to remember that even though the image will be smaller when displayed, the full file size of the larger graphic will have to be downloaded, and little has really been gained.

An important rule to follow:
Whenever possible, use your graphics software to resize your images to exactly the size that you want to display them on your Web page, ensuring the best resolution and load time. Avoid resizing your images using the HEIGHT and WIDTH attributes.

Keep in mind that those users with old, slow computers will take a long time to scroll the above image.

One Last Example (because I can't help myself)

What happens if we change the HEIGHT and WIDTH attributes disproportionately? Let's try it and see.

The HTML

```
<IMG WIDTH=300 HEIGHT=100 SRC="newt.jpg">
```

The Result (Figure 9.25)

Figure 9.25

I think that you knew that was going to happen!

Figure 9.26

Graphic Images as Links

Oftentimes you will want to use a graphic as a link to another page. An obvious example would be the use of buttons.

I have created a small button using an image of Hillary Clinton (Figure 9.26). (Examples were getting a little too male dominated.) I want to link from Hillary's button image back to her page on the White House Web site. The URL is:

http://www.whitehouse.gov/WH/EOP/First_Lady/html/HILLARY_Home.html

Example

I first place the button, called "hillary.gif," on the page using the **<IMG>** tag.

The HTML

<IMG SRC="hillary.gif">

Next I enclose the image with the **<A HREF></A>** tags to create a link.

The HTML

<A HREF="http://www.whitehouse.gov/WH/EOP/First_Lady/html/HILLARY_Home.html">
<IMG SRC="hilary.gif"></A>

The Result (Figure 9.27)

Figure 9.27

You will notice that the image now has a blue border around it, indicating that it is a Hyperlink. Clicking on the image causes it to behave like a button and transport you to Hillary's home page.

Thumbnails

Sometimes, if you have a large graphic, it is a good idea to give visitors to your page a choice whether to download and view the larger image. A common way to do this is to create a small version of the graphic, which is placed on your page and linked to the larger version, on another page. This way, the visitor can see a preview of the image and decide whether he or she wants to invest time in loading the larger version. For example, here's a thumbnail of my 80-room, 14-car-garage summer house (Figure 9.28). Since the image and file size are quite large, I present the viewer with a thumbnail preview and offer a choice.

Figure 9.28

Eliminating the Blue Border

Oftentimes you will not want a blue border around a button, particularly if it is an odd shape like the one in Figure 9.29.

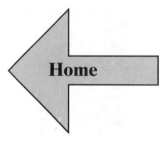

Figure 9.29

Suppose that I want to use the above arrow as a means of navigation on my Web site.

The HTML

<A HREF="index.html"><IMG SRC="home.gif"></A>

The Result (Figure 9.30)

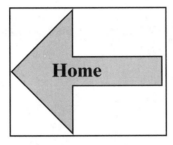

Figure 9.30

The blue border around the image indicates that it is a hyperlink. But it really looks dumb. To get rid of the blue border, we can enter the BORDER attribute into the image tag and give it a value of 0.

The HTML

<A HREF="index.html"><IMG BORDER=0 SRC="leftarrow.gif"></A>

The Result (Figure 9.31)

Figure 9.31

The image will still function as a hyperlink button, even though the blue border is no longer there.

Replacing the Horizontal Rule with a Graphic

Horizontal rules are about as boring as they can be. If you want to spiff up your page, you can use graphics to replace them. You can make horizontal rule graphics yourself or choose from thousands of different ones available on clip art sites.

Here's one that is a favorite among cowboys: (Figure 9.32):

Figure 9.32

To include it, you simply place the image tag linking to your graphic where you would have placed the HORIZONTAL RULE tag **<HR>.**

Visit the Prentice Hall Web site for links to resources for horizontal rules and other related clip art.

Creating Custom Bullets

When making lists, the choice of bullets gets a little boring also. You can replace bullets with any graphic by modifying the definition list, which is normally used for listing terms and definitions.

For example, I want to create a list of important things to do today.

The HTML

Important things to do:

<DL>

<DD><IMG SRC="pin.gif">Eat a big breakfast

<DD><IMG SRC="pin.gif">Eat a big snack

<DD><IMG SRC="pin.gif">Eat a big lunch

<DD><IMG SRC="pin.gif">Lose weight

</DL>

The Result (Figure 9.33)

Important things to do:

Eat a big breakfast

Eat a big snack

Eat a big lunch

Lose weight

Figure 9.33

Visit the Prentice Hall Web site for links to resources for bullets and other related clip art.

Important points of this chapter

- Background images are included within the **<BODY>** tag as in the following example: **<BODY BACKGROUND="backgound.gif">.** Backgrounds are tiled across the screen to fill the window. Depending upon their size, they are tiled either vertically or horizontally.
- Background patterns or textures are a great way to spice up your Web page, but be careful not to use a pattern that is so busy or blends too much with the text color that it is it difficult to read the text.
- It is customary to include the ALT, or alternative, attribute for those whose browsers do not support images, or for those who have disabled the viewing of images. The ALT attribute is included as in the following example:

  <IMG SRC="image.gif" ALT="image">

- Images can be aligned with the text on a page, much like other elements, in that they can be aligned to the LEFT, CENTER, or RIGHT. They can also be aligned to the TOP, MIDDLE, or BOTTOM. An example alignment is as follows:

  <IMG SRC="image.gif" ALIGN=TOP></IMG>.

- Text wrap allows text to wrap around an image to the left or right of the image.
- The image tag also has HEIGHT and WIDTH attributes that can be used to designate variable or precise values for an image.

- Remember to use your graphics software to resize your image to the exact size you intend it to be viewed on your Web page, which will save disk space and loading time.

- Graphic images can also be used as links by including the **<IMG></IMG>** tag within the **<A HREF></A>** tags. When an image is used as a link, it usually has a blue border around it, unless it is turned off by the author by including the BORDER attribute as follows:

    ```
    <IMG BORDER=0 SRC="image.gif"></IMG>
    ```

- It is generally a good idea to have thumbnail images if you have a site that contains several large file images. This gives the user the choice of whether to take the time to view the larger image. Thumbnails can be created in your graphics software program.

- Horizontal rules can be replaced with a graphic horizontal rule to spice up your page and make it more visually interesting.

- Custom bullets can be created from existing graphics or from images you create yourself. They can be used as graphics, hyperlinks, or both.

Visit the Prentice Hall Web site

- For links to sources for background images.
- For links to sources for bullets.
- For links to sources for horizontal rules.
- There is a list of recommended activities and assignments to improve your skills working with background images, text alternatives, alignment, image sizes, images as links, thumbnails, eliminating the blue border, horizontal rules, and creating custom bullets.
- There is a short quiz to test your knowledge on the information in this chapter.

Editing Graphics

Web page development requires an interesting combination of computer skills and a sense of aesthetics. One needs a reasonable level of technical ability and background to create a Web page, create the links, and make it all work. One also needs to have a sense of design and creativity to be able to communicate effectively in this very visual medium.

Building a Web page is an interesting opportunity for technically ori-
ented people to practice their skills at visual communication and for nontech-
nical people to apply their creativity to a somewhat technical endeavor. In
particular, preparing graphics for use on a Web page requires some unique
skills and special software. This chapter addresses some graphics-related concepts on a practical level, as well as step-by-step instructions in using the
graphics software that I recommended in the previous chapter.

Graphics Software

In previous chapters we've covered the basics of how to include graphic images on your Web page. I'd like to now cover some concepts having to do with
optimizing your graphics for use on a Web page. This normally requires doing
some editing to the graphic image, requiring the use of graphics or imaging
software. By editing I mean opening your images in your graphic software,
making the necessary changes, and saving the image in either the GIF or
JPEG format.

There will undoubtedly be many who read this book who will have had
little or no experience working with a graphics program. For this reason, I will
go step by step through the most important editing processes, demonstrating
the use of a Macintosh graphics program called Graphic Converter. It is not
possible to illustrate how all graphics programs work, but most of them are
very similar. This is not intended to be a definitive instruction on editing
graphics; the illustrations in the chapter are intended to be an introduction,
nothing more. If you already have experience working with a graphics program, you can probably go through this chapter rapidly, paying attention to
the types of editing that we will cover and why. Graphics programs are very
similar; it doesn't matter what graphics program you use, as long as it accom-
plishes your goals.

As I pointed out in the previous chapter, links for downloading these
programs are available on the Prentice Hall Web site.

What are your goals?

Your graphics program should be able to do the following:

- Open a number of different file formats and convert them to either GIF
  or JPEG.
- Change the resolution of your image to 72 dpi.
- Change the color depth of your image.
- Resize your image.
- Crop your image.

- Support transparent GIFs.
- Define coordinates on an image for the purposes of an imagemap.

The two shareware programs that I have recommended previously will do all of the above. I will briefly illustrate the steps to accomplish each of the above editing tasks, using the Mac software Graphic Converter. The steps are very similar in PaintShop Pro, but where they differ I will point out the differences. When I illustrate creating transparent GIFS, I will show examples from both types of software, since they are very different from one another in this task.

The step-by-step instructions for this chapter are repeated on the Prentice Hall Web site using PaintShop Pro in a Windows environment.

Opening and Saving a File

Opening a file and converting it to either a JPEG or GIF format.
Any image files that you get off the Internet will of course already be in one of these formats. However, if you are scanning images or getting the images from Clipart CD's, or other locations, you may have to convert the file format to GIF or JPEG to be able to use them on your Web page. This is quite simple to do.

Mac: Using Graphic Converter

Click on the icon to launch your software. At the top of your screen you will get a very simple menu bar.

Go to FILE→Open and you will get a window that looks like the one in Figure 10.1.

Use the selection box on the left to locate your file. When the correct file name is highlighted, the file will show up on the right as a preview. In keeping with the political theme of the last chapter, I have selected the "ape.pict" file, also known as "The Thinker." Click on Open.

Visit the Prentice Hall Web site for full color versions of the examples contained within this chapter.

Converting the File Format

The file that I have opened is in a PICT format, a common Mac graphic format. We cannot use this image on the Web as it is; we must convert it to either GIF or JPEG format first. To convert the file, all we have to do is to save it into the correct format.

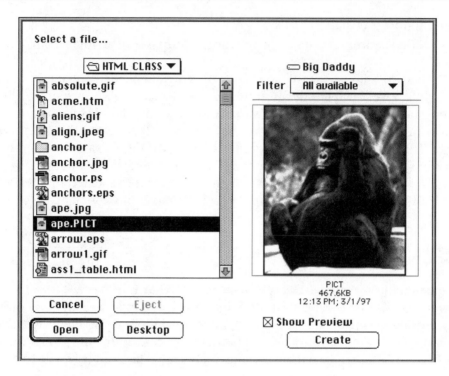

Figure 10.1

But first, let's look at the image as it is seen in the open Graphic Converter window in Figure 10.2. The Information box at the lower left of the image is packed with important information that we will find to be quite valuable shortly.

To save the file as a JPEG, go to the File→Save as... menu. You will get a box that looks like the one in Figure 10.3.

The circled box on the right is the file format in which you are saving the image. It is a dropdown menu with many possible file formats. I selected JPEG, but could have selected GIF from the same menu. Since I have selected JPEG, the program automatically places the suffix .JPG after the file name. (Note that it places the suffix name in caps. File names on the server are case sensitive; I tend to make all file names and suffixes lower-case so I don't have to rely on my memory.)

Select where you want the file to be saved; click Save, and you have just converted the file. It can now be uploaded and used on your Web page. You're probably not even breathing hard!

Figure 10.2

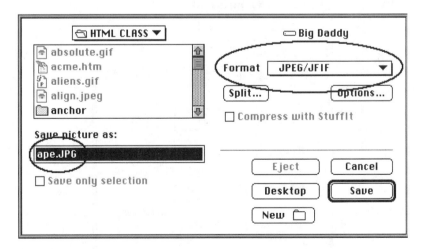

Figure 10.3

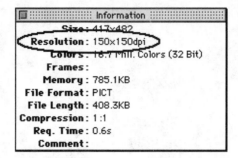

Figure 10.4

File Information

Now that we've converted the image to a JPEG, let's look at the information box to evaluate our image and determine if we can make some other changes to this picture to decrease the file size and improve the download time, without detracting from the quality of the image Figure 10.4.

Resolution

If we look at the resolution of the image we see that it is 150 dpi ×150 dpi (dots per inch). Since we are not going to print with our image, and since a computer monitor's maximum resolution is 72 dpi, we are unnecessarily increasing our file size by including information that we won't even see.

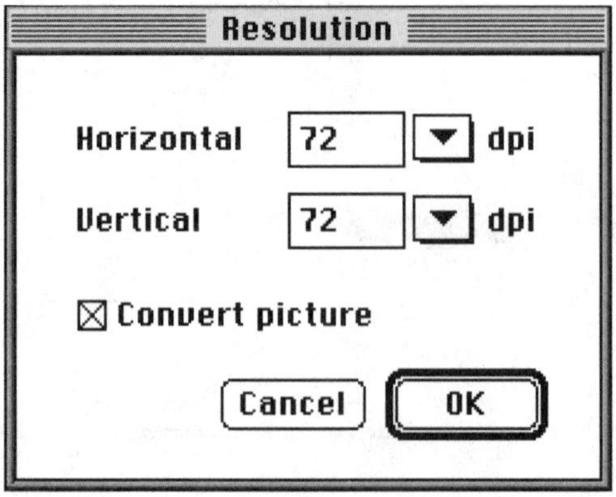

Figure 10.5

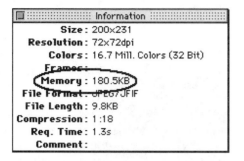

Figure 10.6

To change the resolution:
Go to the Picture Menu on the menu bar and select Resolution. (Picture→Resolution). You will get a small box that looks like the one in Figure 10.5. To change the resolution, use the arrows to move up or down the scale. I have already changed the resolution from 150 dpi to 72 dpi. Click OK.

Now, let's look at the information boxes for the image. Compare the information boxes for the image at the higher resolution, and the box for the image at the lower resolution, to see what has happened to the file size (Figure 10.6).

At 72 dpi the file size is about one-quarter of what it is at 150 dpi, meaning that the image will load four times as fast.

Color Depth

The next area that we should look at is the color depth. Do we really need millions of colors to adequately view this image? The best way to tell is to change the color depth in your graphic program and judge the result. To change the color depth go to the menu bar and select Pictures→Colors. You will get a list of options that allow you to change the color depth of your image. The possibilities are

- Change to B/W (1 bit)
- Change to 4 colors (2 bit)
- Change to 16 colors (4 bit)
- Change to 256 colors (8 bit)
- Change to 32,768 colors (16 bit)
- Change to 16.7 million colors (32 bit)

The option for each color you are currently working in will be grayed out.

In the following tests, I kept the JPEG quality settings constant, and dropped the color depth successively.

Let's look at the results (Figure 10.7).

Figure 10.7

As you can see from the above information boxes, the uncompressed file size is decreased by half each time the color depth is reduced. There is really no discernible difference in the image quality until it is reduced to 16 colors (4 bit), at which point the quality is unacceptable. For this image, 256 colors (8 bit) are acceptable.

The above image is a JPEG. GIF images are always 256 colors. If we wanted to save this image as a GIF, it would have to be reduced to 256 colors. Graphic Converter automatically does this when we select GIF from the File Format options for saving.

Resizing an Image

It is always best to generate your graphic files in the size that you will use them on your Web page. For example: If you are scanning an image, try to scan it in at the exact final size that is needed. While resizing a graphic can be easily accomplished in your graphics program, there will almost always be a loss in quality. If you are unsure of your final size when scanning images, it is far better to make them too large and to scale them down later than to make them too small and have to scale them up. In spite of best-laid plans, you will have occasion to have to resize images.

To resize an image, choose Picture→Size→Scale from the menu bar. You will get a dialogue box like the one in Figure 10.8.

You can resize your image as a percent of the original image by checking Factor and entering a percentage value in X and Y. If Proportional is checked, the values for both Width and Height will be the same. This means that the

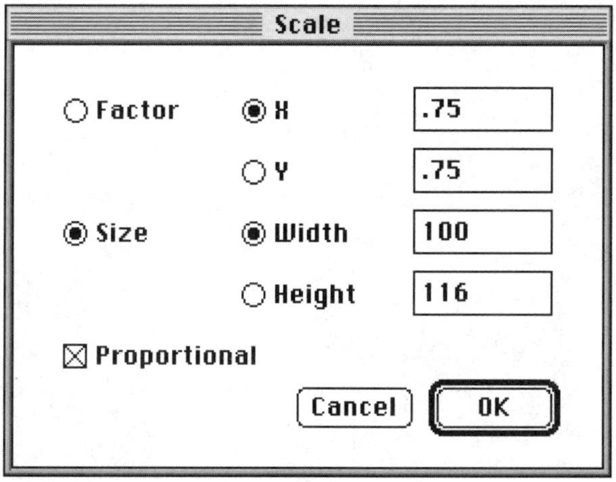

Figure 10.8

image will be Resized, maintaining its original proportions. There is rarely a time that you don't want your image to be resized proportionally. If Size is checked, you can designate the exact size in pixels that you want your image to be. The result of the above settings will be that my image will be scaled down to 75 percent of its original size.

Cropping an Image

In my often ignored opinion, cropping or eliminating unimportant information from an image is the most underused form of file size reduction. I can't even count the times that I have waited what seemed forever to load an image that was 95 percent background and 5 percent content. It is almost always a good idea to crop your image to improve the composition, eliminate unimportant information, or even to get rid of incriminating evidence. Cropping can improve the effectiveness of your images and can lower your file sizes considerably. Let's see if we can make this photograph a little more flattering by eliminating this guy's beer belly. Use the selection tool, as indicated in the picture below, to draw a box around the portion that you want to keep. (Figure 10.9)

Once selected, Choose File→Trim Selection, and your photograph will be cropped, as shown below.

Figure 10.9 Hey Mom, I'm on television!

Figure 10.10

Transparency

Transparent backgrounds on graphics files can be achieved only through the use of GIFs; more specifically the GIF89a format. Both of the graphics programs that I have recommended support the creation of transparent GIF images.

What do I mean by transparent backgrounds, and why are they useful? Let's look at the above example text heading that I have made as a graphic (Figure 10.10):

This would make a great heading for the top of a page, but it looks dumb with that big gray box around it. Transparent GIFS allow us to select one color in an image, usually the background color, and make that color transparent, so that the page's background can show through. If an image has only one background color, it is quite easy to convert it to a transparent GIF.

Select the file that is to be changed and open it in Graphic Converter. In the diagram below I have opened the same example file as shown above (Figure 10.11).

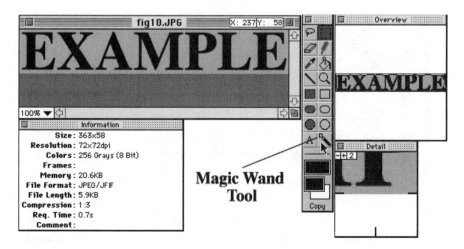

Figure 10.11

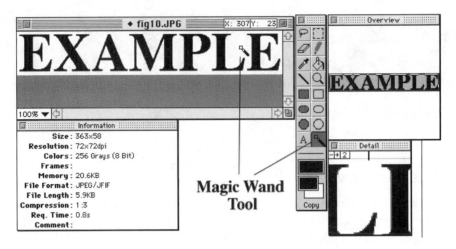

Figure 10.12

In the toolbar, where I have drawn the black line, you will see a tool that looks like a Magic Wand. Select the Magic Wand tool and click inside the area of the color that you want to be transparent.

In the diagram in Figure 10.12 I have clicked inside the gray area with the Magic Wand tool, and it has turned white, taking on the color of my desktop and indicating that it is now a transparent color.

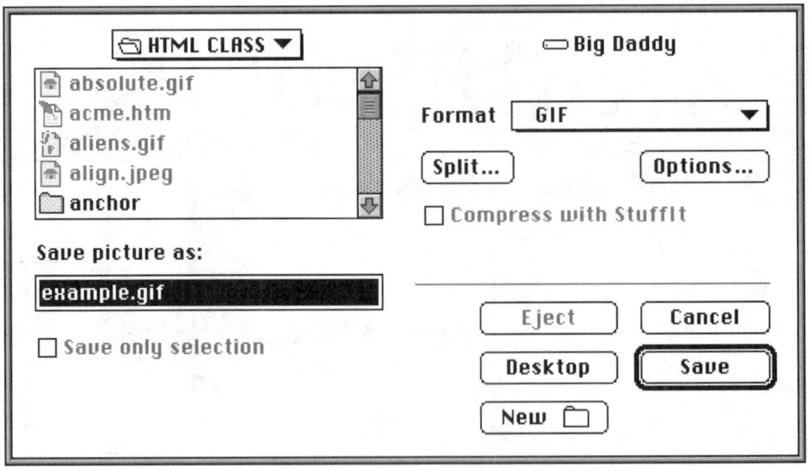

Figure 10.13

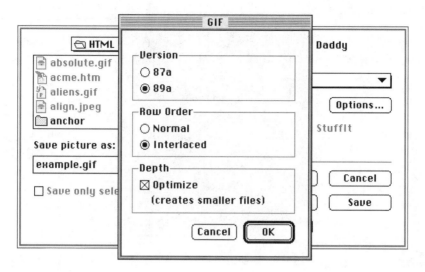

Figure 10.14

When the image is ready to be saved, choose File→Save As... from the menu bar, and you will get the dialog box shown in Figure 10.13. Select the correct file format; in this case, GIF. Name your file and designate where it should be stored. Before saving the file, click on the Options... button as shown in Figure 10.13.

You will get a window that looks identical to the one in Figure 10.14. For the transparency to work, you must click on the 89a button. Interlacing is optional. Remember, interlacing has to do with the image being displayed gradually as it downloads.

Click OK and Save. When you open your image on your Web page, it will look like the following image. The gray background of the graphic is now transparent, allowing the color and pattern of the page background to show through (Figure 10.15).

EXAMPLE

Figure 10.15

Figure 10.16

Converting Backgrounds

As I mentioned during the section on transparency, we can only make one color, the background color, transparent. But what if we have an image whose background is made up of many colors, such as the driver's license photo of our friend Elvis, seen below (Figure 10.16)?

There are several tools in graphics programs that will allow you to change the background. The eraser tool, the selection tool, or the paintbrush will all enable you, in one way or another, to create a uniform color background such as we see in Figure 10.17.

Figure 10.17

Figure 10.18

Once you have created a background with a uniform color, making that background transparent is a matter of a few simple steps, as has been demonstrated previously.

The result will be our good friend stripped of his background (Figure 10.18).

Important Points of this Chapter

- It doesn't matter which graphics program you use, but it should be able to perform a certain number of functions, such as convert file formats, change resolution and color depth, resize or crop an image, support transparent GIFs, and define coordinates for imagemaps.
- To convert a file from one format to another the basic steps are to open the image file and then save it in the preferred format.
- To view file information, you must open the file information window in your graphics software. Then make and save any desired changes.
- The resolution of an image to be used on a Web page doesn't need to be greater than 72 dpi, which is the screen resolution of computer monitors.
- Another way to reduce the file size of an image is to reduce the color depth.
- It is always best to create your image in the size you plan to have it displayed on your Web page. If it is larger than you want, you can resize the image to fit your requirements. It is better to go from larger to smaller than smaller to larger when resizing graphics.

- Another way to resize an image is to crop the image down to the essential information. Cropping can increase the effectiveness of your image while decreasing the file size and download time.
- Transparent images are a valuable tool when you want to have a odd-shaped graphic appear on your screen without a gray box surrounding it. This also works well for text images, such as graphic headers or logos.

Visit the Prentice Hall Web Site

- For links to download graphics software.
- For tutorials in this chapter, which are repeated using PaintShop Pro in a Windows environment.
- For full-color versions of the examples contained within this chapter.
- There is a list of recommended activities and assignments to improve your skills working with your graphics software to edit images for use on your Web page.
- There is a short quiz to test your knowledge on the information in this chapter.

Imagemaps

In previous chapters we learned to use graphics as hyperlinks, which, when clicked upon would take us to other information. Imagemaps are images that contain links to more than one other location. This chapter will cover the development of imagemaps and provide instruction on how to create a client-side imagemap.

Purpose

Imagemaps provide yet another way to visually enhance your Web page by providing a means of navigating pictorially, using visual analogies. For example: Let's say that I need to design a Web page that links to all of the state capitals' home pages for the entire United States. I could make a list of their names and create links using the text.

Or I could use a graphic of the United States to create an imagemap and make each image of a state a clickable link (Figure 11.1). When I click on the state of California, it takes me to the Sacramento Home Page. Which sounds more interesting to you? Which is going to be more useful for users and sustain their interest?

Another example of a good use of an imagemap would be to create a virtual catalog for a business. Let's say that I'm selling shoes. I might have an image-map showing the various shoes that I am selling. Each shoe image would be a link to more information about that style shoe, such as price, ordering information, or testimonials.

Yet another example would be to use an imagemap for instructional purposes. For an anatomy lesson, I might create an imagemap of the human body, with the various organs of the body linked to more specific information about the function of each organ.

Visit the Prentice Hall Web site for additional information regarding imagemaps.

Figure 11.1

There are two types of imagemaps: server-side and client-side. This book will deal only with the development of client-side imagemaps, because they are easiest to set up and use. However, it is important to understand the differences between the two.

Server-Side Imagemaps

As you will soon see, an imagemap is made by taking the coordinates of the parts of a graphic image and linking them to a URL. For example, in the map image in Figure 11.1, if I wanted to make the state of California a hotspot, which it already has a reputation of being, I would record the coordinates of the state boundaries and associate a URL with those boundaries. How to actually do this will become clearer as we move along. The important point is that there will be a relationship between the shape of the state and the URL to which it is linked, telling the browser where to go when the state is clicked upon. The primary difference between server-side and client-side imagemaps is where the information resides and how the hyperlink is activated.

When creating a server-side imagemap, we need to take the coordinates for the state of California and create a separate file called a map file. (It is not called a map file because we are working on a map image. It doesn't matter what the image is, it is still called a map file.) The map file is placed on the server and when an area in the graphic is clicked upon, a message goes to the server and calls a CGI (Common Gateway Interface) script, which is like a small program configured to handle the map file information. The CGI script reads the map file and enables the browser to create a link to the new information.

The advantage of using server-side imagemaps is that they have been in use for quite some time and are almost universally supported by browser software.

One of the big disadvantages is that server-side imagemaps require an extra level of coordination with your Internet Service Provider to be able to use them. Not all Internet Service Providers support imagemaps. An additional disadvantage is that server-side imagemaps cannot be tested until they are loaded onto the server. While not difficult to accomplish, server-side imagemaps require additional steps beyond what are required by client-side imagemaps.

Client-Side Imagemaps

Client-side imagemaps are constructed in a very similar fashion to server-side imagemaps. Going back to our original example, using the State of California, I take the coordinates of the state's boundaries and associate those coordinates with the URL to which I want to link. Rather than having to create a separate map file with the information and place it on the server, I can put all of the information into the HTML of the page. Client-side imagemaps are completely contained within the HTML of a page and do not depend upon special files or scripts on the server for functionality. When an area is clicked upon within an image, the browser looks within the HTML for the URL associated with that area as defined by its coordinates. This also means that client-side imagemaps can be tested without being loaded onto the server. The difference between the two types of imagemaps is transparent to the user—they both function the same. The difference lies in how they are handled by the browser.

Since client-side imagemaps arrived a little later on the HTML scene, they are not supported by older browser software. Browsers that don't support client-side imagemaps will still see the image, but the links will not function. We must also remind ourselves that there are people out there who are using text only browsers and won't even see the graphic. For both of the above reasons, it is advisable to add redundant text links at the bottom of the imagemap.

As I have mentioned above, for the purposes of this book, we will only work with client-side imagemaps. It seems to me that unless you have a driving need, like money, to reach absolutely everyone in the world with your Web page, client-side imagemaps are adequate for most purposes.

A Few Cautions

A few cautions about imagemaps in general are appropriate. Imagemaps don't work for every situation. Your graphic should be carefully selected or designed to ensure that the areas you will be designating as links are clearly defined. A complex, busy graphic image is likely to make a very busy and confusing imagemap.

Sometimes it is not obvious that a graphic is an imagemap. For example, look at the map of the United States in the above examples. Is there anything about the image that suggests that you should click on it? Consider adding instructions when the purpose of the image as an imagemap is not obvious. For example, we might say, "Click on the state of your choice to visit the state capital."

Be careful not to make an imagemap too large. An imagemap should not exceed what will fit into a standard screen size of 640 × 480, otherwise the viewer will have to scroll the page in order to see the whole image. Also, consider the added download time of a large graphic and whether the benefits of the imagemap are negatively offset by the speed at which it will load.

Now that all of that is said, let's create an imagemap!

Figure 11.2

Making an Image

The graphic for a client-side imagemap can either be a JPEG or a GIF. I have created the image below to be used as a Web page navigation bar. Living in the scenic Mojave Desert at the foot of the Sierra Nevada, I want to link to some information about my local area. Additionally, I want to create a return to the home page and create an e-mail link. Finally, since my primary interest is art, I also want to link to a page full of art-related sites on Yahoo. The image in Figure 11.2 has been designed so that it has distinct shapes, making it should be clear to viewers which shape will take them to where. It is larger than what I would normally put on a Web page, but this will make it easy to convert it into an imagemap.

This image is located on the Prentice Hall Web site in color. Feel free to download it and, using your graphic software, adapt it to your own needs.

Marking the Coordinates

The next step is to mark the coordinates of the clickable areas in your imagemap. We're going to use a graphic program to do this, although there are many freeware and shareware mapping programs that make this part easier.

If you want to download some software for working with imagemaps, I recommend the following shareware programs:

- For the Mac: WebMap
- For the PC: Mapedit

They're easy to use and come with adequate documentation.

Visit the Prentice Hall Web site for current links to the programs men- tioned. The software names are linked to locations where the software can be downloaded.

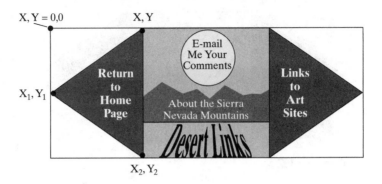

Figure 11.3

What are Coordinates?

Coordinates are locations or points within an image, and in the case of imagemaps, they are used to outline shapes in designating hotspots or linked areas on an image. Coordinates are measured relative to the upper left corner of the image, which is 0,0. If you look at our image (Figure 11.3), the upper left point of the image is marked **X,Y=0,0.**

0,0 are the coordinates for that point on the image. X is the horizontal position and Y is the vertical position measured in pixels. To describe the area for the triangle on the left labeled "Return to Home Page," the coordinates are located at each corner of the triangle and are each indicated by a small black dot. The coordinates would be: X,Y,X_1Y_1,X_2,Y_2

Region Types

Region types refer to the types of shapes that are available for mapping the various shapes that are used within an imagemap. Each region type must have the coordinates listed in a specific way, and the region type must be defined in the HTML.

We can use the following imagemap region types for mapping the coordinates of our image or any imagemap.

Rectangle Region Type (Figure 11.4)

To map a rectangular shape, the coordinates of the upper left corner and the lower right corner are needed.

The number will be: X,Y,X_1,Y_1.

When included in the HTML, the value for the SHAPE attribute will be "RECT."

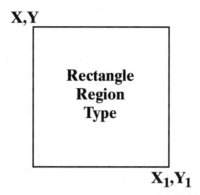

X,Y

Rectangle
Region
Type

X₁,Y₁

Figure 11.4

Circular Region Type (Figure 11.5)

To map a circular shape, the coordinates of the center point and the length of the radius are required.

The number will be: **X,Y,Radius.**

When included in the HTML, the value for the SHAPE attribute will be "CIRCLE."

Polygon Region Type (Figure 11.6)

To map a polygon, or many-sided shape, the coordinates for each point in the shape are required and must be listed in order. The coordinates for the polygon above will be: $X,T,X_1,Y_1,X_2,Y_2,X_3,Y_3,X_4,Y_4.$

Irregular shapes are mapped using the polygon. As many coordinates as necessary to define the shape can be used.

When included in the HTML, the value for the SHAPE attribute will be "POLYGON."

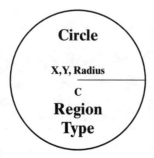

Circle

X,Y, Radius

C

**Region
Type**

Figure 11.5

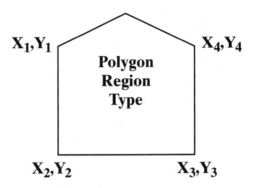

X_1,Y_1 X_4,Y_4

Polygon Region Type

X_2,Y_2 X_3,Y_3

Figure 11.6

Mapping the Coordinates

So where do we get these coordinates? What do we do with them once we have them?

First, we need to open the image in a graphics program. The picture in Figure 11.7 shows my navigation bar graphic as it looks when opened in Graphics Converter. PaintShop Pro displays the coordinates in an almost identical fashion, the only difference being that the coordinates appear in the bottom of the window rather than the top.

On the left, you will see that I have placed my cursor on the left point of the triangle shape. If you look at the far upper right, you will see that the X,Y coordinates for the position of my cursor are being displayed: 5,95. This means that the cursor is located 5 pixels to the right, and 95 pixels below the upper left corner of the graphic, which has the coordinate 0,0.

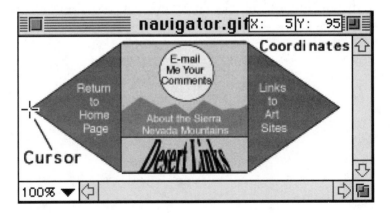

Figure 11.7

Map the Triangle Shape

To map out the coordinates of the triangle shape on the left labeled "Return to Home Page," I simply move the cursor to the three points of the triangle shape and write down the numbers or coordinates that appear in the boxes in upper right corner of the window.

I mapped the coordinates of this triangle to be: **5,95,137,5,137,181.** This gives us a good start on the imagemap. Mapping the triangle on the right is basically the same operation.

Map the Sun Shape (Circular)

To map out the circular coordinates of the sun shape, I start by placing my cursor in the center of the circle as you can see in Figure 11.8. At the top right of the window you can see that the coordinates are 227,44. I now need the length of the radius of the circle. This can be determined by subtracting the coordinate at the right edge of the circle, which I have marked "A," from the X coordinate at the center of the circle.

I have mapped the coordinates of this circle to be: **227,44,39.**

Map the Mountain Shape (Polygon)

The process for mapping the mountain shape is basically the same as mapping the triangle shape. In Figure 11.9, I have placed a white dot at each point on the mountains where we will need a coordinate. Eleven coordinates are required to define the mountain shape. There is no limitation to the number of coordinates that can be used, but they must be listed in the correct order, either from left to right around the shape or right to left.

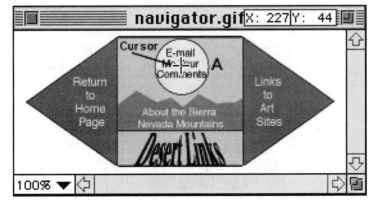

Figure 11.8

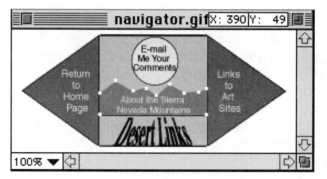

Figure 11.9

Map the Rectangular Shape (Rectangle)

The last area to map for the coordinates is the rectangular shape below the mountains labeled "Desert Links." The coordinates required for a rectangle are the upper left corner and the lower right corner as shown in Figure 11.10.

Coordinates

My final list of coordinates turns out to be:

- Left Triangle (Polygon): 5,95,137,5,137,181
- Right Triangle (Polygon): 313,6,442,89,313,180
- Mountains (Polygon): 138,99,165,75,191,94,213,87,231,100,252,82,278,96, 300,93,311,90,311,132,139,132
- Circle (Circle): 227,44,39.
- Rectangular (Rectangle): 138,131,312,180

Now that we have this crazy list of numbers, what do we do with them?

Figure 11.10

HTML

The next step is to start to put our graphic image and the coordinate information together using HTML.

The MAP Tags

The coordinates that I have defined for the imagemap constitute a numerical map of the various shapes within the image. It makes sense that this map be enclosed within the **MAP** tags, **<MAP></MAP>.**

Naming the MAP

Our first step is to give our **MAP** a name, just as we gave an anchor a name in order to link to other parts of a Web page. Since my image file is called "navigator.gif," I will name my **MAP** "navigator." The NAME attribute is entered into the **MAP** tag followed by an equal sign (=) and the name of the **MAP** in quotations.

The HTML

```
<MAP NAME="navigator">

</MAP>
```

Area Tags

Each set of coordinates that we developed describes an area. There are five areas in our imagemap, so there are five AREA tags included within our map. AREA tags do not require closing tags.

```
<MAP NAME="navigator">

<AREA>

<AREA>

<AREA>

<AREA>

<AREA>

</MAP>
```

SHAPE Attribute

The areas have different shapes, and we need to tell the browser what shape we are working with for the browser to make sense of the coordinates. The SHAPE attribute goes within the AREA tag. The shape is determined by the region type that was used to develop the coordinates. For the above im-agemap we have three polygons, a circle, and a rectangle.

```
<MAP NAME="navigator">

<AREA SHAPE="POLYGON"> (the left triangle)

<AREA SHAPE="POLYGON"> (the right triangle)

<AREA SHAPE="POLYGON"> (the mountains)

<AREA SHAPE="CIRCLE"> (the circular sun shape)

<AREA SHAPE="RECT"> (the rectangular shape)

</MAP>
```

Coordinates

Each area of our image is represented by a different set of coordinates. The "COORDS" attribute is entered for each area, followed by an equal sign and the appropriate coordinates enclosed in quotations:

```
<MAP NAME="navigator">

<AREA SHAPE="POLYGON"
COORDS="5,95,137,5,137,181">
(the left triangle)

<AREA SHAPE="POLYGON"
COORDS="313,6,442,89,313,180">
(the right triangle)

<AREA SHAPE="POLYGON"
COORDS="138,99,165,75,191,94,213,87,231,100,252,82,278,96,300,93,311,90,311,132,
139,132">
(the mountains)

<AREA SHAPE="CIRCLE"
COORDS="227,44,39">
(the circular sun shape)

<AREA SHAPE="RECT"
COORDS="138,131,312,180">
(the rectangular shape)

</MAP>
```

URL

Next, the browser needs to know the URLs to which these coordinates are linked.

- The left triangle is linked to the Cerro Coso College Home Page: http://www.cc.cc.ca.us
- The right triangle is linked to a page on Yahoo that lists art categories: http://www.yahoo.com/Arts/
- The mountains are linked to the Sierra Club: http://www.sierraclub.org/ ecoregions/sierranevada.html
- The sun is a "mailto:" e-mail link in order to send me comments: mailto:pmeyers@cc.cc.ca.us
- The rectangle is linked to the Maturango Museum, a local natural history/art museum: http://www1.ridgecrest.ca.us/~matmus/default.html

The URL is entered into the AREA tag after the coordinates. Begin with the HREF attribute followed by an equal sign, followed by the URL in quotations. In other words, HREF="URL." Notice that there is no **<A>** or anchor at the beginning of the HREF.

The completed MAP information follows.

The HTML

```
<MAP NAME="navigator">

<AREA SHAPE="POLYGON"
COORDS="5,95,137,5,137,181"
HREF="http://www.cc.cc.ca.us">

<AREA SHAPE="POLYGON"
COORDS="313,6,442,89,313,180"
HREF="http://www.yahoo.com/Arts/">

<AREA SHAPE="POLYGON"
COORDS="138,99,165,75,191,94,213,87,231,100,252,82,278,96,300,93,311,90,311,132,
139,132"
HREF="http://www.sierraclub.org/ecoregions/sierranevada.html/">

AREA SHAPE="CIRCLE"
COORDS="227,44,39"
HREF="mailto:pmeyers@cc.cc.ca.us">

<AREA SHAPE="RECT"
COORDS="138,131,312,180"
HREF="http://www1.ridgecrest.ca.us/~matmus/default.html">

</MAP>
```

I have now completed the MAP information, including all of the information needed for my imagemap. I have included the region types, or SHAPES, the numerical coordinates, or COORDs, and the URLs to which the imagemap is linked. The next step is to include the graphic image on the Web page and link it to the MAP information.

Linking the Image

We have already covered how to include an image on a Web page. The name of my image is "navigator.gif" and I include it on the page with the following HTML:

```
<IMG SRC="images/navigator.gif">
```

To link the image and the MAP information, I must tell the IMG SRC tag to use the MAP information that I have created. To accomplish this, the USEMAP attribute is included into the IMG SRC tag. USEMAP is followed by an equal sign, followed by the name that we gave to the map, preceded by a pound sign (#), and enclosed in quotation marks.

The HTML

```
<IMG SRC="navigator.gif"
USEMAP="#navigator"
BORDER="0">
```

(Notice that I have also added a BORDER="0" since I am using an irregular-shaped graphic and do not want a rectangular border around it.)

The completed IMG SRC tag is included in the HTML at the location where the image is to be seen. The MAP tag containing the MAP information does not have to be included in the same location.

In Figure 11.11 we have the completed imagemap. If you were online and were to move your mouse over the image, you would see the URLs change at the bottom of your screen.

The image doesn't look any different than it did before we started this whole process, and that can be a drawback if viewers don't get the idea that they're supposed to click on the various areas. Sometimes it's necessary to put

Figure 11.11

Click Above
[Return to Cero Coso Home Page]
[Links to Information about the Sierra Nevada]

[Links to Information about the Desert]
[E-mail Your Comments][Links to Art sites]

Figure 11.12

a message such as "Click above to visit other links" to make sure that viewers understand how to use the imagemap.

The Result

Visit the Prentice Hall Web site for the complete imagemap, including the full HTML.

Text Links

It has already been pointed out in a previous section on linking graphics that some people use text-only browsers, or turn the images off in their browsers' preferences to speed up load time. It's a good idea to accommodate those folks by including your links in text form under your imagemap to provide an alternative form of navigation.

See my final imagemap above in Figure 11.12.

Overlapping Images

One last, but important, point. What if we have a graphic that we want to use for an imagemap, but the shapes will necessarily overlap? For example, I made this dumb little image to illustrate the problem (Figure 11.13).

The coordinates for the square shape will cover the the coordinates for the circular shape, and the coordinates for the circular shape will cover the co-ordinates for the triangular shape.

To enable all of the shapes to be used as clickable links, we must list the AREA tags in order from smallest to largest, with the largest shape being last. The HTML for this example follows.

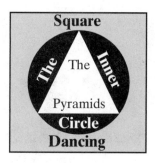

Figure 11.13

The HTML

```
<MAP NAME="square">

<AREA SHAPE="POLYGON"
COORDS="76,32,120,107,31,104"
HREF="http://www.parascope.com:80/en/pyramids.htm">

<AREA SHAPE="CIRCLE"
COORDS="76,76,52"
HREF="http://nmc.uoregon.edu:80/~jmk/HInnerCircle.html">

<AREA SHAPE="RECT"
COORDS="0,0,150,150"
HREF="http://www.prospernet.com:80/artsscience/arts/dance/square_dancing.html">

</MAP>

<IMG SRC="squarecirclepyr.gif"
USEMAP="#square">
```

The Result (Figure 11.14)

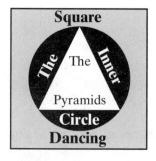

Figure 11.14

Once again, we see no change in the appearance of our image. We haven't really changed the image; we have created a map of the coordinates within the image that will be hotspots. This MAP is included within the HTML, along with the associated URLs. When the user clicks on the hotspots, a link is made to the desired URL.

If you were to go online, you could test this imagemap. You would see that in spite of the shapes being stacked, each one works as a separate clickable link. If the order had been reversed, only the square shape would have worked. (I have to admit that the links are not particularly exciting.)

Visit the Prentice Hall Web site to see how the above example works in action, and even appropriate the image for yourself.

Important Points of This Chapter

- Imagemaps are images that contain links to more than one location. They are an effective means of navigation, with the possibility of being visually interesting at the same time.

- In server-side imagemaps the information resides on the server, where the information is contained in a map file that has within it the coordinates and URLs for the related information. Server-side imagemaps require the use of a CGI script and much more coordination with your Internet Service Provider.

- In client-side imagemaps all the information needed to make the MAP work, that is the coordinates and the URLs, are contained within the HTML of the page. They do not require CGI scripts or contacting your ISP.

- An imagemap can be created from existing graphics or from images you create yourself in a graphics program.

- To define or map the coordinates that outline the designated hotspots or linked areas, use your graphics program to find the X and Y values. By moving the cursor over the boundary points in the image, you can determine the coordinates for your image.

- The three imagemap region types are rectangle, circle, and polygon.

- Remember when mapping the polygon coordinates to start at one point and go either clockwise or counterclockwise around the image to map the subsequent coordinates.

- The HTML for imagemaps includes the imagemap tags **<MAP></MAP>,** the NAME attribute nested inside the **<MAP>** tag, and the **<AREA>** tags, which define the map areas that are to be linked. The SHAPE attribute is contained within the **<AREA>** tag and defines the region type, such as RECTANGLE, CIRCLE, or POLYGON. The COORDS, or coordinates, are also contained within the **<AREA>** tag.

- You can create imagemaps with overlapping images by entering the co-ordinates in order from smallest to largest, with largest being last.

Visit the Prentice Hall Web site

- For additional information regarding imagemaps.
- For current links to the imagemap programs mentioned.
- For the complete imagemaps including the full HTML as shown in this chapter.
- There is a list of recommended activities and assignments to improve your skills in creating imagemaps.
- There is a short quiz to test your knowledge on the information in this chapter.

Tables

For the longest time, I avoided trying to work with tables. There seemed to be so many tags involved, and it looked so complicated. I finally took the plunge, out of necessity, and I discovered that tables are not only easy to use, but are the most useful tool in the limited repertoire of HTML for organizing materials on a Web page. Tables are not only useful for organizing data on a

Web page, they have become the standard method of organizing the entire Web page layout.

While tables may be easy to use, they're not all that easy to explain, but I'll do my best to make this as clear as possible. Please keep in mind that a real understanding and facility in using any features of HTML comes through practice and experience.

I should warn those with older browsers, such as Netscape 2.0, that this chapter will cover table features that may not be supported by your browsers. Why not take this opportunity to upgrade your browser.

Description of Tables

Tables provide a means of organizing and presenting information in columns and rows for the purpose of clarity. For example, let's look at the following list of items that are on sale this month at the college bookstore.

```
Bookstore Sale Items
    Ladies
        Black Lipstick
        False Eyebrows
    Men
        Chainsaws
        Red Heels
    Teachers
        Flack Jackets
        Torture Devices
```

This list could also be presented in the form of a table as shown in Figure 12.1. The table above consists of three Rows and three Columns. At the top of the table is a Caption, "Bookstore Sale Items." In the first row of the table, all of the Headings are bold and centered. The items listed underneath the headings are plain type and are aligned left. The table has a Border that

Bookstore Sale Items

Ladies	Men	Teachers
Black Lipstick	Chainsaws	Flack Jackets
False Eyebrows	Red Heels	TortureDevices

Figure 12.1

defines the rows, columns, and Cells. In other words, this table has all of the qualities of a typical HTML table.

The examples used in this chapter are very simple for the purposes of clarity and brevity. You should not underestimate the value that tables have in organizing large amounts of complex data for a clear and cohesive presentation. In fact, a very common and valuable use of tables is to place the entire contents of a page into a table, enabling a controlled placement of text and graphic elements.

TABLE Tags

The actual HTML to create a basic table is quite simple, using only a few different tags. We start with, you guessed it, the TABLE tags **<TABLE> </TABLE>**. The **</TABLE>** tag indicates the end of the table.

Table Rows Tags

A table must have at least one row. To create rows we use the Table Row tags **<TR><TR>**.

The **<TR></TR>** tags are enclosed or nested in the **<TABLE></TABLE>** tags. **</TR>** indicates the end of a row and is like using a **
** tag with text; it creates a break to the next row of the table.

There are three rows in Figure 12.1, so the initial HTML would look like this:

```
<TABLE>

    <TR></TR>

    <TR></TR>

    <TR></TR>

</TABLE>
```

Notice that I have indented the **<TR>** tags. Since the HTML for tables can get quite complicated, indenting helps keep the HTML organized and facilitates troubleshooting later. Indenting the tags in the HTML will not have any impact on my table.

Table Cells

The places where the rows and columns intersect are called cells (Figure 12.2).

Cells result from making columns by introducing data using the Table Header **<TH></TH>** or the Table Data **<TD></TD>** tags.

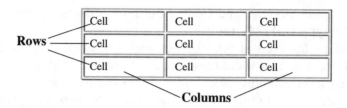

Figure 12.2

Table Header Tags

If the data is to be a heading, such as the Ladies, Men, and Teachers, the **<TH></TH>** or Table Header is used. The result is that the information will be bold and centered in the cell.

Table Data Tags

If the information is not to be a heading, then the **<TD></TD>** or Table Data tags are used, and the information will appear in plain text and be aligned to the left.

The **<TH></TH>** and **<TD></TD>** tags are enclosed or nested in the **<TR></TR>** tags.

Entering Data

Some of the confusion regarding tables results from the fact that when writing the HTML, information is entered into the table in one specific way. The way that we enter the data may be very different from how we intend to read the data (Figure 12.3).

As you can see from Figure 12.3, all of the information is entered row by row from left to right, rather than in columns, from top to bottom. In other words, the information is entered

Row 1,a,b,c
Row 2,a,b,c
Row 3,a,b,c

Row 1	→ **Ladies** a	**Men** b	**Teachers** c
Row 2	Black Lipstick → b	Chainsaws b	Flack Jackets c
Row 3	False eyebrows → c	Red Heels b	Torture Devices c

Figure 12.3

<TABLE>				
<TR>	**<TH></TH>**	**<TH></TH>**	**<TH></TH>**	</TR>
<TR>	<TD></TD>	<TD></TD>	<TD></TD>	</TR>
<TR>	<TD></TD>	<TD></TD>	<TD></TD>	</TR>
				</TABLE>

Figure 12.4

This diagram illustrates the structure of the HTML to create the three-row, three-column table and shows the order in which the data is organized (Figure 12.4).

In practice the structure of the table would be written as follows.

The HTML

```
\TABLE>

   <TR>

        <TH></TH>

        <TH></TH>

        <TH></TH>

   </TR>

   <TR>

        <TD></TD>

        <TD></TD>

        <TD></TD>

   </TR>

   <TR>

        <TD></TD>

        <TD></TD>

        <TD></TD>

   </TR>

</TABLE>
```

Note that I have indented the HTML for clarity as pointed out above.

The actual data is entered between the **<TH></TH>** and **<TD></TD>** tags. The table with data entered looks like the following.

The HTML

```
<TABLE>

  <TR>

      <TH>Ladies</TH>

      <TH>Men</TH>

      <TH> Teachers</TH>

  </TR>

  <TR>

      <TD>Black Lipstick</TD>

      <TD>Chainsaws</TD>

      <TD>Flack Jackets</TD>

  </TR>

  <TR>

      <TD>False Eyebrows</TD>

      <TD>Red Heels</TD>

      <TD>Torture Devices</TD>

  </TR>

</TABLE>
```

The Result (Figure 12.5)

Ladies	**Men**	**Teachers**
Black Lipstick	Chainsaws	Flack Jackets
False Eyebrows	Red Heels	Torture Devices

Figure 12.5

Table BORDER Attribute

Hey, wait a minute! What happened to that cool border that was around the first table?

To have a table with a border, the BORDER attribute must be entered into the **<TABLE>** tag.

The HTML

```
<TABLE BORDER>
```

The Result (Figure 12.6)

Ladies	Men	Teachers
Black Lipstick	Chainsaws	Flack Jackets
False Eyebrows	Red Heels	TortureDevices

Figure 12.6

Tables don't always look their best with borders, so you should look at your table with and without borders and decide. This is especially true if you are using a table for page layout.

Important: A small mistake in a table's HTML can cause it to go bonkers. I have been to the absolute edge of darkness trying to figure out why a table was behaving so crazily. At one point I was strangling my mouse in one hand and had a lethal dose of L.A. water in the other hand, when I realized the following: I have found that when developing a table, always leave the Border turned on. Seeing the border will make it infinitely easier to troubleshoot your problems than if the border is not seen. Sounds simple, but some day you will thank me for that small bit of advice.

Later, I will describe how to change some of the values for the borders.

CAPTIONS Tag

The truly remarkable among us will at this point be impatiently asking, "What happened to the caption that was in the original example? The one that said 'Bookstore Sale Items.'"

Captions can be added to tables at top or the bottom of the table by using the CAPTION tag **<CAPTION></CAPTION>.** The caption tag is placed after the TABLE tag and before the first ROW tag.

The HTML

```
<TABLE BORDER>

<CAPTION> Bookstore Sale Items</CAPTION>

  <TR>...
```

The Result (Figure 12.7)

Bookstore Sale Items

Ladies	Men	Teachers
Black Lipstick	Chainsaws	Flack Jackets
False Eyebrows	Red Heels	TortureDevices

Figure 12.7

Notice that by default the caption appears at the top of the table.

If we want the caption at the bottom of the table, we can include the ALIGN attribute in the CAPTION tag, as in the following.

The HTML

```
<TABLE BORDER>

   <CAPTION

   ALIGN=BOTTOM> Bookstore Sale

   Items</CAPTION>

   <TR>...
```

The Result (Figure 12.8)

Ladies	Men	Teachers
Black Lipstick	Chainsaws	Flack Jackets
False Eyebrows	Red Heels	TortureDevices

Bookstore Sale Items

Figure 12.8

Later, I will show you how to include the caption into the table by adding another row and spanning the cells with the caption.

Alignment

Let's go through some of the alignment possibilities for the various table elements.

Table

An entire table can be aligned to the left margin, centered on the page, or aligned to the right margin. The default alignment is to the left and usually does not have to be entered. To change the alignment of a table, we can use the new DIVISION **<DIV></DIV>** tag along with its ALIGN attribute. This DIVISION tag is a new feature included in HTML 3.2 that will prove to be very useful.

For example, let's work with this small, one-celled table.

The HTML

```
<TABLE BORDER>

    <TR>

        <TD>SUNSHINE</TD>

    <TR>

</TABLE>
```

The Result (Figure 12.9)

SUNSHINE

Figure 12.9

The table is a aligned to the default left alignment. To change the alignment of the table, we enclose the TABLE tags **<TABLE></TABLE>** within the DIVISION tags **<DIV></DIV>.** The ALIGN attribute is included in the **<DIV>** tag, followed by an equal sign and the alignment we want, either LEFT, RIGHT, or CENTER. For example, to align the table to the center of the screen, the HTML would look like the following.

The HTML

```
<DIV ALIGN=CENTER>

<TABLE BORDER>

  <TR>

    <TD>SUNSHINE</TD>

  <TR>

</TABLE>

</DIV>
```

The Result (Figure 12.10)

SUNSHINE

Figure 12.10

To align the same table to the right of the screen, here is the HTML.

The HTML

```
<DIV ALIGN=RIGHT>

<TABLE BORDER>

  <TR>

    <TD>SUNSHINE</TD>

  <TR>

</TABLE>

</DIV>
```

The Result (Figure 12.11)

SUNSHINE

Figure 12.11

The use of the DIVISION tags is not limited to the alignment of tables. Any HTML element enclosed in the DIVISION can have its alignment defined using the align attribute.

Blank Cells

If there is no data entered into the **<TD>** tag, a cell will still be created, but it will be left blank. The following HTML shows an example.

The HTML

```
<TABLE BORDER>

<CAPTION> Child Names of the 60s</CAPTION>

  <TR>

    <TD>Sunshine</TD>

    <TD></TD>

    <TD>Moonbeam</TD>

  </TR>
```

```
<TR>

  <TD></TD>

  <TD>Cactus Flower</TD>

  <TD>Watta Trip</TD>

<TR>

</TABLE>
```

The Result (Figure 12.12)

Child Names of the 60s

Sunshine		Moonbeam
	Cactus Flower	WattaTrip

Figure 12.12

When creating tables, you should have the same number of **<TD>** or **<TH>** tags in each row, even if they do not contain information. Otherwise, the browser will create a blank cell to even out the table and it may not be where you want it to be.

Table Row Alignment

The Align attribute can be used within the **<TR>** tag to specify the alignment of the row contents. ALIGN LEFT, RIGHT, or CENTER can be specified, with LEFT being the default. For example, all of the text in the following table (Figure 12.13), by default, aligns to the left of each cell.

Horizontal Alignment

To specify the horizontal alignment of the data within a row, include the ALIGN attribute within the **<TR>** tag and specify either LEFT, RIGHT, or CENTER. Remember, the default alignment, LEFT, is not normally specified.

Child Names of the 60s

Sunshine		Moonbeam
	Cactus Flower	WattaTrip

Figure 12.13

The HTML

```
<TABLE BORDER>

<CAPTION>Child Names of the 60s</CAPTION>

    <TR ALIGN=RIGHT>

        <TD>Sunshine</TD>

        <TD></TD>

        <TD>Moonbeam</TD>

    </TR>

    <TR ALIGN=CENTER>

        <TD></TD>

        <TD>Cactus Flower</TD>

        <TD>Watta Trip</TD>

    </TR>

</TABLE>
```

The Result (Figure 12.14)

Child Names ot the 60s

Sunshine		Moonbeam
	Cactus Flower	WattaTrip

Figure 12.14

You can see that the data in the first row of the table is is aligned to the right of the cells, and the data in the second row is aligned to the center of the cells.

Note: You may have noticed that I cheated a little in this example to illustrate alignment. I made the cells a little bigger, otherwise you would not have been able to see the shift in alignment. I did not include the HTML required to change the cell size in the above HTML to avoid confusion. How to change and define cell sizes will be covered in the next chapter.

Vertical Alignment

To specify the vertical alignment of the data within a row, include the VALIGN attribute within the **<TR>** tag and specify either TOP, MIDDLE, or BOTTOM. The default vertical alignment is MIDDLE.

The HTML

```
<TABLE BORDER>

<CAPTION> Child Names of the 60s</CAPTION>

  <TR ALIGN=CENTER VALIGN=TOP>

       <TD>Sunshine</TD>

       <TD></TD>

       <TD>Moonbeam</TD>

  </TR>

  <TR ALIGN=CENTER VALIGN=BOTTOM>

       <TD></TD>

       <TD>Cactus Flower</TD>

       <TD>Watta Trip</TD>

  </TR>

</TABLE>
```

The Result (Figure 12.15)

Child Names ot the 60s

Sunshine		Moonbeam
	Cactus Flower	Watta Trip

Figure 12.15

You can see that the first row is vertically aligned to the top of the cell, and that the second row is vertically aligned to the bottom of the cells.

Note: Once again I have cheated by making the cells a little larger in order to see the vertical alignment.

Table Data Alignment

The same alignment possibilities can be applied to the **<TD>** and the **<TH>** tags. If an alignment has already been specified for a row in the **<TR>** tag, the alignment for the **<TD>** tag will override the row alignment for that particular cell. An example of this is shown in the following HTML.

The HTML

<TABLE BORDER>

<CAPTION> Child Names of the 60s</CAPTION>

  <TR VALIGN=TOP>

       <TD>Sunshine</TD>

       <TD></TD>

       <TD ALIGN=BOTTOM>Moonbeam</TD>

  </TR>

  <TR VALIGN=BOTTOM ALIGN=LEFT>

       <TD></TD>

       <TD>Cactus Flower</TD>

       <TD VALIGN=TOP ALIGN=RIGHT>Watta Trip</TD>

  </TR>

</TABLE>

The Result (Figure 12.16)

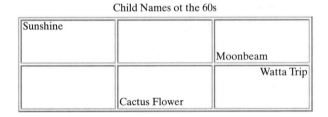

Figure 12.16

In the HTML I have specified a TOP alignment for row 1; however, I have specified a bottom alignment for the third cell in row 1 by including ALIGN=BOTTOM in the **<TD>** tag.

In the second row, I have specified a lower left alignment, which appears in the second cell, but have changed that to a top right alignment for the third cell by changing the alignment in the **<TD>** tag.

If you look carefully at the above HTML, and compare the results, it should become rapidly apparent that tables offer a tremendous amount of control.

Column Span and Row Span

How do we span columns and rows? Your first response might be, "Why would we want to?"

Let's take the following example (Figure 12.17).

It looks kind of dumb having the heading scrunched up in one cell in the middle of the table with empty cells to either side. It would look a lot better if the heading were in a single cell, the width of the table. To accomplish this we would need to span the two empty cells, making one long cell.

Column Span

This can be accomplished by using the COLUMN SPAN attribute **<COLSPAN>** inside of the **<TH>** or the **<TD>** tag. In this case it is the **<TH>** tag. But first let's look at the HTML for the above table (Figure 12.17).

The HTML

```
<TABLE>

  <TR>

        <TH></TH>

        <TH>Gourmet Restaurants in My Town</TH>

        <TH></TH>

  </TR>

  <TR ALIGN=CENTER>

        <TD>The Hamburger Stand</TD>

        <TD>Burger King</TD>

        <TD>Taco Bell</TD>

  </TR>

</TABLE>
```

	Gourmet Restaurants in My Town	
The Hamburger Stand	Burger King	Taco Bell

Figure 12.17

Notice that we have three columns in each row. What we want to do is make the text heading span all three columns. This can easily be accomplished by eliminating the two empty **<TH>** tags and placing the COLSPAN attribute in the remaining **<TH>** tag, with a value that corresponds to the number of cells we are spanning, in this case three. The HTML for this example follows.

The HTML

```
<TABLE>

 <TR>

        <TH COLSPAN=3>Gourmet Restaurants in My Town</TH>

 </TR>

 <TR ALIGN=CENTER>

        <TD>The Hamburger Stand</TD>

        <TD>Burger King</TD>

        <TD>Taco Bell</TD>

 </TR>

</TABLE>
```

The Result (Figure 12.18)

Gourmet Restaurants in MyTown		
The Hamburger Stand	Burger King	Taco Bell

Figure 12.18

Row Span

Let's say that we want to use the same information, but we want to set the table up a little differently.

For example, we want it to read as shown in Figure 12.19.

	The Hamburger Stand
Gourmet Restaurants in My Town	Burger King
	Taco Bell

Figure 12.19

But, we want to get rid of the empty cells on the left and have our heading span the three rows. This can be accomplished by using the ROWSPAN attribute in the **<TH>** tag of the heading, followed by a value indicating the number of rows to be spanned; in this case three. Let's look at the HTML for the above table first.

The HTML

```
<TABLE>

  <TR ALIGN=CENTER>

        <TD></TD>

        <TD>The Hamburger Stand</TD>

  </TR>

  <TR ALIGN=CENTER>

        <TH>Gourmet Restaurants in My Town</TH>

        <TD>Burger King</TD>

  </TR>

  <TR ALIGN=CENTER>

        <TD></TD>

        <TD>Taco Bell</TD>

  </TR>

</TABLE>
```

Please spend a few moments comparing the above HTML for this table to the HTML for the previous table that was formatted differently.

Our goal is to span the three rows in the first column with the heading "Gourmet Restaurants in My Town." To accomplish this, I remove the **<TD></TD>** tags from the first row and the third row and place the **<TH></TH>** tags into the first row. The **<TH>** tag includes the ROWSPAN attribute followed by the number of rows that I want to span, which in this case is three.

The Revised HTML

```
<TABLE>

  <TR ALIGN=CENTER>

        <TH ROWSPAN=3>Gourmet Restaurants in My Town</TH>

        <TD>The Hamburger Stand</TD>

  </TR>
```

```
<TR ALIGN=CENTER>

        <TD>Burger King</TD>

</TR>

<TR ALIGN=CENTER>

        <TD>Taco Bell</TD>

</TR>

</TABLE>
```

The Result (Figure 12.20)

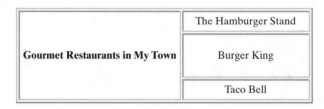

	The Hamburger Stand
Gourmet Restaurants in My Town	Burger King
	Taco Bell

Figure 12.20

It is essential when using column span and row span to keep careful track of the numbers of rows and columns with which you are working. Otherwise, you can create some real interesting problems for yourself. I've seen information spread all over a Web page like bugs on a windshield during a summer drive, all because of one small error in a table. It's not a pretty sight!

Well, we took a big bite out of tables. I hope that the chapter was clear enough and that you feel comfortable trying out tables. It doesn't take too much imagination to see the possibilities that tables provide for controlling not only the presentation of data, but whole page layouts. We'll get into additional possibilities in the next chapter.

 Visit the Prentice Hall Web site to see some examples of effective uses of tables and how they can be used to format your entire page.

Important Points of This Chapter

- Tables are an effective means of organizing information and even formatting entire pages in HTML.
- The table tags are actually quite simple, containing only a few basic tags. The main tags, **<TABLE></TABLE>,** enclose tags, which define columns, rows, and data, as well as headers and captions.

- All tables must have at least one row, which is defined by the table row tags **<TR></TR>**.
- Information is contained within cells of the table, which are created by the **<TD></TD>** or **<TH></TH>** tags.
- The information contained within the **<TH></TH>** tags will be displayed as bold and centered in the cell, and the information contained within the **<TD></TD>** tags will be plain text and aligned to the left.
- Table captions appear above or below the table.
- Table borders are an optional element that can be turned off or on by indicating the size in the **<TABLE>** tag as follows: It is always a good idea to have the border turned on when writing and previewing tables as borders make it much easier to see the structure of the table and identify any problems.
- It is a good idea to indent each element of a table in the HTML to make it easier to read the table HTML when editing and writing tables.
- Table alignment can be controlled by using the division tags **<DIV></DIV>.** The Align attribute has the values of LEFT, RIGHT, or CENTER.
- Blank table data cells can be used for formatting.
- It is possible to control the dimensions of either a row or a column by using the ROWSPAN or COLSPAN attribute within the **<TH>** or **<TD>** tags.

Visit the Prentice Hall Web site

- To see examples of effective uses of tables and how they can be used to format your entire page.
- There is a list of recommended activities and assignments to improve your skills working with tables.
- There is a short quiz to test your knowledge on the information in this chapter.

CHAPTER 13

More on Tables

Border Widths

Cellspacing

Cellpadding

Additional Alignment

Additional Table Attributes

Nesting Tables

Color

Page Layout

Table Alternatives

In this chapter we will continue to work with tables, exploring additional means of using them and of controlling the way that tables, and the information within them appear.

In addition to writing this book, let's say that I am also doing some serious research on extraterrestrial visitations. I have collected data from numerous resources that describe alien body types. I am putting all of this information into table form, hoping to identify the archetypal alien poster person. Part of my table is included in Figure 13.1.

I will use this table to illustrate some additional possibilities regarding tables.

Alien Characteristics	
Heads	
Number of Heads Reported	% Reported (sampling 2 million sightings)
1	12%
2-5	22.5%
5 or	65%

Figure 13.1

Border Widths

As we learned in the last chapter, to have a border around a table, the BOR-DER attribute must be included in the **<TABLE>** tag. The result will be a table border width, or thickness, having a default value of 1. The thickness of the border around a table can be changed by giving the the BORDER attribute a specified value. Any value greater than 1 will make the border thicker. Giving the BORDER attribute a value of 0 will turn the border off. The HTML follows for an exaggerated example.

The HTML

```
<TABLE BORDER=10>
```

The Result (Figure 13.2)

Alien Characteristics	
Heads	
Number of Heads Reported	% Reported (sampling 2 million sightings)
1	12%
2-5	22.5%
5 or more	65%

Figure 13.2

The border is now 10 pixels wide. Notice that this change only applies to the border that surrounds the table, not the borders within the table, between the cells.

Here's the HTML for another example.

The HTML

```
<TABLE BORDER=0>
```

The Result (Figure 13.3)

Alien Characteristics
Heads

Number of Heads Reported	% Reported (sampling 2 million sightings)
1	12%
2-5	22.5%
5 or more	65%

Figure 13.3

Now we have no border, yet the alignment of the text remains the same. The same thing can be accomplished by leaving the BORDER attribute out of the **<TABLE>** tag all together.

This is a clear case where a table without the border doesn't read very well.

Cellspacing

To change the width, or thickness, of the borders within the table, or the space between the cells, we can use the CELLSPACING attribute within the **<TABLE>** tag. The default value is 1. Another exaggerated example follows.

The HTML

```
<TABLE BORDER CELLSPACING=10>
```

The Result (Figure 13.4)

Alien Characteristics	
Heads	
Number of Heads Reported	% Reported (sampling 2 million sightings)
1	12%
2-5	22.5%
5 or	

Figure 13.4

The distance between the cells has changed considerably.

Cellpadding

If you look at the space around the text within the cells in my original table, it looks a little squeezed. More space can be created between the text and the table borders by including the CELLPADDING attribute in the **<TABLE>** tag followed by a value for the space that is desired. Default CELL-PADDING is 1. Here is the HTML for another exaggerated example

The HTML

```
<TABLE BORDER CELLPADDING=10>
```

The Result (Figure 13.5)

Alien Characteristics	
Heads	
Number of Heads Reported	% Reported (sampling 2 million sightings)
1	12%
2-5	22.5%
5 or	

Figure 13.5

Notice that there is now considerably more space around the text within the cells.

Just for the heck of it, let's increase value of all of the preceding attributes to 10.

The HTML

<TABLE BORDER=10 CELLSPACING=10

CELLPADDING=10>

The Result (Figure 13.6)

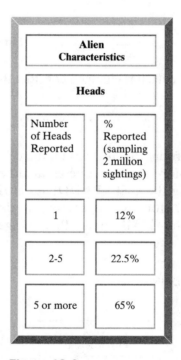

Figure 13.6

Now there's a table that an alien with 5 or more heads could appreciate!

Additional Alignment

Tables can be aligned to the left or right by including the ALIGN attribute in the **<TABLE>** tag. As when aligning images, ALIGN=LEFT aligns the table to the left margin of the page, and the text that follows will wrap to the right of the table. Here's the HTML for this example.

The HTML

```
<TABLE BORDER ALIGN=LEFT>
```

The Result (Figure 13.7)

Alien Characteristics	
Heads	
Number of Heads Reported	% Reported (sampling 2 million sightings)
1	12%
2-5	22.5%
5 or	65%

The information on the left can result in only one of two conclusions:

- By far, the greater number of aliens that have made human contact through extraterrestrial visitation have 5 or more heads.

  or

- Alcoholism is a far more serious problem than had previously been suspected.

Figure 13.7

ALIGN=RIGHT aligns the table to the right margin of the page, and text that follows will wrap to the left of the table. For example

The HTML

```
<TABLE BORDER ALIGN=RIGHT>
```

The Result (Figure 13.8)

The information on the right can result in only one of two conclusions:

- By far, the greater number of aliens that have made human contact through extraterrestrial visitation have 5 or more heads.

  or

- Alcoholism is a far more serious problem than had previously been suspected.

Alien Characteristics	
Heads	
Number of Heads Reported	% Reported (sampling 2 million sightings)
1	12%
2-5	22.5%
5 or	65%

Figure 13.8

Using the ALIGN attribute is limited to ALIGN=RIGHT and ALIGN =LEFT. If you want to place your table in the middle of the page, surround the **<TABLE></TABLE>** tags within the **<CENTER></CENTER>** tags.

Additional Table Attributes

Width

The width of a table can be controlled by including the WIDTH attribute within the **<TABLE>** tag. Width can be defined as either a percentage of the screen width, or as an exact number of pixels. Let's take our little table and give it a WIDTH of 100% of the screen width to see what happens.

The HTML

```
<TABLE BORDER WIDTH=100%>
```

The Result (Figure 13.9)

Alien Charactertistics	
Heads	
Number of Heads Reported	% Reported (sampling 2 million sightings)
1	12%
2-5	22.5%
5 or	65%

Figure 13.9

It wouldn't matter if we stretched or compressed the screen, the table would maintain the same size relative to the size of the screen.

Let's do another experiment and give the table a specific width in pixels. We'll make it 150 pixels wide.

The HTML

```
<TABLE BORDER WIDTH=150>
```

The Result (Figure 13.10)

Alien Characteristics	
Heads	
Number of Heads Reported	% Reported (sampling 2 million sightings)
1	12%
2-5	22.5%
5 or more	65%

Figure 13.10

If we stretched or compressed the screen we would find that the table would stay a fixed width regardless of the width of the screen.

It is usually best to specify your table size in percentages rather than pixels, since you don't know how wide the browser window will be.

Column Width

The WIDTH attribute can also be applied to columns by including the WIDTH attribute into the **<TH>** or **<TD>** tags and giving them a width value in either percentages or in pixels.

For example, let's take the small table with which we've been working and stretch it out to 300 pixels.

The HTML

```
<TABLE BORDER WIDTH=300>
```

The Result (Figure 13.11)

Alien Charactertistics	
Heads	
Number of Heads Reported	% Reported (sampling 2 million sightings)
1	12%
2-5	22.5%
5 or more	65%

Figure 13.11

Let's say for some bizarre reason, as if we needed one, that I want to make the column showing the "Number of Heads Reported" 80% of the table width leaving 20% for the remaining column. I have included the entire HTML for this table below. The change will be entered into the **<TD>** tag that includes "Number of Heads Reported." For example:

<TD WIDTH=80%> Number of Heads

Reported </TD>

The Complete HTML

```
<TABLE BORDER WIDTH=300>

  <TR>

        <TH COLSPAN=3>Alien

        Characteristics</TH>

  </TR>

  <TR>

        <TH COLSPAN=3>Heads</TH>

  </TR>

  <TR>

        <TD WIDTH=80%>Number of Heads Reported</TD>

        <TD WIDTH=20%>% Reported (sampling 2 million sightings)</TD>

  </TR>

  <TR ALIGN=CENTER>

        <TD>1</TD>

        <TD>12%></TD>

  </TR>

  <TRALIGN=CENTER>

        <TD>2-5</TD>

        <TD>22.5%</TD>

  </TR>

  <TR ALIGN=CENTER>

        <TD>5 or more</TD>
```

```
        <TD>65%</TD>

    </TR>

</TABLE>
```

The Result (Figure 13.12)

Alien Charactertistics	
Heads	
Number of Heads Reported	% Reported (sampling 2 million sightings)
1	12%
2-5	22.5%
5 or more	65%

Figure 13.12

The column on the left now occupies 80% of the table width. Notice that I have defined the column on the left as 80% by including the WIDTH attribute in the **<TD>** tag for the cell containing, "Number of Heads Reported." Not leaving anything to chance, I have also defined the width of the column on the right by including the WIDTH attribute and a value of 20% in the **<TD>** tag for the cell containing "% Reported (sampling 2 million sightings)."

Nesting Tables

We can actually include tables within tables by nesting them. In fact, any other HTML element can be nested inside a table. Let's look at a very simple example (Figure 13.13).

In Figure 13.13 I have nested two tables in a larger table in order to organize all of the information with a very specific alignment. Notice that the text "Alien Characteristics" is also a hyperlink (linked to the alien capital of the world, Roswell, New Mexico). The picture that I have included is an authentic photo, enclosed in a handsome border, of an extraterrestrial(s), taken outside of the sheep cloning clinic in Scotland.

The following diagram (Figure 13.14) illustrates the arrangements of the tables.

To nest a table inside of a table, an additional set of **<TABLE> </TABLE>** tags is added within the **<TD>** or **<TH>** cell that is to include the

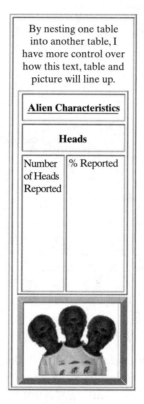

Figure 13.13

new table. In the following example, I have simplified the HTML to illustrate how to nest tables.

The HTML

```
<TABLE BORDER>

  <TR ALIGN=CENTER>

    <TD>Table One<P>
```

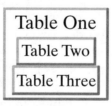

Figure 13.14

```
<TABLE BORDER>

  <TR>

    <TD>Table Two</TD>

  </TR>

</TABLE><P>

<TABLE BORDER>

  <TR>

    <TD>Table Three</TD>

  </TR>

</TABLE>

  </TD>

</TR>

</TABLE>
```

The Result (Figure 13.15)

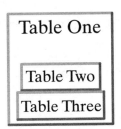

Figure 13.15

Right now you're probably saying, "That's a lot of typing for that dumb little table," and you have vowed never to have a reason to nest tables. Actually, the ability to nest tables and to nest information inside of tables is quite valuable.

There are additional examples of tables and nesting tables on the Prentice Hall Web site.

Color

A new feature of tables is the ability to create background colors. Introduced first by Microsoft, colored tables are now also supported by Netscape. However, beyond that, colored tables are not widely supported by other browsers.

It's not something that I would build my site around at this point, but colored tables do offer some interesting possibilities for the future.

The background color of an entire table and/or individual cells can be changed by including the BGCOLOR attribute within the **<TABLE>, <TR>, <TH>,** or **<TD>** tags. The value of the BGCOLOR will be expressed as hexadecimal colors. If the table is given a color in the **<TABLE>** tag, it will override the color of the page background. If a table row is given a different color than the table background in the **<TR>** tag, the table row color will override the color of the table background. If a table cell is given a different color than the table or the table row that it is in, by designating the color in the **<TD>** or **<TH>** tag, the table cell color will override the color of the table or table row.

You cannot color a cell unless it has some content. Placing a **
** tag in the otherwise empty cell will solve the problem. Remember to take your text color into consideration when changing the color of cells. If you are using red text and change the color of the cell to red, your text will disappear.

 I have repeated this example on the Prentice Hall Web site, so that it can be viewed in color.

Let's give some color to our earlier alien example.

The HTML

```
<TABLE BORDER=1 WIDTH=300 BGCOLOR="#FFFFFF">

  <TR>

    <TH COLSPAN=3 BGCOLOR="#FF0033">Alien Characteristics</TH>

  </TR>

  <TR>

    <TH COLSPAN=3 BGCOLOR="#66FFFF">Heads</TH>

  </TR>

  <TR>

    <TD WIDTH=80% BGCOLOR="#FFFF00">Number of Heads Reported</TD>

    <TD WIDTH=20% BGCOLOR="#66FFFF">% Reported (sampling 2 million sight-
    ings)</TD>

  </TR>

  <TR>

    <TD BGCOLOR="#FF9900">1</TD>

    <TD BGCOLOR="#66FFFF">12%</TD>

  </TR>
```

```
<TR>

  <TD BGCOLOR="#FF9900">2-5</TD>

  <TD BGCOLOR="#66FFFF">22.5%</TD>

</TR>

<TR>

  <TD BGCOLOR="#FF9900">5 or more</TD>

  <TD BGCOLOR="#66FFFF">65%</TD>

</TR>

</TABLE>
```

The Result (Figure 13.16)

Alien Charactertistics	
Heads	
Number of Heads Reported	% Reported (sampling 2 million sightings)
1	12%
2-5	22.5%
5 or	65%

Figure 13.16

Page Layout

You have probably already noticed that one of the serious limitations in developing Web pages is the ability to place text and graphics where you choose on the page. You can't just move elements around in the same way that you can when working directly on a sheet of paper. One of the most powerful ways to use tables is to be able to control your page layout. Up until now our approach to tables has been working with little boxes or tables to organize the way that information is presented. Now try to picture your Web page as a big table, made up of rows and cells. All of the elements that you want to have on your page can be placed in various cells in order to position them exactly the way that you want them to appear on the page, giving you almost exact control over the layout of your page. This in fact has become the most important use of tables: page layout.

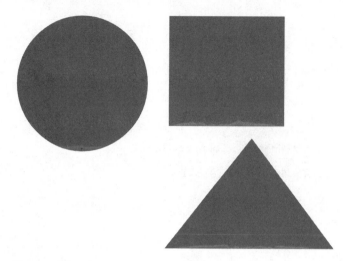

Figure 13.17

Let's go through a little exercise to illustrate this point. In Figure 13.17 I have created three simple shapes.

The shapes are dutifully lined up on the page, like good soldiers. In previous chapters we have explored a few alignment possibilities for moving the shapes around or having text wrap around the shapes. But, I think you will agree that our ability to put these shapes anywhere on the page, in any relationship to each other or to other elements, such as text, is somewhat limited up until now. Let's see what we can do with tables.

I took the above shapes and put them into a large table. Using column span, row span, and the alignment options, I moved the shapes into positions that would not otherwise have been possible without tables. The result is the Web page shown in Figure 13.18.

The shapes above could really be any element that might be used on a Web page: graphics, text, horizontal rules, and so on. The important point is that tables allow us to organize our page with excellent control. In the above diagram I have left the borders visible in order to see how the table functions. I strongly recommend that when you are working with tables that you always include the borders until you have finished your table. When you have completed the table, you can eliminate the border by changing the BORDER attribute to zero.

Figure 13.19 shows the same page with the borders turned off.

Nearly all pages of any complexity on the World Wide Web use tables to organize the composition of the page. If you really want to learn about Web page design, I recommend the following exercise. Visit a number of sites looking for pages with interesting and complex organization. Select a page and

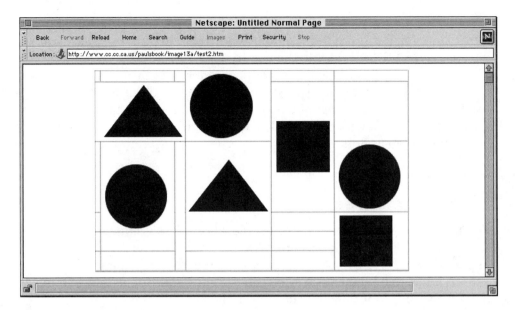

Figure 13.18

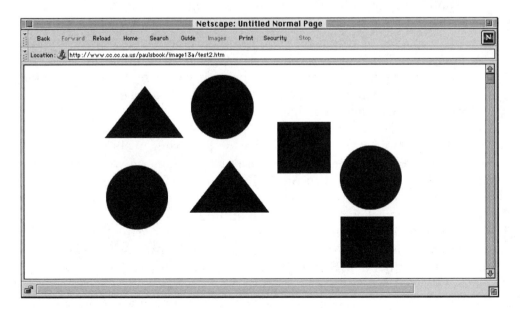

Figure 13.19

save the source code to your hard drive. Using your text editor, open the source code for the saved page, and look for table tags. Every place you see the tag, enter BORDER=1 into the tag. In other words, turn the borders back on. Save the changes and then view the page using your browser. It's a lot like the spy movies when the guy sprays dust in the air in order to see the otherwise hidden laser beams. All of the sudden you will see the table or tables in which the page has been organized. It's an excellent way to learn the secrets of the big-time Webmasters.

Table Alternatives

We must once again consider those people who will be visiting your site using a browser that does not support tables. Since tables have become more widely supported, there is less to worry about in this regard. I will admit that my suggestions here are a little half-hearted, since I have have found tables to be absolutely one of the most important tools in the HTML arsenal.

Some of the possibilities

- If you are using tables to chart information, you can often use lists for similar effects. In other words, you can try to organize your information so that tables are not needed. Most of the information included in this chapter could have been presented in an organized format by using lists. Another option is to create a table-like appearance using preformatted text.
- Use a graphic of your table. You could develop a table in your graphics program and save it as a GIF or JPEG. Instead of using the table, you could include the graphic on your page. If you want to save some time here's a good trick that you might want to try: Create a graphic that looks like an HTML table (see Figure 13.20).

Create a table using HTML and view it in your Web browser. Do a "screen capture"; meaning take a picture of everything on your screen. Mac people can do this easily with the keyboard command "Command/Shift/3." PC people can easily find a shareware program that will do the same.

On the Mac, when you hold down all three keys at once, you will hear what sounds like the shutter on a camera. A file called Picture 1 will show up on your hard drive. Open that file with your graphic program, crop the image, and save it as either a GIF or a JPEG. (Remember, if you make it too big, it will load slowly.)

Figure 13.20 is an example of a table that was done as a screen capture. It looks identical to the real thing.

Alien Characteristics	
Heads	
Number of Heads Reported	% Reported (sampling 2 million sightings)
1	12%
2-5	22.5%
5 or more	65%

Figure 13.20

The only drawback that I see to using tables is having to write the code to create them. The HTML for a table of any size can be somewhat complex and confusing. Remembering the following suggestions will make it easier to keep track of what you are doing

- Keep the border turned on until your table is completed.
- Indent your HTML so that you can easily see where the **<TABLE>, <TR>,<TH>,** and **<TD>** tags begin and end.

The drawbacks to tables are far outweighed by the potential that tables have for providing the maximum amount of control over the precise formatting and organization of information on Web pages. For those who would really like to continue to develop their Web pages in new and exciting ways, I highly recommend a book called Creating Killer Web Pages, by David Siegel. The book is loaded with great examples of designing entire Web pages within table structures. While tables might seem cumbersome to construct, they are quite liberating in terms of organizing space on a Web page for more effective communication.

Important points of this chapter

- To change the thickness of a table border, you enter a value of 1 or greater as follows: **<TABLE BORDER= # in pixels>**. A value of 0 will turn the border off.

- To change the width or thickness of the borders within a table, the CELLSPACING attribute is used within the **<TABLE>** tag.
- To change the width, or thickness, of the space around the text within the cells, the CELLPADDING attribute is used within the **<TABLE>** tag.
- Tables, as with images, can have text wrap to the left or right of them by using the alignment, ALIGN, attribute within the **<TABLE>** tag.
- You can control the width of the entire table by designating the WIDTH, in pixels or percentages, in the **<TABLE>** tag. You can also control the width of columns by using the WIDTH attribute in the **<TH>** or **<TD>** tags and giving the WIDTH attribute a value in either percentages or in pixels.
- Nesting tables within other tables allows further control over the formatting of a page and the information contained within it.
- A new feature of tables is background color, which can be used for the entire table, individual rows, or cells.

Visit the Prentice Hall Web site

- For additional examples of tables and nesting tables.
- For color versions of the examples shown in this chapter.
- There is a list of recommended activities and assignments to improve your skills working with tables and using tables for formatting.
- There is a short quiz to test your knowledge on the information in this chapter.

Forms

It seems that we are constantly filling out forms. Visa, MasterCard, American Express, and after that, we fill out bankruptcy forms. We complete tax forms, survey forms, missing cat reports; the list is endless. From the time that we awake, until the time that we go to bed, our lives consist of nothing more than filling out one form after another. What's the answer?

Outlaw forms, ban them from our society, punish the perpetrators of forms?

No! The answer is to get even; we must learn to make forms ourselves. That is what this chapter is about: How to make a form for your Web page.

Until now we have been in the business of delivering information. We've all worked hard to make our web pages interesting, well organized, and entertaining. What do we get out of all of that work? The answer is feed-back. Now we want to ask people what they thought of all of our work. We are going to create a guest book for our site. We want not only feedback about our pages, but we also want to know things about our guests, personal things, things that they wouldn't even tell their best friends. All of this will be possible through our guest book form.

Actually, forms can be used for all sorts of noble and or greedy purposes. Perhaps you are running a Web page that attempts to find out if people think that Congress is doing a good job. You could run an informal survey from your page. Maybe you have a product line, and you want to enable customers to order over the Internet from an online catalog. A form is the perfect mechanism.

This chapter demonstrates how to create a simple guest book for your web site.

Now that I have gotten you all excited about creating forms for your page, I must bring a little reality to the picture before we get started. Forms involve interactivity between the viewer and your Web page.

There are two important aspects to the development of forms.

- To create a form is to add special components to a Web page that allow the viewer to enter information by typing in text or making selections from a number of options presented to them.
- Once the form is completed, means must be provided for the results to be transmitted back to you, otherwise the form is of no value.

You will see shortly, that the development of a form through HTML is really pretty easy. An understanding of how to construct forms is basic to the study of HTML, which is why it is included in this book.

Getting the information back from a form is a little more problematic, often requiring some programming knowledge. It is outside the intent of this book to provide you with the programming skills required to write a program that processes forms. Frankly, I don't have the skills either. However, I will discuss various options, from my own experience, for making your forms functional, including several practical solutions that sidestep programming requirements.

So, first we focus on creating the form. Then we turn our attention to retrieving the information.

FORM Tags

Let's deal with the basic form tags first. How many of you have already guessed **<FORM></FORM>**? (This stuff gets easier each time.) Everything that is in the form will be placed between the **<FORM></FORM>** tags.

We start our form by asking for the person's name (assuming that it is a person). To do so we must create a box, called a Text Field, within which his or her name can be typed. To accomplish this we will use the <INPUT> tag between the **<FORM></FORM>** tags.

The HTML

```
<FORM>

<INPUT>

</FORM>
```

Notice that the **<INPUT>** tag is a singlet, requiring no closing tag.

The Result: (Figure 14.1)

Figure 14.1

We now have a box, but we need to add some attributes to make it functional.

NAME Attribute

Form elements (with the exception of SUBMIT and RESET) must be given a name using the NAME attribute in the <INPUT> tag. When we receive our results back from the form, it won't be adequate to just receive the answer. We will also want to know what question is being answered. The name represents the question and will be returned to us along with the answer. When you select the name, be sure to select a name that is descriptive of the question that you are asking. In this case, since I am asking for the guest's name, I will call the text field "Name:" Clever?

The HTML

```
<FORM>

<INPUT NAME="Name">

</FORM>
```

The Result (Figure 14.2)

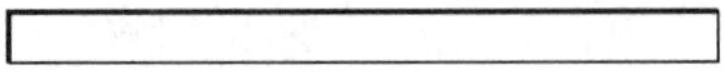

Figure 14.2

It doesn't look any different, but now that it has a name, it feels different. It's really the age-old question, "If an input field doesn't have a name, does it really exist?"

TYPE Attribute

There are several possible TYPES of INPUT. The default TYPE is TEXT. To avoid confusion, TYPE="TEXT" should be entered as an INPUT attribute.

The HTML

```
<FORM>

<INPUT TYPE="TEXT" NAME="Name">

</FORM>
```

The Result (Figure 14.3)

Figure 14.3

Again, no visible change. We're dealing with the "inner" text field right now.

VALUE Attribute

We need to tell our guest what we want entered into the text area. To do so, we can just type a label in front of the box.

The HTML

```
<FORM>

Name:<INPUT TYPE="TEXT" NAME="Name">

</FORM>
```

The Result (Figure 14.4)

Name: [   ]

Figure 14.4

An alternative is to put text into the box that your guest can type over. This is accomplished by including the VALUE attribute followed by the text that you want to appear.

The HTML

```
<FORM>

Name:<INPUT TYPE="TEXT" NAME="Name"

VALUE="Yes, your name, here, now!>

</FORM>
```

The Result (Figure 14.5)

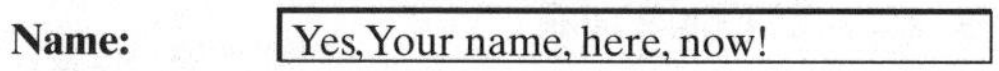

Name: [Yes, Your name, here, now!]

Figure 14.5

Sometimes it doesn't hurt to be real clear about what you want. After all, this is your form!

SIZE Attribute

Let's suppose that we expect a lot of visitors from one of those foreign countries where they have real long names, with no vowels. No problem; our guests can type as many characters as they need, up to 255, into the text area. They will only be able to see 30 characters at time.

If we want to give them a little more room, we can change the size of the text area, by using the SIZE attribute.

The HTML

```
<FORM>

:Name:<INPUT TYPE="TEXT" NAME="name"

SIZE="60">

</FORM>
```

The Result (Figure 14.6)

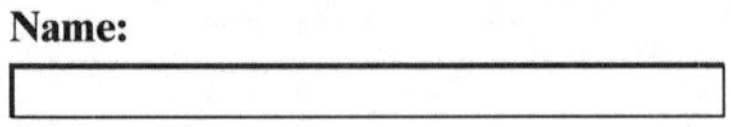

Name:

Figure 14.6

That should work for most names!

Maximum Length

We can also control the length of the information that our guest puts into the text area. For example, if we want to create a box for middle initials and don't want to allow guests to enter their whole middle names, we can use the MAXLENGTH attribute.

The HTML

```
<FORM>

Your Middle Initial:<INPUT TYPE="TEXT"

NAME="Initial" SIZE="2" MAX LENGTH="2">

</FORM>
```

The Result (Figure 14.7)

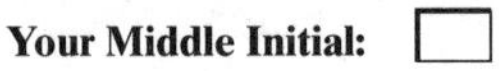

Your Middle Initial:

Figure 14.7

Try to enter more than two characters in that box and the stock market will probably crash! (Notice that I changed the size of the text field at the same time with the SIZE attribute.)

Simple Form

Now that we have covered the various possibilities for the text area, let's build a simple form that asks some basic questions.

The HTML

```
<FORM>

Name:<INPUT TYPE="TEXT" NAME="Name"

SIZE="35"><BR>
```

Address:<INPUT TYPE="TEXT"

NAME="Address" SIZE="35">

E-mail:<INPUT TYPE="TEXT" NAME="E-mail"

SIZE="35">

Shoe Size:<INPUT TYPE="TEXT" NAME="Shoe

Size" SIZE="4">

</FORM>

The Result (Figure 14.8)

Name:	
Address:	
E-mail:	
Shoe Size:	

Figure 14.8

Notice that each INPUT field has a different name, corresponding to the information within that field. This is essential! Also, notice that I have followed each field with a <BR> tag, forcing a line break so that the form doesn't just string itself across the page.

Forms and Tables

Right now, our form looks disorganized and unprofessional. It would be nice to line up the text fields so we look like we know what we're doing, like the IRS. Combining forms and tables is an excellent way to organize the form elements.

The HTML

```
<FORM>
 <TABLE BORDER=0>
  <TR>
   <TD>Name:</TD>
   <TD><INPUT TYPE="TEXT" NAME="Name"
```

```
    SIZE="35"></TD>

  </TR>

  <TR>

    <TD>Address:</TD>

    <TD><INPUT TYPE="TEXT" NAME="Address"

    SIZE="35"></TD>

  </TR>

  <TR>

    <TD>E-mail:</TD>

    <TD><INPUT TYPE="TEXT" NAME="E-mail"

    SIZE="35"></TD>

  </TR>

  <TR>

    <TD>Shoe Size:</TD>

    <TD>INPUT TYPE="TEXT" NAME="Shoe Size"

    SIZE="4"></TD>

  </TR>

  </TABLE>

</FORM>
```

The Result (Figure 14.9)

Name:	
Address:	
E-mail:	
Shoe Size:	

Figure 14.9

A completed form! Not quite. The form still needs a way for the guest to SUBMIT the form.

SUBMIT and RESET

Submit

To complete our form we will need to include a button for the guest to send the information to us. This is accomplished by once again using the INPUT tag. In this case we want to change the TYPE attribute to SUBMIT.

The HTML

```
<FORM>

<INPUT TYPE="SUBMIT">

</FORM>
```

Notice that the type-"SUBMIT" Input does not require a name.

The Result (Figure 14.10)

Submit

Figure 14.10

The default text for the SUBMIT button is "Submit Query." I don't know about you, but that sounds a little stuffy. The text on the button can be changed by using the VALUE attribute followed by the name that you want to appear on the button.

The HTML

```
<FORM>

<INPUT TYPE="SUBMIT" VALUE="Sock it to

me!">

</FORM>
```

The Result (Figure 14.11)

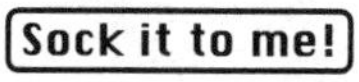

Sock it to me!

Figure 14.11

Notice that the button automatically stretches to accommodate the longer text.

Graphic SUBMIT Button

We could also substitute a graphic for the SUBMIT button. First we need to change the TYPE from SUBMIT to IMAGE. Then we need to replace the VALUE attribute with the SRC attribute, followed by the location of the graphic that we want to use.

The HTML

```
<FORM>

<INPUT TYPE="IMAGE" SRC="send.gif">

</FORM>
```

The Result (Figure 14.12)

Figure 14.12

Notice that the button has a border around it, indicating that it is a hyperlink. We can eliminate the border by including BORDER="0" in the INPUT tag.

The HTML

```
<FORM>

<INPUT TYPE="IMAGE" SRC="send.gif"

BORDER="0">

</FORM>
```

The Result (Figure 14.13)

Figure 14.13

RESET

What if our guest wants to clear the form and start over again? We will need to include a RESET button. We use the INPUT tag once again, and for the TYPE we enter RESET.

The HTML

```
<FORM>

<INPUT TYPE="RESET">

</FORM>
```

The Result (Figure 14.14)

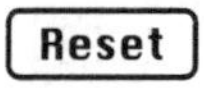

[Reset]

Figure 14.14

The word "Reset" may not make it clear to everyone what the button actually does. We can change the label on the button by including the VALUE attribute followed by the name that we want the button to have.

The HTML

```
<FORM>

<INPUT TYPE="RESET" VALUE="Clear

Form">

</FORM>
```

The Result (Figure 14.15)

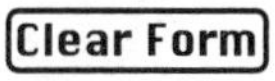

[Clear Form]

Figure 14.15

Notice that the RESET button, like the SUBMIT button, does not require a NAME attribute.

Complete Form

Let's combine our form with the text fields and the buttons (Figure 14.16).

If we were online, we could give the form a try. We would fill it out carefully, being honest about our shoe size, and hit the SUBMIT, or "Sock it to me!" button.

Whoops!! Nothing happens. We have not yet told the Web browser what to do with the form. There is some important information that must still be entered into the <FORM> tag.

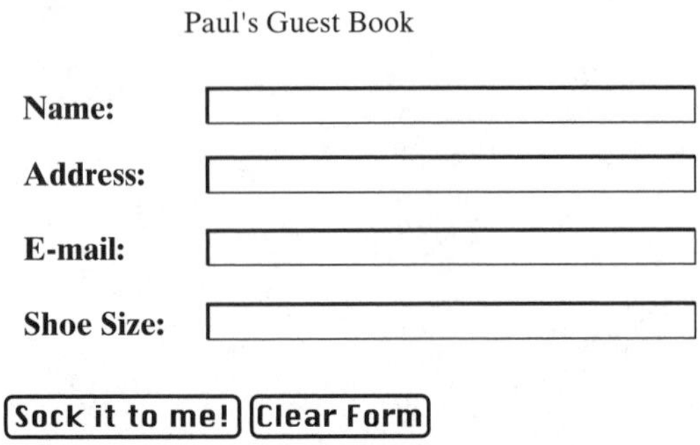

Paul's Guest Book

Name:

Address:

E-mail:

Shoe Size:

Sock it to me! Clear Form

Figure 14.16

METHOD Attribute

The form must include information about how we want the information sent. There are two possible METHODS, GET or POST. The most common METHOD is POST, and without getting into the differences, that is what we will use here. The METHOD is entered in to the **<FORM>** tag followed by POST.

The HTML

    <FORM METHOD=POST>

ACTION Attribute

The Browser also needs to know where to send the information for it to be processed. Normally, forms are sent to a CGI (Common Gateway Interface) script that processes the information in some designated manner.

CGI Scripts

 There is additional information regarding CGI scripts on the Prentice Hall Web site.

A CGI is a small program that resides on the server and acts as an interface between the server and other applications that might be required to process the form. In our case, we might want the results of our form to be organized so that we have the name of the text fields combined with the information provided and returned to us in the form of an e-mail.

We would want to read the result of our form like this

Name: Paul Meyers

Address: 3000 College Hts. Blvd

E-mail: pmeyers@cc.cc.ca.us

Shoe Size: 16

Since each form is unique in the information that is requested, each form requires a separate script to be written or adapted to handle the information.

I have included a guest book on the Prentice Hall Web site. You are welcome to copy it. While you are there, please fill out the form and submit it. The results are automatically entered onto a guest book Web page, which you can visit to see your entry and the entries of other visitors.

Fortunately, many scripts are available on the Internet and in books that can be adapted to meet most needs, without having to learn to program in one of the CGI scripting languages. Once you find a script that is designed for processing a form in the way that you choose to have it processed, it is possible, with very little knowledge, to change or adapt the script to specifically meet your needs.

Using a CGI script does require some contact with the system administrator to set things up. (The system administrator is the person who is responsible for the Web server.) Most Internet Service Providers provide a directory for CGIs, although they might not provide much help in setting up your script.

An in-depth look at CGIs is outside of the realm of this book, and beyond my expertise. However, at the beginning of this chapter, I did say that I would suggest several practical alternatives for posting forms. One of those alternatives is to use FrontPage, a Web editing program developed by Microsoft. FrontPage goes well beyond the ability of most Web editing programs, in that it allows you to build interactivity into your pages. Forms are particularly well implemented in FrontPage and are very easy to construct. If your Web page resides on a server that has FrontPage extensions installed, your form processing problems are over. FrontPage extensions have built in CGIs specifically for processing your form in almost any manner that you choose. Because of the popularity of FrontPage, its low cost, and the increased functionality that it provides, many ISPs are now providing FrontPage extensions on their servers.

Before we move on, I am sure that you are curious to see what the information from our form will look like when it is returned to me. Figure 14.17 is an example of the way a script processes the form data and e-mails it to me.

On the left, I have bracketed all of the names that I gave the INPUT fields. Each name is followed on the right by the information that was entered into the field and submitted.

Figure 14.17

Mailto:

Remember, I said that I would give you several alternatives for handling forms without having any programming knowledge. I already talked briefly about the use of FrontPage and its extensions.

Using the MAILTO: protocol is another option. You might remember way back in one of the earlier chapters I introduced MAILTO: to create a link that would send you mail from your home page.

MAILTO: can also be used in forms. By placing the ACTION attribute within the **<FORM>** tag, followed by MAILTO: plus an e-mail address, I can send the results of the form to myself. An example follows.

The HTML

```
FORM METHOD="POST"

ACTION="MAILTO:pmeyers@cc.cc.ca.us"
```

When the SUBMIT button is clicked on my form, the results will automatically be mailed to the address supplied.

The Advantages of MAILTO

- The nice thing about the MAILTO: is that it is so easy. It does not require access to the server, nor does it require knowledge about CGI scripts.
- Another advantage is that you can test it right from your desktop. Open your page in Netscape, fill out your form, and hit the SUBMIT button. Check your e-mail, and you will have received your form.

The Disadvantages of MAILTO:

Right now you are probably saying, "Why did we go through all of the discussion about CGIs if MAILTO: is so simple?"

- One of the obvious shortcomings of MAILTO: is that it can only mail you the information. CGIs, on the other hand, can be set up to process forms in a number of very useful ways.

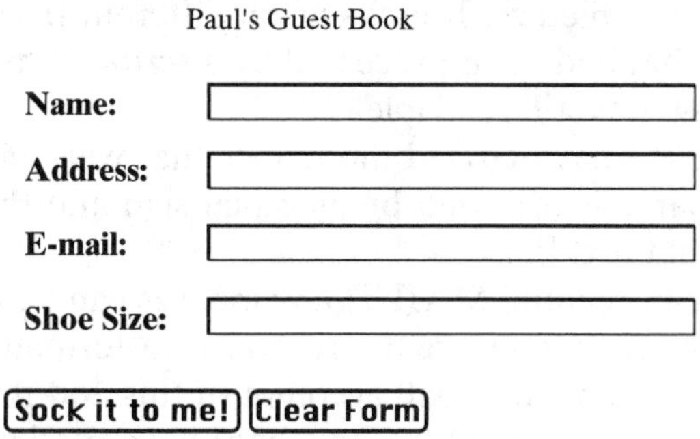

Paul's Guest Book

Name:

Address:

E-mail:

Shoe Size:

[Sock it to me!] [Clear Form]

Figure 14.18

- Another shortcoming of MAILTO: is that your form will be limited to guests with browsers that have an e-mail program built into the browser, such as Netscape. As of this writing, Internet Explorer does not support MAILTO: forms. If your guest book is primarily for feedback about your personal Web page, then it probably isn't too important if you miss a certain percentage of people. If, however, your Web page is for business purposes, you don't want to miss anyone, particularly if you are using your page to take orders.
- Another drawback to MAILTO: is the somewhat unclear format in which you will receive the information, making it more difficult to understand. I will elaborate on this shortly.

This form is available to test on the Prentice Hall web site.

However, let's give it a try and see if it actually works. The completed form is shown in Figure 14.18. You can fill it out online if you like and send me your shoe size, just to see how it works.

You will notice that when you submit the form you receive a warning that you are about to reveal your e-mail address. Also, you will not get any confirmation of the form having been sent, as you normally do when submitting a form that is processed by a CGI.

I filled out the above form and sent it to myself. Figure 14.19 is what the information looks like in my e-mail.

```
&name=Paul+Meyers&address+3000+College+Hts.+Blvd&email=pmeyers@cc.cc.ca.us.&shoe=14.5
```

Figure 14.19

Not a very pretty picture. It looks much different from the earlier example that I showed that had been processed by a script. While it may appear to be a little confusing, it is still readable.

In Figure 14.20 I have circled the names that were given to each of the text fields. Each name is followed by an equal sign and the information that was entered into that text field.

The difficulty in reading MAILTO: responses can be overcome by using an additional program to convert the response to formatted text. There are many shareware programs that will accomplish this and make the MAILTO: easier to read and save to a text file. One that I have tried for the Macintosh is called Mailto: Converter. It works okay and costs $5.00. I have posted the Web address for this program and a few other such programs on the Prentice Hall Web site.

The HTML

The following is the complete HTML for the above fully functional form, combining the use of a table to format a form using MAILTO

```
<FORM METHOD=POST

ACTION=MAILTO:"pmeyers@cc.cc.ca.us">

<TABLE BORDER=0>

        <TR>

            <TD>Name:</TD>

            <TD><INPUT

            TYPE="TEXT"

            NAME="Name"

            SIZE="35"></TD>

        </TR>

        <TR>

            <TD>Address</TD>

            <TD><INPUT
```

&name=Paul+Meyers&address=3000+College+Hts.+Blvd&email=pmeyers@cc.cc.ca.us&shoe=14.5

Figure 14.20

```
            TYPE="TEXT"

            NAME="Address"

            SIZE="35"></TD>

      </TR>

      <TR>

            <TD>E-mail</TD>

            <TD><INPUT

            TYPE="TEXT"

            NAME="E-mail"

            SIZE="35"></TD>

      </TR>

      <TR>

            <TD>Shoe Size</TD>

            <TD><INPUT

            TYPE="TEXT"

            NAME="Shoe size"

            SIZE="4"></TD>

      </TR>

</TABLE>

<INPUT TYPE="SUBMIT"

VALUE="Sock it to me!">

<INPUT TYPE="RESET"

VALUE="Clear Form">

</FORM>
```

Hopefully, you now have a clear idea of how to create a simple form. Before you actually start slapping a form together, you should do some careful planning. What information do you really want to get? Make it as simple as possible, so that guests do not have to spend a lot of time with it. Frankly, if it is too long, people won't bother to complete your form. You should carefully plan the layout of your form. It should appear logical and nicely organized.

You are asking people to give you information, usually with no expectation of a return response. If you don't have too high a volume of traffic, you might consider sending a short e-mail thanks for filling out your form. Another possibility is to copy and paste the contents of the form messages onto a Web page and link to it from your form page. In that way, visitors can see the comments of previous visitors.

The next chapter will cover the use of some other possibilities for your form, such as checklists, selection boxes, and text areas.

Important points of this chapter

- Forms are a means of receiving feedback on your Web page and acquiring information for a wide variety of reasons, such as business.
- The basic form tags are **<FORM></FORM>.**
- The **<INPUT>** tags are contained within the **<FORM></FORM>** tags and are used to create text fields in which information can be entered.
- All of the form elements (with the exception of SUBMIT and RESET) must be given a name using the NAME attribute in the **<INPUT>** tag.
- There are several possible TYPES of INPUT. The default TYPE is TEXT. To avoid confusion, TYPE="TEXT" should be entered as an INPUT attribute.
- To designate the size of the text field, the SIZE attribute is used. If a maximum length is desired the MAXLENGTH attribute is entered into the **<INPUT>** tag.
- Combining forms and tables is an excellent way to organize form elements.
- To receive the information entered into your form, you must supply the user with a SUBMIT button, which is a value for the TYPE attribute in the **<INPUT>** tag.
- To give the user the ability to alter the information by clearing the form completely, we use the RESET button which is a value for the TYPE attribute in the **<INPUT>** tag.
- The METHOD attribute is used to tell the form what to do with the information entered into the form. The two possible METHODS are POST and GET.
- The browser also needs to know where to send the information for it to be processed as indicated by the ACTION.
- A CGI script is normally used to process form information. It requires some knowledge of programming.

- One of the alternatives to a CGI script is MAILTO:. By entering the ACTION attribute into the **<FORM>** tag followed by MAILTO: and an e-mail address, the results of the form will be sent to that address. MAILTO: is a simple and easy way to get information via forms; however, it is not currently supported by all browsers.

Visit the Prentice Hall Web site

- For additional information regarding CGI scripts.
- For a sample guest book that you are welcome to copy.
- To try out a test form and see how it works.
- There is a list of recommended activities and assignments to improve your skills working with forms and their related attributes and elements.
- There is a short quiz to test your knowledge on the information in this chapter.

CHAPTER **15**

More on Forms . . .

INPUT Tags

Password Field

Checkboxes

Radio Buttons

Pop-up Menu

TEXTAREA

To review a little:
In the last chapter we completed a form using only the **<INPUT>** tag enclosed in the **<FORM></FORM>** tags.

To create a text field, we made the INPUT TYPE="TEXT." To make a SUBMIT button, we made the INPUT TYPE="SUBMIT." To make the RESET button, we made the INPUT TYPE="RESET."

For example

```
<INPUT TYPE="TEXT">
```

The Result (Figure 15.1)

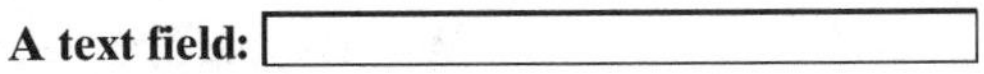

A text field: [_____]

Figure 15.1

```
<INPUT TYPE="SUBMIT">
```

The Result (Figure 15.2)

A SUBMIT button [**Submit**]

Figure 15.2

```
<INPUT TYPE="RESET">
```

The Result (Figure 15.3)

A reset or clear button: [**Reset**]

Figure 15.3

Finally, we covered how to have the form submitted.

Right now, you're probably asking yourself, "Is that all there is to forms—a short one line text area, a quick submit, and goodbye?"

This chapter will cover additional ways for us to probe the minds of the visitors to our pages. We will cover selection lists, text areas, radio buttons, and checkboxes.

INPUT Tags

Since we left off with **<INPUT>** tags, let's stay with them. Remember, the **<INPUT>** tag is a singlet; it does not have a closing tag.

Password Field

Let's start out with the simplest thing that I can show you, the Password Field. Let's suppose that you have been admitted to a witness protection program as a result of having testified against the head of a crime syndicate that was making a fortune by reselling dog coffins from a pet cemetery. While you feel that you still have a right to lead a normal life, including the right to have your own Web page, you certainly don't want every yahoo in the world coming and going, and finding out all about your identity change, new address, and so on.

You'd like a login procedure that includes a login name and a password. And I am going to show you how to make the form for this purpose.

The login name is the simple one: We just create a text field, like the following HTML:

The HTML

```
<FORM>

Login Name:<INPUT TYPE="TEXT"

NAME="Login">

</FORM>
```

The Result (Figure 15.4)

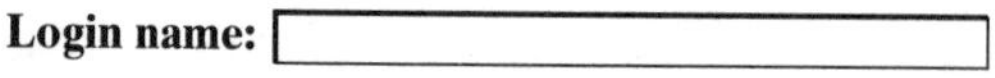

Login name: [   ]

Figure 15.4

Pretty simple, huh? Now we want to create a place to enter the password, but we don't want to have it show up as text. What if the mob was looking through our window with high powered, infrared, heat seeking missile type of binoculars. They would be able to read the password, login to your web page, find your location, and the rest is best left up to your imagination. We all know what they do to snitches.The answer is to create a Password Field.

By changing our INPUT TYPE from TEXT to PASSWORD, when we type into the field, little dots show up instead of text. For example

```
<FORM>

Login Name: <INPUT TYPE="TEXT"

NAME="Login"><P>

Password: <INPUT TYPE="PASSWORD"

NAME="password">

</FORM>
```

The Result (Figure 15.5)

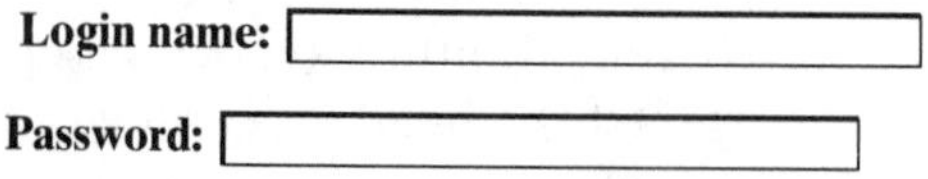

Login name: [   ]

Password: [   ]

Figure 15.5

If you could type into the above password field, you would see that little bullets show up instead of characters. (I wish that they had this stuff when I was a kid!) The form with the login and password filled in would look like Figure 15.6.

Login name: [Paul Meyers   ]

Password: [•••••••   ]

Figure 15.6

How can we use it? I have no idea. I just felt obligated to pass on this widely documented bit of form information. You may need to know how to use it someday. This is another case where you would have to be working with a system administrator, or someone with programming knowledge to make the password field functional.

Now, to move on to something that has more immediate practical use.

Checkboxes

A single checkbox is useful when you want to ask a question for which there is only one answer, such as a yes or no, true or false answer. This type of question is called Boolean, meaning, "there are no two ways about it."

To create a checkbox, we once again use the **<INPUT>** tag within the **<FORM></FORM>** tags. We change the TYPE of INPUT to "CHECK-BOX."

The HTML

```
<FORM>

<INPUT TYPE="CHECKBOX">

</FORM>
```

The Result: (Figure 15.7)

☐

Figure 15.7

Now we need to ask a question. We also need to indicate to our guest what it means to check the box. Here's the HTML for an example.

The HTML

```
A check will indicate a yes answer:<BR>

Have you stopped driving too fast?
```

```
<FORM>

<INPUT TYPE="CHECKBOX">

</FORM>
```

The Result (Figure 15.8)

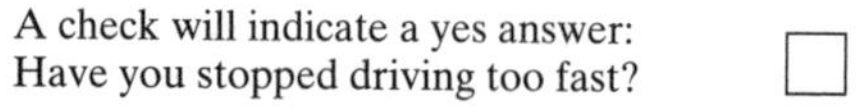

A check will indicate a yes answer:
Have you stopped driving too fast?

Figure 15.8

Now we have to enter additional information into our **<INPUT>** tag that will enable us to interpret the answer when the form is returned. A NAME attribute is essential. Additionally, we need to have a VALUE attribute, that is sent to us with the name if the box is checked. To complete the form we will need a SUB-MIT button and a RESET button. We will use MAILTO: to submit the form.

The HTML

```
<FORM METHOD="POST"

ACTION="MAILTO:pmeyers@cc.cc.ca.us>

A check will indicate a yes answer:<BR>

Have you stopped driving too fast?

<INPUT TYPE="CHECKBOX" NAME="Speeding"

VALUE="YES"><BR>

<INPUT TYPE="SUBMIT">

<INPUT TYPE="RESET">

</FORM>
```

The Result (Figure 15.9)

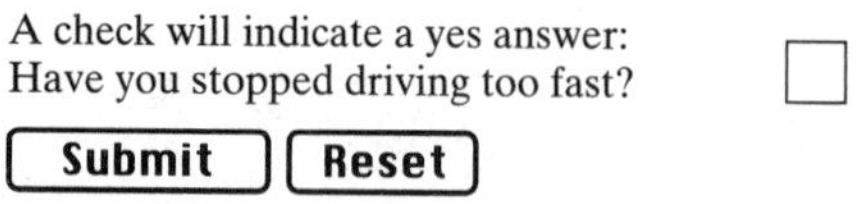

A check will indicate a yes answer:
Have you stopped driving too fast?

| Submit | | Reset |

Figure 15.9

After having checked the box, I submitted this form to myself. The e-mail result is shown in Figure 15.10.

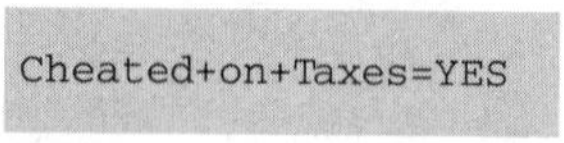

```
Cheated+on+Taxes=YES
```

Figure 15.10

If the box had been left unchecked, it would have been ignored and not included in our result.

If we had not included a VALUE attribute as part of the checkbox, the default value of "ON" would have been returned instead of "YES."

To illustrate this more clearly, I completed and sent myself a form using MAILTO: that includes three checkboxes. I have charted the form below to help better understand the results. Please follow me as I move between the chart and the results and explanation below the chart (Figure 15.11).

What color meat would you eat if you were really hungry?		NAME	VALUE	SELECTED
Red:	☒	red:	yes:	checked:
Green:	☒	green:	default: (ON)	checked:
Blue:	☐	blue:	yes:	unchecked:

Figure 15.11

The Result (Figure 15.12)

```
red=yes&green=ON
```

Figure 15.12

When I submitted the form

- I checked Red, and since it had the VALUE="yes," yes was returned after the NAME.
- I checked Green, but did not give it a value, so the default value "ON" was returned after the NAME.
- I left Blue unchecked, therefore nothing was returned.

Note: In this chapter, I am only going to illustrate how example forms would be returned using ACTION=MAILTO:. Since I assume most of you will not yet have access to CGIs or FrontPage, we will focus on using ACTION=MAILTO: to process them—kind of a poor man's solution to forms. As I have already pointed out, if you want to test MAILTO: forms, you will have to use Netscape to post them. If the forms were being posted to a CGI, the results would depend upon how the CGI was written to process the form.

All of the example forms in this chapter are available on the Prentice Hall Web site.

Multiple Selections

A particularly valuable way to use checkboxes is to give the guest a list of items from which to select. Let's imagine that I'm running a pizza place where you can order over the Internet. On the menu is a list of toppings. An example is shown in Figure 15.13.

Cheese Pizza with:

Roadkill Rabbit ☐
Still Leapin' Lizard ☐
Banana Mustard ☐
Out of Season Mussel ☐
Eye of Newt ☐ (not a political statement)

You can order none, one, or all of the above choices.

Figure 15.13

The HTML

```
<FORM METHOD="POST"

ACTION="MAILTO:pmeyers@cc.cc.ca.us>

Roadkill Rabbit

<INPUT TYPE="CHECKBOX" NAME="rabbit"

VALUE="yes".<BR>

Still Leapin' Lizard

<INPUT TYPE="CHECKBOX" NAME="lizard"

VALUE="yes"><BR>

Banana Mustard

<INPUT TYPE="CHECKBOX"

NAME="mustard" VALUE="yes"><BR>

Out of Season Mussel

<INPUT TYPE="CHECKBOX" NAME="mussel"

VALUE="yes" > <BR>
```

Eye of Newt

<INPUT TYPE="CHECKBOX" NAME="newt"

VALUE="yes" >(not a political statement)

</FORM>

The Result (Figure 15.14)

```
rabbit=yes&lizard=yes&mustard=yes&mussel=yes
```

Figure 15.14

I mailed the above form to myself; the MAILTO: response is included below
As you can see above, everything sounded good to me except Eye of Newt (not a political statement).

Prechecked Boxes

One last point about checkboxes. Let's say that we are asking a question that we assume most people will answer yes. To save people a little time, we can have the box prechecked, and the guest will have to uncheck it if the answer is no. To accomplish this we will include the CHECKED attribute within the **<INPUT>** tag.

The HTML

<FORM>

Do you still owe me $100?

<INPUT TYPE="CHECKBOX" NAME="owe"

VALUE="yes" CHECKED>
check box for yes

</FORM>

The Result (Figure 15.15)

Do you still owe me $100 ⊠
check box for yes

Figure 15.15

This little prompt will help to jog our guest's memory.

Radio Buttons

There are occasions when we do not want to give our guests an opportunity to select more than one choice in a list of items. In these cases we can use radio buttons. Radio buttons are also created by using the **<INPUT>** tag, but in this case the TYPE is RADIO.

The HTML

<FORM>

<INPUT TYPE="RADIO" CHECKED>

<INPUT TYPE="RADIO">

</FORM>

The Result (Figure 15.16)

Figure 15.16

Looks like a winking fish, doesn't it? Notice that one of the buttons is checked. Only one item from a list of radio buttons can be selected. If I were to click on the button on the right, the button on the left would no longer be selected.

Let's say that I have a questionaire that asks you to indicate whether you are driving a domestically made or foreign made automobile.

The HTML

<FORM>

I drive a foreign car

<INPUT TYPE="RADIO" NAME="cars"

VALUE="foreign" CHECKED>

I drive a domestic car

<INPUT TYPE="RADIO" NAME="cars"

VALUE="domestic">

</FORM>

The Result (Figure 15.17)

I drive a foreigh car ◉
I drive a domestic car ○

Figure 15.17

Let's look carefully at the HTML. Notice:

- I have made the TYPE="RADIO" resulting in a radio button.
- I have given both buttons the same NAME. If I were to give them different names, they wouldn't be part of the same list of choices.
- I have given each button a different VALUE that corresponds to the choice that the guest is making. The foreign car button has the VALUE="foreign" and the domestic car button has the VALUE="domestic." The value of the checked button is what will be returned to me in the results.
- I have included the attribute CHECKED in the first choice, making that choice selected by default.
- Only one choice can be selected. When you check on one, the other is deselected.

When I submitted the above form to myself using the MAILTO: I checked the box for domestic cars. The e-mail response is shown in Figure 15.18.

```
cars=domestic
```

Figure 15.18

Notice that the NAME "cars" is submitted and returned with the VALUE "domestic."

Let's complicate matters a little. Not only do I want to know where the car that you drive is made, I also want to know what make of car you drive.

The HTML

```
<FORM>

I drive a foreign car

<INPUT TYPE="RADIO" NAME="cars"
```

VALUE="foreign" CHECKED>

My car is a:

Honda<INPUT TYPE="RADIO" NAME="make"

VALUE="Honda" CHECKED>

Toyota<INPUT TYPE="RADIO" NAME="make"

VALUE="Toyota">

I drive a domestic car

<INPUT TYPE="RADIO" NAME="cars"

VALUE="domestic">

My car is a:

Chevrolet<INPUT TYPE="RADIO"

NAME="make" VALUE="Chevy">

Ford<INPUT TYPE="RADIO" NAME="make"

VALUE="Ford">

</FORM>

The Result (Figure 15.19)

I drive a foreigh car ◉
My car is a:
Honda ◉
Toyota ○
I drive a domestic car ○
My car is a:
Chevrolet ○
Ford ○

Figure 15.19

You should notice in the HTML for this form that I have given the NAME="make " for all of the car makes. The VALUE is the make of the car corresponding to the button's name. Guests will not only be able to indicate whether they drive a foreign or domestic car, they will be able to indicate which make of car they drive from the choice that I have given them.

Once again I have submitted this form to myself using MAILTO:, after checking off "domestic" and "Chevrolet." The results are shown in Figure 15.20.

```
cars=domestic&make=Chevy
```

Figure 15.20

The gifted among us will have already realized a shortcoming in this form. A truly devious person can check off that he or she drives a foreign car, and check off that it is a Chevrolet. There was a day when you didn't have to worry about people like that! Can you redesign the form to prevent this from happening?

Other

We need to consider one other possibility on our form, which is that the person filling it out drives a car that is not included in the choices that I have given. The obvious answer is to include an "other" button as an option. But I still want to know what the person is driving. We can include a text field to indicate what the "Other" car is. In the following example I will work with the foreign choices to simplify the HTML.

The HTML

```
<FORM>

I drive a foreign car

<INPUT TYPE="RADIO" NAME="cars"

VALUE="foreign" CHECKED><BR>

My car is a:<BR>

Honda<INPUT TYPE="RADIO" NAME="make"

VALUE="Honda" CHECKED><BR>

Toyota<INPUT TYPE="RADIO" NAME="make"

VALUE="Toyota"><BR>

Other<INPUT TYPE="RADIO" NAME="make"

VALUE="other"><BR>
```

Please state other:<INPUT TYPE="TEXT"

NAME="other">

</FORM>

The Result (Figure 15.21)

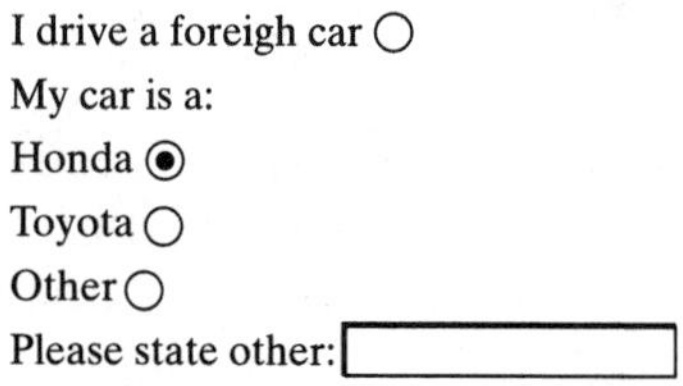

I drive a foreigh car ◯
My car is a:
Honda ◉
Toyota ◯
Other ◯
Please state other: [   ]

Figure 15.21

Using a table would improve the appearance of this form considerably.

Once again, subjecting myself to the perils of the MAILTO: I have submitted this form to myself, after checking off "Other" and filling in the text field. Figure 15.22 is a copy of the e-mail response.

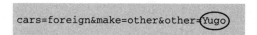
cars=foreign&make=other&other=Yugo

Figure 15.22

The above points out that sometimes you learn things through forms that you don't really want to know.

Pop-up Menu

Another way to handle making selections from a list is the use of the pop-up menu. A list of items is displayed from which one choice may be made. Clicking on the box will display all of the choices in the menu (Figure 15.23).

item one ▼

Figure 15.23

A pop-up menu is accomplished with the **<SELECT></SELECT>** tags included within the **<FORM></FORM>** tags. Notice that they require a closing tag, unlike the <INPUT> tag.

The HTML

```
<FORM>

<SELECT>

</SELECT>

</FORM>
```

The Result (Figure 15.24)

Figure 15.24

OPTION Tag

Kind of an ugly little thing (Figure 15.24), and we can't do much with the above pop-up menu until we add some options. Options are the choices that will appear in the pop-up menu. Options are included within the **<SELECT>** tags by using the **<OPTION>** tag. The **<OPTION>** tag is a singlet and is followed by the text that is to appear in the pop-up menu. For example, a very common question to ask is, "How did you learn about this site?" Once I know this, I can better allocate the $3 million that I spent last year in advertising my Web site.

The HTML

```
How did you learn about this site?

<FORM>

<SELECT>

<OPTION>Surfed In

<OPTION>Search Engine

<OPTION>Advertisement

<OPTION>A Friend

</SELECT>

</FORM>
```

The Result (Figure 15.25)

How did you learn about this site?

Surfed In ▼

Figure 15.25 When we click on the menu all of the other choices will be revealed.

SELECTED Attribute

If we want a different choice to show up as the default in the pop-up window, we can add the SELECTED attribute in the **<OPTION>** tag for the choice that we want to appear. For example, the HTML that follows makes "Friend" the default choice.

The HTML

How did you learn about this site?

<FORM>

<SELECT>

<OPTION VALUE="surfed">Surfed In

<OPTION VALUE="search">Search Engine

<OPTION VALUE="ad">Advertisement

<OPTION VALUE="friend" SELECTED>A

Friend

</SELECT>

</FORM>

The Result (Figure 15.26)

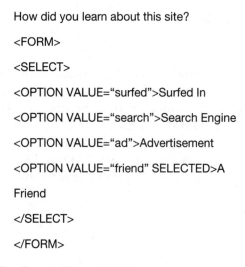

How did you learn about this site?

A friend ▼

Figure 15.26

VALUE Attribute

We now want to enter some values into the **<OPTION>** tag that will be sent back to us when the form is submitted. This is accomplished by using the VALUE attribute.The value does not have to be the same as what the guest sees as a choice. In the above case, since the choices have long names, it would be best to make the value different, yet related.

The HTML

How did you learn about this site?

<FORM>

<SELECT>

<OPTION VALUE="surfed">Surfed In

<OPTION VALUE="search">Search Engine

<OPTION VALUE="ad">Advertisement

<OPTION VALUE="friend" SELECTED>A

Friend

</SELECT>

</FORM>

NAME Attribute

The last step in making the pop-up menu fully functional is to give it a name with the NAME attribute within the <SELECT> tag followed by the name. A pop-up menu is similar to a list of radio buttons, in that all of the choices have the same NAME. For example, here's the HTML for the completed pop-up menu.

The HTML

How did you learn about this site?

<FORM>

<SELECT NAME="learn">

<OPTION VALUE="surfed">Surfed In

<OPTION VALUE="search">Search Engine

<OPTION VALUE="ad">Advertisement

<OPTION VALUE="friend" SELECTED>A

Friend

```
</SELECT>

</FORM>
```

The Result (Figure 15.27)

How did you learn about this site?

Figure 15.27

The pop-up menu doesn't look any different, but will now return the information that we require. Using MAILTO: to submit the form to myself, I received the following results after selecting Search Engine from the choices. (Figure 15.28).

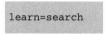

Figure 15.28

SIZE Attribute

If we would like to view more than one choice at a time in a pop-up menu, we can include the SIZE attribute within the **<SELECT>** tag. Until now we have been working with the default, seeing one item on the list at a time. This would be the same as we would see if we set the SIZE to 1. If we set the SIZE to 2, not only will we see two choices, but our window will change from a pop-up window to a scrolling window (Figure 15.29).

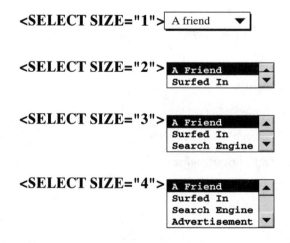

Notice below, that if I increase the size beyond the number of choices, I will end up with a blank line. If that line is selected, no data will be returned.

<SELECT SIZE="5">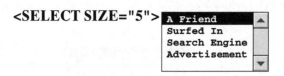

Figure 15.29

Multiple Selections

We might want to give our guest the opportunity to make multiple selections from our window. This is accomplished by including the attribute MULTIPLE within the **<SELECT>** tag. For example: **<SELECT MULTIPLE>**. If MULTIPLE is specified, then a scrolling window will automatically appear.

The HTML

How did you learn about this site?

<FORM>

<SELECT NAME="learn" MULTIPLE>

<OPTION VALUE="surfed">Surfed In

<OPTION VALUE="search">Search Engine

<OPTION VALUE="ad">Advertisement

<OPTION VALUE="friend">A Friend

</SELECT>

</FORM>

The Result (Figure 15.30)

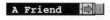

Figure 15.30

Notice that I have not included SIZE, so I get the default all choices showing. Since I have included MULTIPLE, my pop-up window now appears as a scrolling list. When there are only a few choices, it is usually best to have all of your options showing for multiple selections as shown in Figure 15.30.

When there are numerous choices it can be a good idea to use the SIZE attribute within the **<SELECT>** tag to limit the size of the menu, allowing only a few choices to be seen at once. In Figure 15.31 I have set the SIZE attribute to "3" so that now I have to scroll to my fourth choice.

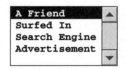

Figure 15.31

Hold down the SHIFT key to make multiple choices that are adjacent to one another on the list. To select non-adjacent items hold down the COMMAND key on the Mac , the CONTROL key on the PC.

To test the above scrolling list, I have submitted it to myself using MAILTO: after I selected "A Friend," "Search Engine," and Advertisement. Figure 15.32 shows the e-mail response that I received.

```
learn=friend&learn=search&learn=ad
```

Figure 15.32

Notice that all of the values refer to the same NAME , "learn."

TEXTAREA

There is one last form possibility to cover, and that is the "mother of all form features," the TEXTAREA. So far, all we've offered our guests is the one line text field. What if we have some special need, such as entering whole Web pages or an entire encyclopedia?

The TEXTAREA is created by using the **<TEXTAREA></TEXTAREA>** tags, within the **<FORM></FORM>** tags.

The HTML

```
<FORM>

<TEXTAREA></TEXTAREA>

</FORM>
```

The Result (Figure 15.33)

Figure 15.33

ROWS and COLS

By default the TEXTAREA is created with a field that is 40 characters wide and 4 rows high. The size of the field can be changed by using the ROWS and COLS attributes in the **<TEXTAREA>** tags and specifying the size.

The HTML

```
<FORM>

<TEXTAREA ROWS=10 COLS=10></TEXTAREA>

</FORM>
```

The Result (Figure 15.34)

Figure 15.34

The result is this rather impractical shape. By adjusting the values for ROWS and COLS , we can make the TEXTAREA any size that we require.

Default Text

Any text that is included between the **<TEXTAREA></TEXT AREA>** tags will appear in the TEXTAREA.

The HTML

```
<FORM>

<TEXTAREA>Type your life story into this TEXTAREA</TEXTAREA>

</FORM>
```

The Result (Figure 15.35)

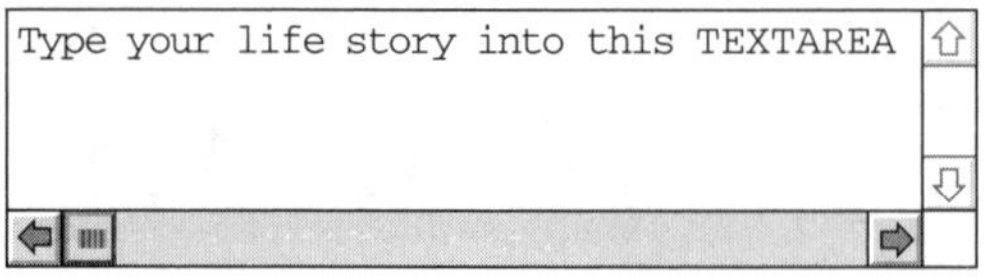

```
┌──────────────────────────────────────────┬───┐
│Type your life story into this TEXTAREA    │ ⇧ │
│                                           │   │
│                                           │   │
│                                           │ ⇩ │
├─┬───┬──────────────────────────────────┬──┼───┤
│⇦│ ▥ │                                  │⇨ │   │
└─┴───┴──────────────────────────────────┴──┴───┘
```

Figure 15.35

NAME

One last step: we need to include the NAME attribute within the TEXTAREA tags. This tells us which data is associated with the TEXTAREA when it is submitted to us.

The HTML

<FORM>

<TEXTAREA NAME="lifestory">

Type your life story into this TEXTAREA

</TEXTAREA>

</FORM>

The Result

Once more, I have tested the results of the above form that includes the TEXTAREA by submitting it to myself using MAILTO: Figure 15.36 is from the e-mail response that I received.

```
names=Type+your+life+story+into+this+TEXTAREA
```

Figure 15.36

As you can see, if this were a very large body of text, all of the + signs would be quite annoying, particularly if we wanted to use this input for some other purpose. Software like Mailto: Converter will take out the unwanted characters.

This not only concludes this chapter, but also concludes our work with forms. I have tried to show all of the possibilities that I could find documented. If I left something out, please let me know.

Important points of this chapter

- The INPUT tag is a singlet and does not require a closing tag.
- The password field is used when you want to protect information from being viewed by others.
- A single checkbox is useful when you want to ask a question that can have a yes or a no, true or false, answer. The checkbox is created by including **<INPUT TYPE="CHECKBOX">** within the **<FORM></FORM>** tags.
- CHECKBOXES can be used for multiple selection lists, and prechecked boxes can be used to indicate a popular selection.
- Radio buttons are used only when one selection is allowed from a list of choices, and are created by including **<INPUT TYPE="RADIO">** within the **<FORM></FORM>** tags.
- The pop-up menu displays a list of options from which one choice may be made. Clicking on the box will display all of the choices in the menu. The pop-up window is created by including the **<SELECT></SELECT>** tags within **<FORM></FORM>** tags.
- Options are the choices that will appear in the pop-up menu. Options are included within the **<SELECT>** tag by using the **<OPTION>** tag. The **<OPTION>** tag is a singlet and is followed by the text that is to appear in the pop-up menu.
- The VALUE attribute is entered into the **<OPTION>** tag with a name that will be returned with the form, identifying the information returned.
- The SIZE attribute within the **<SELECT>** tag allows viewing more than one choice in the pop-up menu.
- The MULTIPLE attribute used within the **<SELECT>** tag allows multiple choices from a pop-up menu.
- The TEXTAREA is a text field for entering large amounts of information. It is created by entering the **<TEXTAREA></TEXTAREA>** tags within the **<FORM></FORM>** tags.
- The size of the TEXTAREA can be changed with the ROWS and COLS attributes in the **<TEXTAREA>** tag.
- Text that is included between the **<TEXTAREA></TEXTAREA>** tags will appear in the TEXTAREA when viewed in the browser.
- The NAME attribute within the **<TEXTAREA>** when it is submitted to us.

Visit the Prentice Hall Web site

- For links to more information about password fields.
- To see the example forms used in this chapter and test them.
- There is a list of recommended activities and assignments to improve your skills working with forms and their related attributes and elements.
- There is a short quiz to test your knowledge on the information in this chapter.

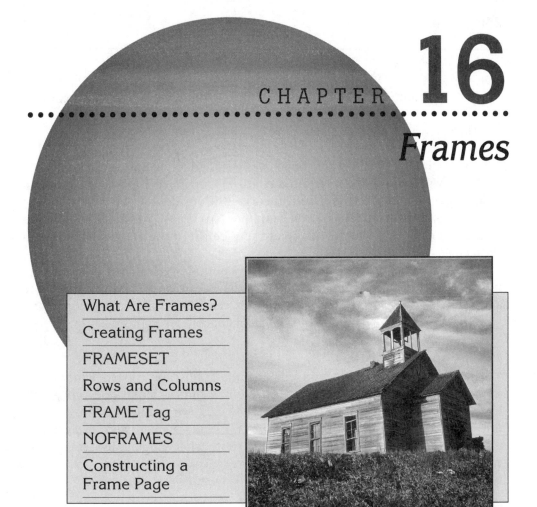

Additional information and links regarding frames have been posted on the
Prentice Hall Web site.

The use of frames is particularly controversial on the World Wide Web. In spite of their popularity with some Web designers, there are others who feel that they should be outlawed. In this chapter, rather than my going into the specific issues surrounding the use of frames, I recommend that you read the following articles, which list the pros and cons. Links to these articles are also available on the Prentice Hall Web site.

- "Frames, Heaven or Hell," WebSchrift No. 11, December 1996.
  http://home.suxess.co.at/suxess/webschrift/Webschrift_11_e.html
- "Why Frames Suck (Most of the Time)," Jakob Nielson's Alertbox for
  December 1996.
  http://www.useit.com/alertbox/9612.html

My opinion? Frames have been overused and have most often been used
poorly in ways that make navigation confusing, negatively affect visual design
of Web pages, and take the focus off content. Considering that about 13% of
the users on the Internet cannot view frames (from: "Why Frames Suck (Most
of the Time)"), one should think carefully before using frames as part of a
Web page.

Why do I present frames here? The news about frames is not all bad.
Frame design is improving and gaining wider acceptance. Additionally, there
are instances where frames, done correctly, can be useful for improving navigation. I'll present an example of such an instance later in this chapter.

Important

When working with frames, you will learn that Netscape is particularly obsti-
nate about loading changes. Often, the reload button alone does not work.
Closing the browser window and opening a new window works most of the
time. Clearing the cache works sometimes. Placing a small stick of dynamite
into your floppy disk slot, and leaving the room while giggling hysterically, always works.

What Are Frames?

We all know what a picture frame is. It is like a window that a picture fits behind. Typically, a picture frame will have one window with one picture, in the
same way that a Web page normally consists of one window with one Web
page at a time (Figure 16.1).

There are also picture frames that are designed to hold a number of pictures in different windows within the same frame. The picture frame below is
an example, with pictures of some relatives on my wife's side of the family
(Figure 16.2).

With the addition of frames to HTML, we can create a Web page that is
like a picture frame in which we can see more than one Web page at a time.

The image in Figure 16.3 is a Web page using frames. Each one of my
family pictures is in a separate Web page that is being displayed in its own
frame within the larger frame page. Notice how each small frame has its own
set of scrollbars.

Figure 16.1

The HTML frame page above is very much like the picture frame that I showed earlier. The frame is separate from the pictures; the pictures are loaded into it.

Creating Frames

Just as a picture frame is constructed differently than the pictures that go in it, the frame page is constructed differently than a standard HTML Web page and is separate from the pages that go into it. The frame page is technically

Figure 16.2

Figure 16.3

called the "frame definition document" and contains the layout information, as well as the names of the Web pages that will occupy the frame.

FRAMESET

By now, everyone is comfortable with the basic tags for a Web page. You could probably write the following HTML in your sleep and, in fact, probably have.

The HTML

```
<HTML>

<HEAD>

<TITLE>Typical Web Page HTML</TITLE>
```

```
</HEAD>

<BODY>

</BODY>

</HTML
```

The most important difference between a standard HTML document and a frame page is that the **<BODY></BODY>** tags are replaced by the **<FRAMESET></FRAMESET>** tags. The following HTML will define a Web page as a "frame definition document." (We will refer to "frame definition document" as the frame page for the remainder of the chapter.)

The HTML

```
<HTML>

<HEAD>

<TITLE>Frame Web Page HTML</TITLE>

</HEAD>

<FRAMESET>

</FRAMESET>

</HTML
```

(If the **<BODY>** tags are included along with the **<FRAMESET>** tags, the page will not work correctly. Horrible things will happen that will threaten continued peace and prosperity in the Western World)

You'll try it, I know you will!

Rows and Columns

The **<FRAMESET>** tag must include either the ROW attribute or the COLS attribute or a combination of both. The use of the attributes in as indicated below.

To divide the page into row frames

```
<FRAMESET ROWS>
```

To divide the page into column frames

```
<FRAMESET COLS>
```

To divide the page into both row and column frames

```
<FRAMESET ROWS COLS>
```

ROWS Attribute

The ROWS attribute indicates that the frame-page is to be divided into rows. How the page is to be divided into rows is indicated by including values that specify the number of rows and their sizes. The values are enclosed by quotations and each value for each row is separated by a comma. There are several ways to set the values.

Absolute Values

Let's say that we want a screen with three rows and we want each row to be 125 pixels high.

The HTML

```
<FRAMESET ROWS="125,125,125">
```

The Result (Figure 16.4).

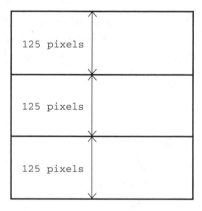

Figure 16.4

Figure 16.4 illustrates how the screen would be divided with the above ROW values.

The fact that I have three values for the ROWS attribute will result in the creation of three separate rows. If I had four values, four rows would have been created, and so on. The value of 125 will make each of the rows 125 pixels high. It is generally considered bad practice to give columns or rows absolute values, because there is no guarantee how they will be seen on different-sized screens.

Relative Values

Rather than dividing the screen with absolute values, it makes more sense to divide the screen with relative values. If I want three rows and all of them to be the same height, I can enter the values as percentages.

The HTML

```
<FRAMESET ROWS="33%,33%,33%">
```

The Result (Figure 16.5)

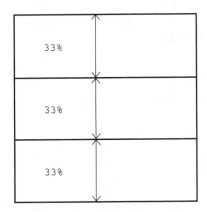

Figure 16.5

No matter how the screen is resized the rows will stay in the same relative size.

The HTML to make a screen that has a top row that is 25% of the screen, a middle row that is 50%, and a bottom row that is 25% looks like the following.

The HTML

```
<FRAMESET ROWS="25%,50%,25%">
```

The Result (Figure 16.6)

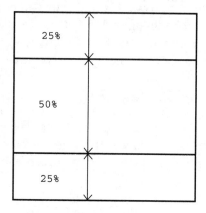

Figure 16.6

Proportional Values

Another way to enter the values is proportionally. Proportional values are also relative. When the screen size is changed, the rows will stay the same relative size to one another. Using an asterisk (*) to indicate each part of the screen, separated by commas, a value indicating three equal rows would be as shown is the following HTML.

The HTML

```
<FRAMESET ROWS="*,*,*">
```

The Result (Figure 16.7)

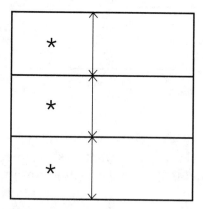

Figure 16.7

If we want three rows, with the middle row twice the height of the top and bottom row, the values could be written like this:

The HTML

<FRAMESET ROWS="*,2*,*">

The Result (Figure 16.8)

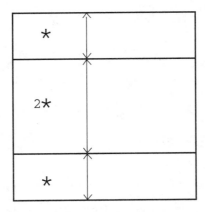

Figure 16.8

COLS Attribute

To divide the screen into columns, the COLS attribute is entered into the **<FRAMESET>** tag. The number of columns and their sizes are determined by the values given to the COLS attribute. The values are entered for the COLS attribute in the same way as they are entered for the ROWS attribute. Figure 16.9 summarizes the various ways in which values can be entered for the COLS attribute.

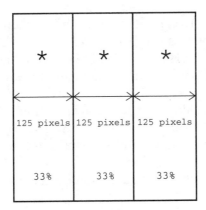

Figure 16.9

In order to make a frame page that consists of both columns and rows, we enter both the ROWS and COLS attributes into the **<FRAMESET>**. For example: What if we want to create a frame divided into four equal parts? It would require two columns and two rows. The HTML could be written, with the same result, in the following ways.

The HTML

```
<FRAMESET COLS="50%,50%"

ROWS="50%,50%">
```

or

```
<FRAMESET COLS="*,*" ROWS="*,*">
```

The result (Figure 16.10)

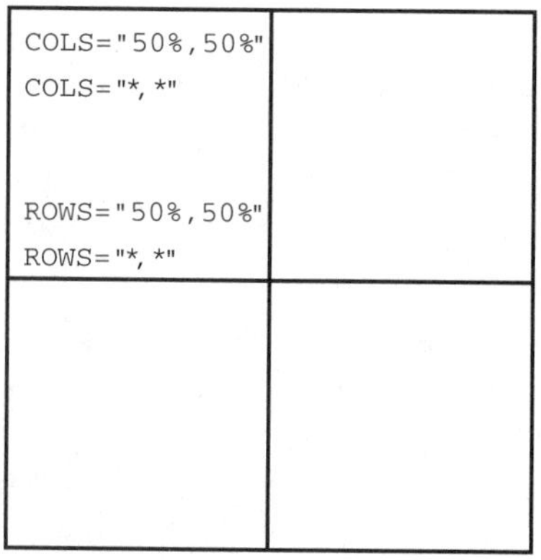

Figure 16.10

FRAME Tag

I am confident that someone got halfway through the above examples and said," I want to try this and see if it works." That person quickly threw together a test page with the HTML that I have covered and viewed it through a browser—and it didn't work! Nothing appeared. I have yet to cover one essential element of frames—the **<FRAME>** tag.

The **<FRAME>** tag defines each individual frame. The **<FRAME>** tag is enclosed by the **<FRAMESET></FRAMESET>** tags. There must be one **<FRAME>** tag for each frame defined in the COLS and ROWS attributes in the **<FRAMESET>** tag.

For example, if we want to create a screen that is divided into three equal column frames

```
<FRAMESET COLS="*,*,*">
```

Since each value represents a different frame and there are three values, I must have three **<FRAME>** tags for my frame page to function.

The Complete HTML

<HTML>

<HEAD>

<TITLE>Frame Test</TITLE>

</HEAD>

<FRAMESET COLS="*,*,*">

<FRAME>

<FRAME>

<FRAME><

</FRAMESET>

</HTML>

The Result (Figure 16.11)

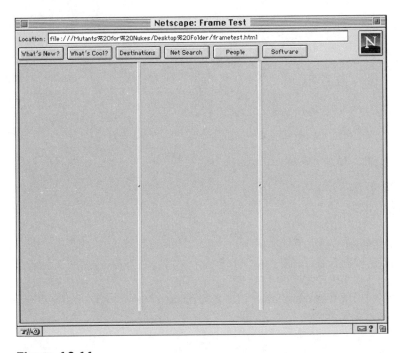

Figure 16.11

Please notice some important points

- There is no **<BODY>** tag in the frame page HTML.
- There are the same number of **<FRAME>** tags as the number of VALUES indicated in the COLS attribute, resulting in the same number of frames (3).
- There is no information in the three frames at this point.
- Frame pages are saved the same as other HTML documents, with an .html or .htm suffix.

SRC Attribute

In order to have something appear in the individual frames we have to tell the **<FRAME>** tag which pages to load into each frame. This is accomplished by entering the SRC attribute followed by the URL of the HTML document to be included. For example, in the following HTML I have repeated the same URL for our college home page as a demonstration.

The HTML

```
<HTML>

<HEAD>

<TITLE>Frame Test</TITLE>

</HEAD>

<FRAMESET COLS="*,*,*">

<FRAME SRC="http://www.cc.cc.ca.us">

<FRAME SRC="http://www.cc.cc.ca.us">

<FRAME SRC="http://www.cc.cc.ca.us">

</FRAMESET>

</HTML>
```

The Result (Figure 16.12)
A few other points to notice

- Each of the frames is now like a separate browser window within a large browser window.
- Each frame has a set of scroll bars.
- Each frame can be resized by the user.

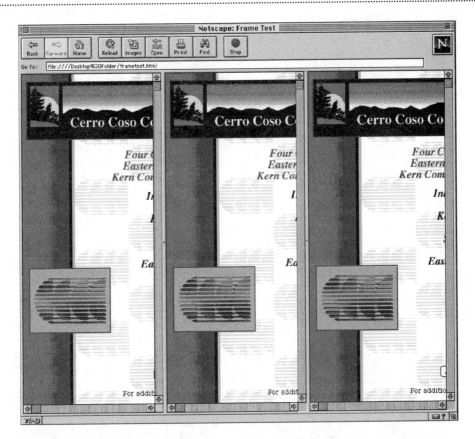

Figure. 16.12   Déjà vu, déjà vu, déjà vu!

Other Frame Attributes

In addition to the SRC attribute we can control other attributes of our frame windows.

SCROLLING

Scroll bars will automatically be created for a frame if the content that has been specified is too large to fit within the frame. Scroll bars can be controlled by including the SCROLLING attribute within the **<FRAME>** tag and indicating either "YES," "NO," or "AUTO." "YES" will force scrollbars to appear. "NO" will eliminate the scrollbars, and "AUTO" is the same as the default. The scrollbars will appear if the content exceeds the size of the screen.

The HTML

<HTML>

<HEAD>

<TITLE>Frame Test</TITLE>

</HEAD>

<FRAMESET COLS="*,*,*">

<FRAME SCROLLING="YES" SRC="http://www.cc.cc.ca.us">

<FRAME SCROLLING="NO" SRC="http://www.cc.cc.ca.us">

<FRAME SCROLLING="AUTO" SRC="http://www.cc.cc.ca.us">

</FRAMESET>

</HTML>

The Result (Figure 16.13)

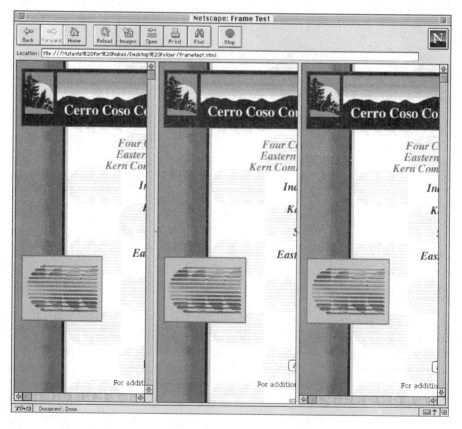

Figure 16.13

You will notice that the first frame still has a scroll bar, because it is required by the "YES" value in the HTML. In the second frame the scroll bar has been eliminated because of the "NO" value in the HTML. Because of the "AUTO" value in the HTML, the third frame continues to have a scroll bar as a result of the content of the page being too large for the frame.

Margins

The margins of a frame can be modified by using MARGINWIDTH and MARGINHEIGHT attributes within the **<FRAME>** tag, followed by the desired margin value in pixels. In the following example, I have changed the URL and increased the MARGINWIDTH and MARGINHEIGHT values for each frame to illustrate the changes.

The HTML

```
<HTML>

<HEAD>

<TITLE>Frame Test</TITLE>

</HEAD>

<FRAMESET COLS="*,*,*">

<FRAME MARGINWIDTH="10" MARGINHEIGHT="10"

SCROLLING="YES" SRC="http://www.cc.cc.ca.us/html98">

<FRAME MARGINWIDTH="50"

MARGINHEIGHT="50" SCROLLING="NO"

SRC="http://www.cc.cc.ca.us/html98">

<FRAME MARGINWIDTH="100"

MARGINHEIGHT="100" SCROLLING="AUTO"

SRC="http://www.cc.cc.ca.us/html98">

</FRAMESET>

</HTML>
```

The Result (Figure 16.14)

You should notice that the page contents have been shifted increasingly as the margin values have increased.

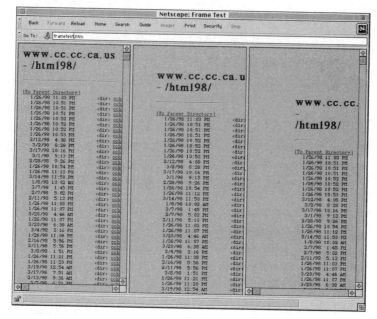

Figure 16.14

NORESIZE

Frames have the odd feature that they can be resized. If you pass your cursor over the border of a frame you will get a double arrow cursor as shown in Figure 16.15.

You can use the mouse to move the borders of the frame, resizing it.

The reason for resizing is that frames will appear differently when seen in different browsers, and resizing allows the viewer to expand the frame if it is blocking part of the content. If you have tested your frame page on a number of different browsers and platforms and want to prevent users from having this capability, the NORESIZE attribute should be included in the **<FRAME>** tag.

<FRAME NORESIZE>

Figure 16.15

NAME

The final FRAME attribute is the NAME attribute. The NAME attribute gives the frame a name. In this way the FRAME can be "Targeted" from other links within the frame page. This is very important. I will demonstrate how it applies later in the chapter.

NOFRAMES

I pointed out earlier that about 13% of the users of the World Wide Web are using frame-deficient browsers. Additionally, there are also a large number of users who just don't like frames and would prefer not to be bothered with them. Unless we want to miss that 13% that can't see the frames and annoy the visitors that don't want to see them, we need to provide them an alternative to frames when they come to our site.

Including the **<NOFRAMES></NOFRAMES>** tags within our **<FRAMESET>** tags provides us a means of giving the viewer an alternative. When the viewer encounters our page, using a browser that does not support frames he or she will see whatever we have included within the **<NOFRAMES>** tags. That information can take the following forms

We could include a simple statement like:

```
<NOFRAMES>Sorry, this page can only be viewed by a FRAMES enabled browser
</NOFRAMES>
```

We could include an entire HTML document so that viewer would see a complete Web page of information as an alternative

```
<NOFRAMES>

Entire HTML document, creating a Web page containing the same information in a no-frames version.

</NOFRAMES>
```

Or we could include a URL that would link to the individual pages within our frames:

```
<NOFRAMES>

<A HREF="http://www.cc.cc.ca.us/student">Frame

ONE</A>

<A HREF="http://www.cc.cc.ca.us/student">Frame

TWO</A>
```

<A HREF="http://www.cc.cc.ca.us/student">Frame

THREE</A>

</NOFRAMES>

Another possibility, one that I use, is to give the viewer a choice to select the frames version or the no-frames version. For example: When I create the Web page for the schedule of classes for the college, I always create one version using frames and another using no frames. When the visitor clicks on a link to see the schedule, he or she first gets a page asking if he or she would like the frames or no-frames version. It takes little extra time to do, but is a very courteous approach.

Constructing a Frame Page

In the following pages we will go step by step through the construction of a frame page. I have seen only a few frame designs that I felt improved navigation. The frame design that I will cover here is one that I feel is an effective use of frames: a clickable index.

The following tutorial is repeated in an online format on the Prentice Hall Web site.

Nesting Frames

So far, we have covered some basic frame configurations, all of which could easily be created within a single FRAMESET . Let's create something a little more complex, but also very useful. I would like to have a frame page that looks like Figure 16.16. The purpose of the page will be to view the student Web pages during the online HTML class that I teach at the college.

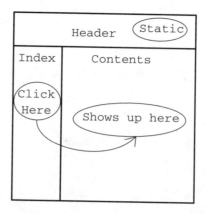

Figure 16.16

The top frame is a header for the page. It will remain static. The frame on the left will contain an index of the class's student Web pages. When we click on a name in the index, we want the contents of the directory to appear in the frame on the right.

The above frame design consists of two rows, with the second row divided into two columns. To create the above frame configuration we must "nest" frames. We will first create a FRAMESET that has two rows. We will then create a nested FRAMESET within the second row that has two columns. Sound a little like tables?

We start by making the two rows: the header frame being 25% of the frame page and the Contents frame being the remainder

```
<FRAMESET ROWS="25%,*">
```

Since the header frame will have a fixed content we define it as no scrolling

```
<FRAMESET ROWS="25%,*">

<FRAME SCROLLING="NO" >
```

Next, we create two columns in the second row by nesting another FRAMESET. The first column is 20% of the width and the second column is the remaining 80% of the width.

The HTML

```
<FRAMESET ROWS="25%,*">

<FRAME SCROLLING="NO">

<FRAMESET COLS="20%,80%">

<FRAME>

<FRAME>

</FRAMESET>

</FRAMESET>
```

The Result (Figure 16.17)

It looks pretty close to the plan that I diagrammed above. The next step is to link to the pages that will fill the frames.

I have created three pages to use for this exercise. My goal is to be able to click on an index of my students' home page directories in the frame on the left side of the screen and have them appear in the frame in the center of the screen. In the header, located in the frame at the top of the page, I have a link

Figure 16.17

to take me back to my home page. When I click on the home page link, I want my home page to load and replace the frame page in the browser window.

The page to be loaded into the header frame (see Figure 16.16) is called "header.html" Notice that it has a link, "Return to Home," to take me back to my home page (Figure 16.18)

The page to be loaded into the index frame, the frame on the left (see Figure 16.16), is called "student.html"

It consists of a list of hyperlinks to the students' directories in my HTML class (Figure 16.19).

The page to be initially loaded into the Contents frame (see Figure 16.16) is called "content.html." When I click on a link in the index, I want the new page to replace this page (Figure 16.20)

The stage is set and all of the characters are ready. Let's give it a try. When I write the HTML for this frame page I am going to include the NAME attribute in the frame tag and give each of the frames a name. The reason for this will become clear shortly.

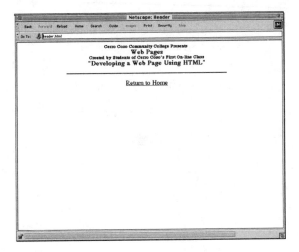

Figure 16.18

The HTML

<FRAMESET ROWS="25%,*">

<FRAME SCROLLING="NO" SRC="header.html" NAME="header">

<FRAMESET COLS="20%,80%">

<FRAME SRC="student.html" NAME="student">

<FRAME SRC="content.html" NAME="content">

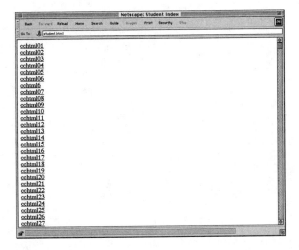

Figure 16.19

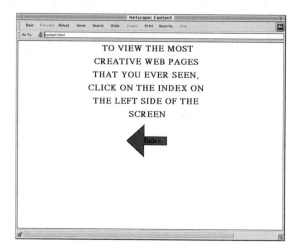

Figure 16.20

</FRAMESET>

</FRAMESET>

The Results (Figure 16.21)

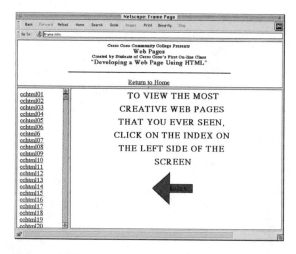

Figure 16.21

Success! All of the our pages ended up in the correct frames, and our frame page looks exactly the way we wanted it to look.

There are still some problems, however. If you were to click on one of the links in the index or student.html frame, the new page would load into that same frame, instead of loading into the Contents frame where we want it. We need to tell the index links that they are to load into the proper frame, and to do so we need to introduce a new concept called Targeted Windows. Before our project is complete, we will use Targeted Windows in several different ways.

TARGET Attribute

Normally, when we click on a link, we expect the new page to load into the same window, replacing the page from which we linked. When we are working with frames, we have more than one window open at once. We have a choice of where the pages load. Using the TARGET attribute within our **<A HREF>** tag we can specify a different window, or frame, where we want the new page to appear. To accomplish this, we must first use our text editor to open the page containing the links, in this case "student.html." The first directory name on our hyperlink index list is "cchtml101." The HTML for the link to the directory looks like this:

The HTML

```
<A

HREF="http://www.cc.cc.ca.us/html98/cchtml0l">

cchtm101</A>
```

If we want this page to appear in the Contents frame, we can target the frame by including the TARGET attribute followed by the frame name.

The HTML

```
<A

HREF="http://www.cc.cc.ca.us/html98/cchtml0l"

TARGET="content"> cchtm101</A>
```

The very bright among us are already asking, "But how does the Contents frame know that it is called the Contents frame. If you remember, a little while back, when I wrote the HTML for the frame page, I gave each of the frames a name using the NAME attribute as part of the **<FRAME>** tag. Each frame can be targeted by including the TARGET attribute in the hyperlink with the name of the frame into which the new page is to load. The following is the HTML for our frame page.

The Entire HTML

```
<HTML>

<HEAD>

<TITLE> Student Page Directory<TITLE>

</HEAD>

 <FRAMESET ROWS="25%,*">

<FRAME NAME="header" SCROLLING="NO"

SRC="header.html">

<FRAMESET COLS="20%,80%">

<FRAME NAME="student"

SRC="student.html">

<FRAME NAME="content"

SRC="content.html">

</FRAMESET>

</FRAMESET>

 </HTML>
```

Now, when we click on the link cchtml01, the page loads into the Contents frame.

But that's only one name! "You mean we have to add the TARGET attribute to each of the 99 other links?"

No, there is a shortcut...

BASE Tag

When we have a page full of links that we want to appear in the same target frame, we can use the **<BASE>** tag. By including the **<BASE>** tag in the HTML for the index links, on the "student.html" page, we can target the contents frame for all 100 links at once. In this case we would include

```
<BASE TARGET="content">
```

Remember the BASE Tag goes in the HTML of our "index page," or "student.html" page. It can go at the top of the document or can even be included between the **<HEAD></HEAD>** tags.

Magic Target Name

Our project page is almost done. We still have one troublesome link. In the header I have a link back to my home page. When we click it, it loads my home page into that small frame at the top. What I really want is for my home page to be loaded into the entire browser window, replacing the frame page. To accomplish this we can use what is known a Magic Target Name. (Maybe some of these computer engineers do have a sense of humor.)

I first must open my "header.htm" document using my text editor and locate the link to my home page. I then include the TARGET attribute in the **<A HREF>** tag that links to my home page followed by the name we will target, which in this case is "_top". (A designated Magic Target Name will force the page to load into the full browser window.)

An Example

```
<A HREF="index.html"

TARGET="_top">Return to Home</A>
```

The result will be as desired. When the "Return to Home" link is clicked, the home page will take the place of the frame page in the entire browser window.

More Magic Target Names

Listed below are the remainder of the Magic Target Names with a description of what they do. You can test them out and apply them where they suit your needs.

Be sure to visit the Prentice Hall Web site where you can find additional examples of frames and can test out some of the examples from this chapter.

- TARGET="_blank" opens a new untitled window to display the specified document.
- TARGET="_self" opens a link within the same window from which it was called.
- TARGET="_parent" opens a link in the previous window, or it will default to "_self".
- TARGET="_top" as already pointed out, opens a link into the full browser window.

As with all of the features of HTML, the best way to learn to use frames is to experiment with them. I would be very careful about imposing frames in an effort to solve a navigation problem that might be solved more easily.

Important points of this chapter

- Frames are more widely supported than in the past and can be a useful tool for improving navigation on the World Wide Web.
- With the addition of frames to HTML, a Web page can be created that is like a picture frame in which more than one page at a time can be viewed.
- The frame page is constructed somewhat differently than a regular HTML page. It is seperate from the pages contained within it, and it is called the "frame definition document." The frame page containts the layout information as well as the names of the pages that will occupy the frame.
- In a frame page the **<BODY></BODY>** tags are replaced by the **<FRAMESET></FRAMESET>** tags.
- The **<FRAMESET>** tag must include either the ROWS attribute or the COLS attribute, or a combination of both.
- The frame page will be divided according to the value entered into the ROWS or COLS attribute, which can be either an absolute value, meaning a set size in pixels, a relative value, where size is determined by percentages, or a proportional value, where elements are relative in size to each other.
- The **<FRAME></FRAME>** tags are enclosed by the **<FRAME-SET></FRAMESET>** tags and are used to define each individual frame. There must be one set of **<FRAME><FRAME>** tags for each frame defined in the COLS and ROWS attribute in the **</FRAMESET>** tag.
- In order to have a page appear in the individual frames we have to tell each **<FRAME>** tag which page to load into each frame. This is accomplished by entering the SRC attribute followed by the URL of the HTML document to be included.
- Scrollbars will automatically be created for a frame if the content that has been specified is too large to fit within the frame. Scrollbars can be controlled by including the SCROLLING attribute within the **<FRAME>** tag, and indicating either "YES", "NO", or "AUTO."
- The NORESIZE attribute can be included in the **<FRAME>** tag to prevent users from having the capability to resize the frame page.
- The NAME attribute gives the frame a name and allows the frame to be "targeted" from other links within the frame page.
- An alternative to frames can be accomplished through the use of the **<NOFRAMES></NOFRAMES>** tags within the **<FRAMESET></FRAMESET>** tags.

- Nesting frames you can create an effective system of navigation allowing the user to easily move within a Web site.
- Using the TARGET attribute within the **<A HREF>** tag can specify a different window, or frame where the new page is to appear.
- The **<BASE>** tag can be used to cause multiple links on a page to appear in the same target frame.
- The Magic Target Name can be used to link to a page from a frame page and have it fill the entire broswer window.
- There are several different kinds of Magic Target Names, and each performs a different function. Some Magic Target Names are "_blank," "_self," "_parent," "_top".

Visit the Prentice Hall Web site

- For additional information and links regarding frames.
- For the tutorial repeated in an online format.
- There is a list of recommended activities and assignments to improve your skills working with frames and their various attributes.
- There is a short quiz to test your knowledge on the information in this chapter.

Publishing and Advertising Your Web Page

W̱ell, as they say in the movies, "looks like this is where the trail splits off." At the conclusion of this chapter, you'll go your way and I'll go mine. We'll look at each other, stoically, give a quick nod, and then suddenly, without ceremony, double-click on our mice, kick the side of the desk, and ride off into the big sunset of cyberspace.

But before we do: I would like to touch on a few more important bits of information. I assume, that as you have moved through this book, you have been applying the information to the development of your own Web page. Right now, it probably resides on your computer's hard drive, and it's about time the world was able to see it. If you haven't already, you'll need to think about contacting an Internet Service Provider (ISP) to carry your Web page. Additionally, you might want to advertise your page so that more people see it. We'll cover both briefly in this chapter. I will also touch on Web validation services. To top things off, we'll finish with a very brief discussion of some of the new features being used on Web pages that promote interactivity.

The Internet Service Provider

My assumption is that most people who have worked through this book probably already have an ISP that provides them access to the Internet. If you are affiliated with a college or a university, you probably receive your Internet access either free or at a very low cost. Otherwise, you probably subscribe to a commercial ISP and pay a monthly fee, as I do. Once your Web page is ready to put on the Internet, you need to contact your ISP to find out what kinds of services it provides for carrying your Web page. If it doesn't provide the services you need, you will have to try to switch your account to an ISP that does.

If you can't afford to switch, or you can't find an ISP in your area that will carry your pages, you might try contacting Geocities, whose Web address is "http://www.Geocities.com/." Geocities is not an ISP, but is an online service that provides free Web pages and e-mail for noncommercial purposes. After creating a free account, you can use Geocities tools to create a generic Web page-which you, of course won't need—or you can upload your pages to its site. Geocities has a 2-megabyte size restriction on the amount of space that you can use, and some restrictions on how you can use your account. However, Geocities seems like an excellent alternative to be able to display your personal Web page. (The above information is not an advertisement or an endorsement. I'm just suggesting a possibility that you might explore.)

It's impossible to cover all situations that you might encounter placing your home page on the Internet, so let's focus on dealing with a commercial ISP. Some of this information will be relevant to your situation, some may not be.

As I've said, your first step should be to call your ISP and ask what kind of services it provides for carrying personal home pages. Some of the questions you might ask

- Do you provide subscribers space for personal Web pages?
- How much space is allocated?
- What level of technical support do you provide?
- How should the files be transferred to the ISP?
- What would be the path or path name to my home directory where the pages would be loaded?

- What is the URL where my page would be accessed via the World Wide Web?

- What is the policy for the use of CGIs?

- Do you or do you plan to support FrontPage with FrontPage extensions on your server? (Remember the discussion in the chapter on forms about using FrontPage to give them functionality, with no programming knowledge required. If I were making a choice between two ISPs, and one of them offered FrontPage extensions, that one would definitely be my first choice.)

I contacted my ISP and I got the following responses to the above questions

- Yes, it does provide space for personal home pages as part of the normal subscription rate, and since I have an account it had already created a home directory for me.

- I am allowed 5 megabytes of space. If I require more than that, I will have to pay a commercial rate. Five megabytes is a lot of space!

- Regarding the question of technical support, I was told that Web pages and any enhancements to them are the complete responsibility of the subscriber. In other words, if I need help with my Web page, don't call my ISP.

- FTP is required to transfer my file to my home directory. (More on this later in the chapter.)

- I was given the path name to my home directory and also the URL to view my page over the Internet. (More on this later in the chapter.)

- I am allowed to use CGIs. I received guidelines on how they need to be set up and where to put them. I also learned that my ISP has a page counter that I can link to and that it does not provide FrontPage extensions.

- I believe that the above information is very typical of the way that most commercial ISPs operate.

FTP

 There is an FTP tutorial in the Prentice Hall Web site.

When I asked the system administrator how to place my files on the ISP server, I was told to upload-or **FTP**-the files to my home directory.

As you remember, FTP is an acronym for **File Transfer Protocol**. It is a means of transferring files from one computer to another over the Internet, which is what we want to accomplish by transferring our Web pages and associated graphics to the Web server. In order to FTP files you will need an FTP client software.

The standard FTP software for the Macintosh platform is called Fetch. There are current links to a location for downloading Fetch and a good Fetch user's guide on the Prentice Hall Web site.

Equivalent software for the PC platform is WS-FTP95 or WS_FTP, Win FTP, or Cuteftp. This software is available over the Internet. There are links to PC platform FTP client software on the Prentice Hall Web site.

Transferring Files

It is not practical to include a complete tutorial on FTP in this short space. Tutorials are available on the Prentice Hall Web site for both the PC and Macintosh software. However, I will show the most important steps in transferring files to give you some idea of the steps involved. Since I am working on a Macintosh, I will use the Fetch software.

When I launch Fetch, I get the window shown in Figure 17.1.

To make a connection, I need to tell Fetch where to go.

- In the Host field I enter the address for my ISP.
- In the User ID field, I enter my login name.

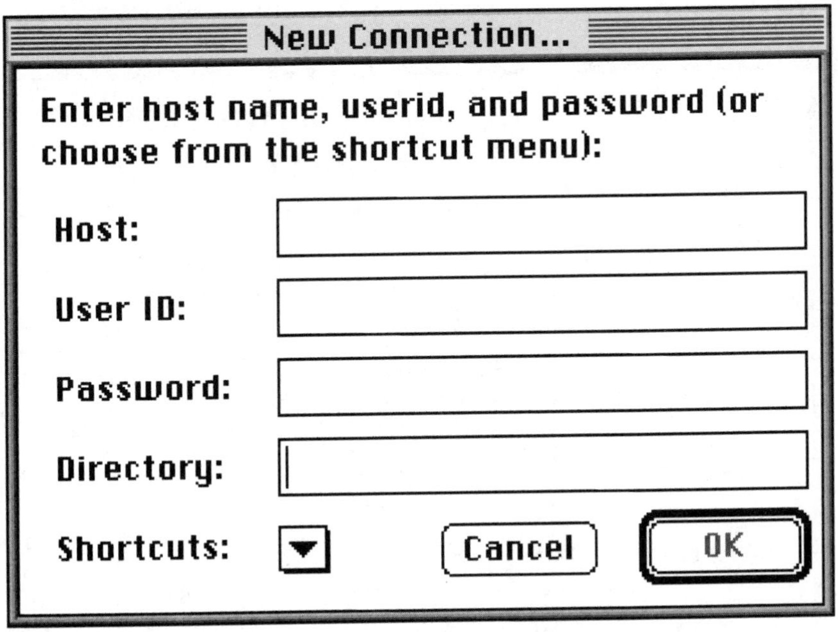

Figure 17.1

- In the Password field I enter my password.
- In the Directory field I enter the path name that was given to me by my ISP. This is the location of my personal directory, where I will place or upload my Web page.

The completed form will look like Figure 17.2.

Click OK and if you have entered the information correctly, you should immediately and magically be looking at your home directory in a window that looks like Figure 17.3.

Notice that there is nothing in my home directory other than a couple of directories put there by my ISP. The first thing that we need to do is create a directory in which to put our images. If you remember, in Chapter 7 I encouraged you to keep your images in a directory called "images" to keep your files organized. When you created links to your images on your home page, you linked to them in the images folder on your hard drive. We now need to have an images folder on the server, and we need to place the images into it. Otherwise, all of your image links will be wrong when you upload your home page.

To create an image folder, go to "Directories" on the main menu bar, and select "Create New Directory." You will get a window asking you to

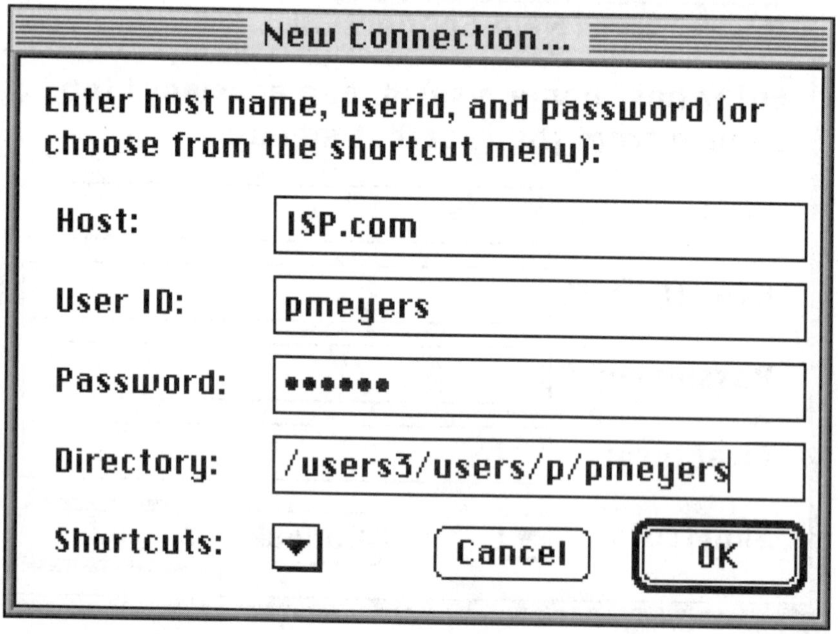

New Connection...

Enter host name, userid, and password (or choose from the shortcut menu):

Host: ISP.com

User ID: pmeyers

Password: ●●●●●●

Directory: /users3/users/p/pmeyers

Shortcuts: ▼ [Cancel] [OK]

Figure 17.2

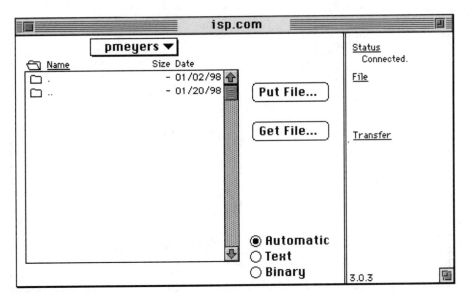

Figure 17.3

name the directory. Type in "images," the same name that you have on your hard drive. Remember to use the same case as on your hard drive as well. Click OK and your new directory will show up in your home directory.

Now let's load our home page. In Chapter 7, I also explained that your home page should be called "index.html." The server, when given a directory name, will look in that directory for an "index.html" and load it automatically. This eliminates your having to include your home page name as part of the URL to your home page. To upload your home page, click on the "Put File..." button. You will get a window that allows you to locate the file on your hard drive that you want to upload to the server. Find your file, select it, click OK, and it will be uploaded. Your home directory should now look like Figure 17.4.

We could load our images in one of two ways.

- We could open the images directory by clicking on it and load each graphic file individually, as we did our home page using the "Put File..." button.

- Or, we can select and load the whole images folder from our hard drive at one time, overwriting the images folder that is already on the server. To do so, go to "Remote" on the main menu and select "Put Folders and Files." You will get a window that allows you to locate and select your images folder. Click OK.

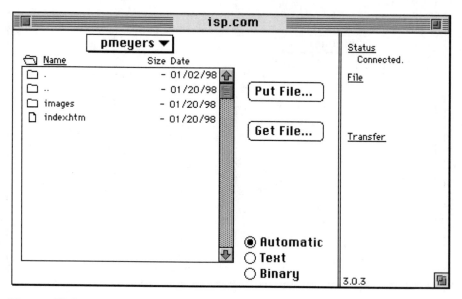

Figure 17.4

File Formats

Before you hit the transfer button you will also be given a choice of file formats. Your HTML page should be transferred as text. To transfer your graphics files you should use "raw data." If your graphic files don't seem to work after being uploaded, you should ask the system administrator which format you should use. If you transfer the files using the wrong file format you may not be able to read them.

You will find that having FTP access to your Web pages is really convenient. Once you are set up, you will enjoy the freedom to alter your pages on a daily basis, at three o'clock in the morning if you like. You will be as one with your Web page, transcending the normal, the mundane, elevating information to previously unheard of cosmic heights. Don't you just like the way that sounds?

URL

The next step is looking at your home page once it is uploaded. You will need the URL that takes you to your Web page. My ISP has set it up so that I can enter its Web address, followed by a tilde (~), and my user name. My browser then takes me to my page without having to list the directory that it is in. This is a very standard setup, but you need to ask your ISP's system administrator the URL to reach your home page over the Internet.

If you need help, you might also ask him or her over for dinner and offer to loan your car. Whatever it takes to get your page up.

Let's assume for the moment that your page is up and running. How is anybody going to know it is there? What if nobody ever sees your Web page? We're going to take care of that possibility in a moment.

Advertising Your Site

John Donne wrote, "No man is an island entire of itself. Every man is a part of the continent, a piece of the whole . . ." (Or was it Kevin Costner in "Waterworld" who said that?)

At any rate, what's the point of having a Web site if it is just going to be an island, unknown to anyone but yourself? You need to make it part of the World Wide Web by letting people know that your page is out there. You need to advertise.

I'm certain that by now everyone has done an Internet search for one topic or another. Did you ever wonder where that information comes from? People like yourself supply it by submitting information about their sites.

There are two primary forms of search resources on the World Wide Web.

Web Directories

Web directories are sites that have organized lists of links to other Web sites classified hierarchically into categories and subcategories. The image in Figure 17.5 is from the Yahoo home page, one of the largest and most famous Web directories. http://www.yahoo.com.

To do a Yahoo search, I start with a major category and work my way down through subcategories until I find a page that meets my research needs. For example, to search for Cerro Coso Community College, where I teach, I would start by first clicking on Education. This takes me to a page with subcategories under Education. The following is the series of subcategories that I went through in my search: Education/Higher Education/Community Colleges/United States/California. Ultimately I ended up with a list of community colleges in California, where a link to the Cerro Coso home page was listed.

Registering

To place information about your home page on the Yahoo Web directory, you will need to register it. The image in Figure 17.6 is the registration page for Yahoo.

You can access this form from a link at the bottom of Yahoo's home page, http:www.yahoo.com. It is just a standard everyday form, which every-

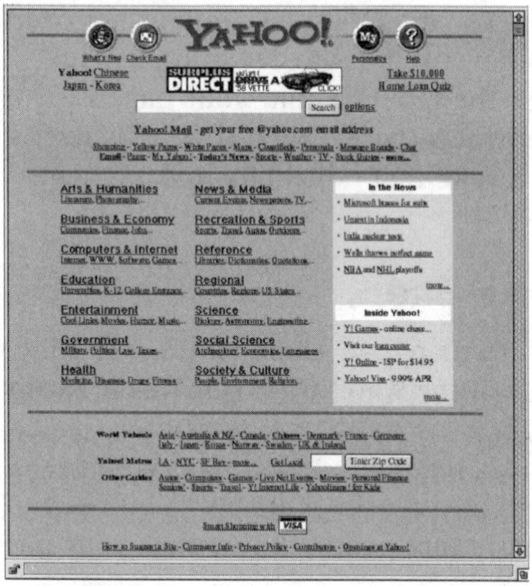

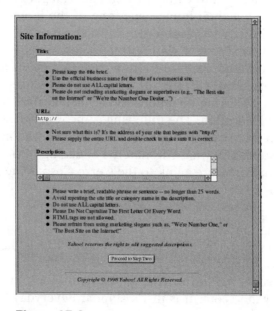

Figure 17.5

one who reads this book could make. All you have to do is fill it out and your site will be registered with Yahoo. It only takes a short time to be officially registered.

There are several other important Web directories.

 Additional links to other Web directories and places to register your Web page are located on the Prentice Hall Web site.

Figure 17.6

Web Indexes

Another category of search resource on the Web is Web index, more commonly known as search engines. These are large databases that are regularly updated through the use of robots, crawlers, spiders, and so on—nicknames for programs that roam the World Wide Web automatically gathering information. They are perpetually following links and recording them, as well as keyword information on Web pages. This information can then be accessed by doing keyword searches.

I did a search for Cerro Coso Community College using Alta Vista, and I was amazed at the results. I received a list of every page on the Cerro Coso Web site, including some pages that are no longer active. Since these old pages had not been deleted from the server, I was able to access very dated information. There is an important lesson to be learned here: keep your files up to date and eliminate obsolete files.

The largest and most well known search engines are

- Alta Vista
- Infoseek
- Lycos
- Web Crawler

This chapter is really not about Web searching, but about how to advertise your site on these Web resources. If you would like more information about search services and resources, I highly recommend visiting the Prentice Hall Web site, which has links to valuable resources related to Web searching and Web research in general, including information on citing resources in academic writing.

There are a large number of search services on the World Wide Web, and the idea of going to each one individually and filling out a form to register a site does not seem all that exciting. There is an alternative, however; you can contact a submission service.

Submission Services

Fortunately, there is an alternative to having to go to dozens of sites to register your page. A submission service is a one-stop registration process where you fill out one form and it is submitted automatically to a number of search services.

A popular submission service is *Submit-it,* located at http://www.submit.com. It has a really excellent Web page using Java buttons and links to other submission services. There are other submission services listed on the Prentice Hall Web site.

The submission services are free to the first 20 to 30 search services, but after that there is a fee, depending upon the amount of exposure that you want to get. The free service is adequate for a personal home page. If you are using the Web commercially, you might consider the commercial service. Or better yet, if you have the time, make the rounds and register the page yourself.

Keywords

However you register your page, you will be asked to submit information about your site. For example, you will be asked for a brief description, the location, and a list of keywords. The keywords, that you register will be what is targeted when a search is made. Lets say that I do a search for the keyword "extraterrestrial" and you have included "extraterrestrial" as a keyword when you registered your site. Your site will probably be listed along with the other 14,309 Web pages that I get as the result of my search-14,309 pages, all of whose owners are convinced that there are alien beings, at this moment, cloning sheep in a hangar somewhere near Roswell, New Mexico.

The META Tag

Since search engines go out and get their own information using Web vermin, such as spiders and robots, it is helpful to provide keywords for them to eat.

Along time ago, in Chapter 3, we talked about what goes into the **<HEAD>** tag. I mentioned that the **<META>** tag could be used for identifying **keywords**. At that time you had no more than your name on your page, and it was a little premature to cover this idea. Now is the time. By now you have developed a comprehensive Web page, and it should be quite easy to select the keywords that best describe the information that a visitor would want to see when viewing your site.

To add keywords to your page, enter the **<META>** tag after the **<HEAD>** tag. (The **<META>** tag is a singlet with no closing tag.) Inside the **<META>** tag, place the attribute NAME followed by the value KEYWORD. Enter an additional attribute, CONTENT, followed by the list of keywords for your site.

The HTML

```
<HEAD>

<TITLE>Keyword</TITLE>

<META NAME="KEYWORD" CONTENTS=beer,

brew, homebrew, lager, ale, draft">

</HEAD>
```

Anyway, to make a long list short, you get the point, and so will one of those creatures who will come around to get information for the search engines.

DESCRIPTION Value

In addition to keywords you can also provide the search engine with a description of your site in the **<META>** tag. The description would be returned to someone who has done a keyword search that brings up your site. To enter a description, add an additional **<META>** tag. Inside the **<META>** tag place the attribute NAME followed by the value DESCRIPTION. Enter the attribute CONTENTS followed by a short description of your site.

The HTML

```
<HEAD>

<TITLE>Keyword</TITLE>

<META NAME="KEYWORD" CONTENTS=beer,

brew, homebrew, lager, ale, draft">

<META NAME="DESCRIPTION" CONTENTS="This

glorious site is a tribute to beer connoisseurs everywhere">

</HEAD>
```

Web Verification or Validation Services

It seems that absolutely everything exists on the Internet; there isn't anything that someone hasn't thought of. And much of it seems to be free. Here's another example.

How would you like to have your Web page evaluated by an expert for correct HTML syntax and to make sure that the links function-for free. Before you answer "Yes!" **I must warn you . . . you may get what you ask for.**

There are a number of Web verification services to which you can submit the URL for your Web page, have your page completely analyzed for correct syntax, and have the results shown to you almost immediately. Before doing this, one little warning. You had better have thick skin, because these services point out every little mistake. It can be like going to the doctor for a cold and finding out you need open heart surgery. Web validation can be quite humbling!

Actually, it's pretty cool. You can enter a specific line of code and have it analyzed. A great way to troubleshoot.

Of the validation services that I surveyed, I like one called Dr. HTML the best. It's located at: http://www2.imagiware.com/RxHTML/> It seemed to be the easiest to use, spell-checked the document, and checked links. I have listed links to additional Web validation services on the Prentice Hall Web site.

Comments

Sometimes an **HTML** page can get so long and complicated that it is almost impossible to figure out where you are and what you could have been thinking when you wrote it. Notes can be a valuable assistance to you and to others when trying to edit or troubleshoot your page. There is a way to enter notes onto a page that will not show when the page is viewed through a browser.

Any text that is placed between the quotes in the following expression, <!— "" —> will be commented out of your HTML page. In other words, you will be able to see the text when viewing the HTML, but it will not be visible when viewing the page with your Web browser. For example, if I wrote a note to myself, such as

<!— Look for a different picture of Mildred. Find one where she's wearing her false teeth !—>

This statement will not show up on the Web page, but it will show up when the source is viewed. (I'd want to be careful that Mildred isn't into viewing source code.)

Test your comments. There are two potentials for embarrassment.

- What you thought was commented out shows up on the Web page.
- Your comment wasn't closed properly and you end up commenting out half of your page. I've done both.

Conclusion

The focus of this book has been the development of an understanding of HTML for the purpose of developing a Web page. We have covered a lot in these seventeen short chapters, but we have also left out a great deal. As we discovered in a previous chapter, the World Wide Web is developing at a staggering pace. Initially, the Web browser was limited to viewing text, linking to other pages, and enjoying the occasional graphic, if you had the time to load it. Increased modem speeds with better data compression are making it feasible to expand the kind of media that we can experience over the Internet. For example, it is now practical and easy to include links to a sound file or a video file on your Web page, turning it into a multimedia experience. Plugins, small proprietary applications that run in conjunction with the Web browser, enable multimedia applications and presentations created on programs such as Macromedia Director and Authorware to be viewed over the Internet. Improved data compression enables real-time streaming of audio and video.

New programming and scripting languages overcome the static qualities of HTML and introduce interactivity to the Web. Java, a cross-platform programming language developed by Sun Microsystems, has had a profound impact on Web design and has increased functionality. Microsoft has developed ActiveX controls and dynamic HTML, and while not widely supported except on Internet Explorer, both promise to have an impact similar to Java's.

In other words, what we have covered in this book is just the beginning. Once you have a sound grasp of HTML, you will want to continue to learn more about the programming and scripting developments. One of the wonderful aspects of the Internet is that it is so full of information about itself. You will find numerous links to resources regarding all of the new innovations in Web development on the Prentice Hall Web site.

Important points of this chapter

- You will want to find an ISP that offers services for carrying your Web page.
- There are several things you should know about an ISP before you subscribe that will help you in planning your Web pages. A list of questions to ask your ISP is provided early in this chapter.
- Most ISPs use FTP to transfer files from a client computer to its server.
- There are several software programs available commercially and over the Internet that make FTP easy and readily accessible.
- Graphics files transferred via FTP are usually transferred as raw data.
- Be sure to find out the URL that will take you to your home page.
- To advertise your site, register it with several Web directories.
- Web indexes, more commonly known as search engines, are large databases that are regularly updated through the use of robots, crawlers, and spiders, which are programs that roam the World Wide Web automatically gathering information.
- Submission services offer a one-stop registration process for automatically submitting a number of search services to a Web site.
- The **<META>** tag can be used to identify keywords that are used in Web searches.

- In addition to keywords a description of your site can be provided in the **<META>** tag. The description will be returned in a keyword search.
- There are a number of Web verification services to which you can submit the URL for your Web page. have your page completely analyzed for correct syntax.
- Any text that is placed between the quotes in the following expression-<!— "" —>—will be commented out of your HTML page.

Visit the Prentice Hall Web site

- For additional links to other Web directories, and places to register your Web page.
- For additional links to Web validation services.
- There is a list of recommended activities and assignments on HTML authoring to get you on the way to authoring on your own.
- There is a short quiz to test your knowledge on the information in this chapter.

Glossary

A

Absolute URL: Is the precise location or address of a resource anywhere on the World Wide Web.

Anchor: A clickable link that takes you to a specific location within the current document, to a separate document, or to a specific location within a separate document. (*see also,* Hyperlink)

B

Background: The color or image that appears behind all the information one sees on a Web page. The background can have a designated color, the default color, or an image that is tiled to fill the viewing area.

Bookmark: Also known as "hotlists," bookmarks are the recorded URLs of visited Web sites that have been saved by the user and are available from session to session. This browser feature allows the user to access favorite Web sites easily and rapidly.

Browser: Also known as "Web browser," a browser is the software that is used on the client computer used to access the World Wide Web, and allows the user to retrieve and view documents. Some common examples of browsers are Netscape Navigator, Internet Explorer.

C

CGI Script: Common Gateway Interface script, which is a small program that resides on the server and acts as an interface between the server and other applications that might be required. This script can be written in C, C++, perl, C Shell, Bourne shell, or Tcl.

Chat Groups: Synchronous forms of communication where real-time discussion can take place in a written format.

Checkboxes: A form property that allows the author to define single or multiple choices of information by giving the viewer options followed or preceded by boxes. The viewer can select or "check" the box(es) that indicates the desired choice.

Client-Side image map: An image map which is completely contained within the HTML of a document and not dependent upon specific files or scripts on the server to function.

Clip art: Image software programs that are used in illustrating documents. Clip art is usually royalty free and comes in many different file formats. Clip art is also available over the Internet and can be found by doing a net search. Be careful when using clip art for commercial purposes that you do not infringe upon copyrights.

CMYK color: The manner in which color is created in the printing process using Cyan, Magenta, Yellow, and Black. Different from the RGB values (Red, Green, Blue), which are used to create color on a computer screen.

Copyrights: The legal rights granted to an author, publisher, artist, musician, and so on, that give them exclusive rights to the use, production, distribution, and sale of the copyrighted material.

D

Data: Information that is represented in a form appropriate for processing by a computer.

Default: The automatically assigned value for a variable that remains in effect until changed by the web author. An example in HTML is the default alignment, which is to the left of the viewing screen. This will automatically be the alignment unless the web author specifies a different alignment.

Digital camera: A camera used to take photographs and store them in a digital format. With the appropriate software pictures taken with a digital camera can be transferred directly to a computer.

Directory pathname: The element in the URL of a Web address that specifies which folder the information is contained within, preceded by the server name and followed by the filename.

Download: The process of transferring a copy of a file(s) that resides on a different computer or server to your computer.

E

Electronic mail (e-mail): Mail which is produced and sent electronically via a computer rather than on paper via a postal service. E-mail programs are available commercially, and many Web browsers come equipped with a built-in e-mail composer and mailer.

Explicit style: A text style that is designated by the web author.

F

Frame: An HTML element that allows multiple documents to be viewed simultaneously in separate viewing areas that are all shown on a single screen. Frames allow for navigation within the displayed documents and allow for linking to separate documents.

File format: Designates the kind of file being viewed by a Web browser. There are many file formats seen on the World Wide Web, of which the most common are HTML format documents, ".htm or .html," and graphic file formats, ".gif or .jpeg."

File name: The name given to a specific file within a web structure to designate it as separate and unique and indicate its format. An example of an HTML document file name would be "index.html."

File Size: The size in bytes of a particular document.

Form: A special kind of HTML document that is used in gathering information, much like paper forms. The information acquired from the form is then sent to the web author via several means of transfer, such as e-mail, posting, or CGI scripting. (*see** Style Sheet; Form Tags)

FTP: An acronym for File Transfer Protocol. FTP is a protocol for transferring files from one computer to another over the Internet. FTP requires client software, of which many versions are available, and can be downloaded from the Internet. FTP is also used as a verb to describe the act of transferring files from one computer to another.

G

Graphic Interchange Format (GIF): A commonly used graphic file compression format, developed by CompuServe, which allows for good quality images. It has a slower download time but a faster decompression rate then JPEGs. Some GIF formats support interlacing and transparency.

Graphic file formats: The two most commonly used graphic file formats used on the Internet are GIF and JPEG. Other graphic file formats include, but are not limited to, RAW, TIFF, PICT, Pixar, PNG, Targa, and Bitmap, but cannot be viewed on the WWW.

Graphics converter: A simple graphics editing program created by IMSI for Macintosh systems.

---

*For all references to "Style Sheet," see HTML Style Sheet, which begins on page 296. The specific topics follow the semicolon in the reference.

H

Hardware: The physical equipment that performs data-processing or communications functions. Some examples of hardware include the keyboard, monitor, modem, computer casing, drives, speakers, and printer.

Hexadecimal color: As used with the Internet, a 6-digit number that describes or dictates the value of a given color. The first two numbers relate to a red value, the second two to green values, and the last two relate to blue values. Hexadecimal color is based on a 16-number system with values ranging from 1-16, with two-digit numbers being replaced by the letters A–F respectively. An example of hexadecimal color would be FF0000, which is the given numerical value for red.

Horizontal rule: ——Commonly used as a means of organizing information on a Web page. (*see* *Style Sheet; Alignment Tags)

HTML: An acronym for Hypertext Markup Language, the language that a Web browser is programmed to recognize as a Web page. It also instructs the browser how to display the information contained therein.

HTML tags:

& Ampersand: & (*see* *Style Sheet; Alternative Characters)
&copy or © Copyright: © (*see* *Style Sheet; Alternative Characters)
> Greater-than symbol: > (*see* *Style Sheet; Alternative Characters)
< Less-than symbol: < (*see* *Style Sheet; Alternative Characters)
  Nonbreaking space (*see* *Style Sheet; Alternative Characters)
" Quotation mark: " (*see* *Style Sheet; Alternative Characters)
&reg or ® Registered TM: ® (*see* *Style Sheet; Alternative Characters)
Number Sign: # (*see* *Style Sheet; Alternative Characters)
% Percent Sign: % (*see* *Style Sheet; Alternative Characters)
+ Plus Sign: + (*see* *Style Sheet; Alternative Characters)
= Equal Sign: = (*see* *Style Sheet; Alternative Characters)
@ Commercial at: @ (*see* *Style Sheet; Alternative Characters)
™ Trademark symbol: ™ (*see* *Style Sheet; Alternative Characters)
<!—Comment—> (*see* *Style Sheet; Miscellaneous)
<A></A>, Anchor (*see* *Style Sheet; Hypertext Link Tags)
<ABBREV></ABBREV>, Abbreviation (*see* *Style Sheet; Text Formatting Tags)
<ACRONYM></ACRONYM>, Acronym (*see* *Style Sheet; Text Formatting Tags)
<ADDRESS></ADDRESS>, Address (*see* *Style Sheet; Text Formatting Tags)
<AREA>, Area (*see* *Style Sheet; Hypertext Link Tags)
<AU></AU>, Author (*see* *Style Sheet; Text Formatting Tags)
<B></B>, Bold (*see* *Style Sheet; Text Formatting Tags)
<BASE>, Base (*see* *Style Sheet; Basic HTML Tags)
<BASEFONT>, Basefont (*see* *Style Sheet; Text Formatting Tags)
<BGSOUND>, Background Sound (*see* *Style Sheet; Sound Tags)
<BIG></BIG>, Big (*see* *Style Sheet; Text Formatting Tags)
<BLINK></BLINK>, Blinking Text (*see* *Style Sheet; Text Formatting Tags)
<BLOCKQUOTE></BLOCKQUOTE>, Blockquote (*see* *Style Sheet; Alignment Tags)
<BODY>, Body (*see* *Style Sheet; Basic HTML Tags)

</BR>, Break (*see* *Style Sheet; Alignment Tags)
<CAPTION></CAPTION>, Caption (*see* *Style Sheet; Table Tags)

---

*For all references to "Style Sheet," see HTML Style Sheet, which begins on page 296. The specific topics follow the semicolon in the reference.

<CENTER></CENTER>, Center (*see* *Style Sheet; Alignment Tags)
<CITE></CITE>, Citation (*see* *Style Sheet; Text Formatting Tags)
<CODE></CODE>, Code (*see* *Style Sheet; Text Formatting Tags)
<DD></DD>, Definition Description (*see* *Style Sheet; List Tags)
<DEL></DEL>, Deleted Text (*see* *Style Sheet; Text Formatting Tags)
<DFN></DFN>, Definition (*see* *Style Sheet; Text Formatting Tags)
<DIR></DIR>, Directory List (*see* *Style Sheet; List Tags)
<DIV></DIV>, Division (*see* *Style Sheet; Alignment Tags)
<DL></DL>, Definition List (*see* *Style Sheet; List Tags)
<EM></EM>, Emphasis (*see* *Style Sheet; Text Formatting Tags)
<EMBED SRC>, Embed Source (*see* *Style Sheet; Graphics Tags, Sound Tags)
<FIG>, Figure (*see* *Style Sheet; Graphics Tags)
<FONT></FONT>, Font (*see* *Style Sheet; Text Formatting Tags)
<FORM></FORM>, Form (*see* *Style Sheet; Form Tags)
<FRAME></FRAME>, Frame (*see* *Style Sheet; Frame Tags)
<FRAMESET></FRAMESET>, Frameset (*see* *Style Sheet; Frame Tags)
<HEAD></HEAD>, Head (*see* *Style Sheet; Basic HTML Tags)
<H?></H?>, Heading ?=size (*see* *Style Sheet; Text Formatting Tags)
<HR></HR>, Horizontal Rule (*see* *Style Sheet; Alignment Tags)
<HTML></HTML>, Hypertext Markup Language (*see* *Style Sheet; Basic HTML Tags)
<I></I>, Italics (*see* *Style Sheet; Text Formatting Tags)
<IMG>, Image (*see* *Style Sheet; Graphics Tags)
<INPUT>, Input (*see* *Style Sheet; Form Tags)
<INS></INS>, Inserted Text (*see* *Style Sheet; Text Formatting Tags)
<ISINDEX>, Searchable Document Tag (*see* *Style Sheet; Basic HTML Tags)
<KBD></KBD>, Keyboard (*see* *Style Sheet; Text Formatting Tags)
<LI></LI>, List Item (*see* *Style Sheet; List Tags)
<MAP></MAP>, Map (*see* *Style Sheet; Hypertext Link Tags)
<MARQUEE></MARQUEE>, Scrolling Marquee (*see* *Style Sheet; Text Formatting Tags)
<MENU></MENU>, Menu List (*see* *Style Sheet; List Tags)
<NOBR></NOBR>, No Break (*see* *Style Sheet; Alignment Tags)
<OL></OL>, Ordered List (*see* *Style Sheet; List Tags)
<OPTION></OPTION>, Option (*see* *Style Sheet; Form Tags)
<P></P>, Paragraph (*see* *Style Sheet; Alignment Tags)
<PERSON></PERSON>, Person (*see* *Style Sheet; Text Formatting Tags)
<PRE></PRE>, Preformatted (*see* *Style Sheet; Alignment Tags)
<Q></Q>, Quotations (*see* *Style Sheet; Text Formatting Tags)
<S></S>, Strike-through Style (*see* *Style Sheet; Text Formatting Tags)
<SAMP></SAMP>, Sample (*see* *Style Sheet; Text Formatting Tags)
<SELECT></SELECT>, Select (*see* *Style Sheet; Form Tags)
<SMALL></SMALL>, Small (*see* *Style Sheet; Text Formatting Tags)
<STRIKE></STRIKE>, Strike-through Style (*see* *Style Sheet; Text Formatting Tags)
<STRONG></STRONG>, Strong Emphasis (*see* *Style Sheet; Text Formatting Tags)
, Subscript (*see* *Style Sheet; Text Formatting Tags)
, Superscript (*see* *Style Sheet; Text Formatting Tags)
<TABLE></TABLE>, Table (*see* *Style Sheet; Table Tags)
<TD></TD>, Table Data (*see* *Style Sheet; Table Tags)
<TEXTAREA></TEXTAREA>, Text Area (*see* *Style Sheet; Form Tags)
<TH></TH>, Table Header (*see* *Style Sheet; Table Tags)
<TITLE></TITLE>, Title (*see* *Style Sheet; Basic HTML Tags)
<TR></TR>, Table Row (*see* *Style Sheet; Table Tags)

<TT></TT>Typewriter Text (*see* *Style Sheet; Text Formatting Tags)
<U></U>, Underlined (*see* *Style Sheet; Text Formatting Tags)
<UL></UL>, Unordered List (*see* *Style Sheet; List Tags)
<VAR></VAR>, Variables (*see* *Style Sheet; Text Formatting Tags)
<WBR>, Where Break (*see* *Style Sheet; Alignment Tags)

HTTP: An acronym for Hypertext Transfer Protocol. HTTP is the protocol used by Web servers and Web clients to exchange information, allowing them to communicate.

Hypertext: Text that is linked or anchored to other information, which, when clicked upon, will transfer the user to the link destination. Hypertext is usually distinguished by being highlighted and underlined.

Hyperlink: The text, graphic, or body of information that connects two documents and is activated when clicked upon; it then takes the user to other information or another location. (*see also* Link, Anchor)

I

Imagemap: A pictorial means of navigation, imagemaps are images that have areas within them that are linked to specific URLs. When one of the areas is clicked, it sends the user to the resource location.

Internet: An internet (lower case i) is a network, where the Internet (capital i) is the largest collection of networks in the world, commonly called the World Wide Web. It is a multiprotocol internet that is built upon a tri-level hierarchy of backbone networks.

Internet Explorer: A Web browser created by Microsoft.

Internet Service Provider (ISP): A company that provides Internet access to consumers.

J

Java: A cross-platform programming language.

Java Applets: Java programs that can be embedded into a Web page that instruct the browser to run a particular program, located on the server, when the page is loaded.

Java Script: A scripting language that is used to write programs that can be included in the HTML of a Web document. They are executed by the client browser, if it supports Java scripts.

Joint Photographic Experts Group (JPEG): An image compression format that is normally used for photographic images. Although JPEGs have a smaller compression ratio, they tend to take longer to decompress than GIFs.

K

Keywords: Words that are listed when registering a Web page with a Web directory as the identifying terms describing the contents of your Web page. These words are targeted when a search is performed.

L

Link: Hypertext connections between Web pages. Also known as "hotlinks," hyperlinks, and anchors.

M

Mailto: An HTML feature that appears in the Web page to be a link, which, when activated by clicking it, launches a mail window, with address already filled in. This feature is not supported by Internet Explorer.

---

*For all references to "Style Sheet," see HTML Style Sheet, which begins on page 296. The specific topics follow the semicolon in the reference.

META: Tags that are used for including information about an HTML document. Keywords can be entered using the META tag and are useful in identifying information when performing Internet searches. (*see also* *Style Sheet; Basic HTML tags)

N

Netscape Navigator: A popular Web browser created by Netscape Communications Corporation.

P

PaintShop Pro: A PC-based, simple graphics editing program created by JASC, Inc.

Password field: A form field that allows the user to enter text that appears as asterisks (*) instead of text to protect the information being entered.

Pathname: Instructs both FTP software and Web browsers where to go in a directory to find a given file.

Plug-in: A small application that can be added to a browser to give it additional functionality. An example might be the including of a Real Audio plug-in that allows for the reception of real audio broadcasts via the Internet, using a browser.

Pop-up menu: Used in forms, a "pop-up" box that is displayed when selected that offers the user a choice of several options.

Preformatted text: In HTML, text that, when surrounded by the **<PRE></PRE>** tags, maintains its original formatting. Preformatted text is usually displayed in a monospaced font. (*see also* *Style Sheet; Text Formatting Tags)

Protocol: The method or procedure used in the transfer of data from one computer to another. In reference to the Internet, there are several protocols used; some examples: File Transfer Protocol (FTP), Hypertext Transfer Protocol (HTTP), gopher, telnet, and news.

R

Radio button: A form field element that, unlike checkboxes, which allow for multiple selections, only allows one item on a list to be selected.

Relative URL: Gives the location of a document or other source within the current directory or on the current server.

Resolution: Resolution refers to the dpi (dots per inch) of an image or graphic. Computer screens have a resolution of 72 dpi. Generally, images intended for use on a Web page should be no more than 72 dpi resolution, as increasing the resolution will not affect the quality of the viewed image but will unnecessarily increase the file size.

Resource file name: The name of the HTML document file that contains the identifying suffix to be loaded by the Web browser. This is the last element in a URL.

RGB color: Red, Green, and Blue, the three colors that, when combined, make up the colors seen on a computer screen.

S

Scanning: The process of electronically recording text or images in a digital format. Scanners, a hardware accessory, are used in conjunction with scanning software to perform this function.

Search engine: A program that "searches" the World Wide Web for information related to a specified topic. Search engines accomplish this through the use of keywords, by subject, and by surfing.

---

*For all references to "Style Sheet," see HTML Style Sheet, which begins on page 296. The specific topics follow the semicolon in the reference.

Server: A computer that stores, manages and provides information and applications requested by client computers. In the realm of the World Wide Web, servers provide information to the requesting Web browser.

Server-side imagemap: An imagemap where the map coordinates reside in a separate file on the server, called a map file. When an area of the map is clicked, the message goes to the server, which activates a CGI script that reads the map file and enables the browser to create a link to the new information.

Software: The programs that control and direct the functioning and operation of hardware.

Source code: The plain text script that contains the instructions for an HTML document, which directs how the Web page will be displayed by a Web browser.

Submission services: A submission service is a Web site that provides an online registration service that then sends the entered information to multiple Web directories, saving the user a good deal of time and effort.

T

Table: An HTML feature that provides a means of organizing and presenting information in columns and rows for the purposes of clarity.

Thumbnail: A small version of a larger graphic that allows the viewer to see a preview of the larger version and choose whether to spend the time to download the larger file.

Transparency: Transparent GIFs make one color in an image, usually a solid background color, invisible or transparent, so that the Web page can show through.

U

Uniform Resource Locator (URL): Also known as the "address" of a Web page. The URL contains the information that directs the server to the desired location by a string of terms that designate the path that the server is to follow to locate the resource. A URL is written as follows: *protocol://server name directory pathname/filename.*

Upload: The term used to describe the transferring of files from a client computer to a server computer.

V

Validation service: A group that provides a Web page evaluating service where HTML pages can be submitted and analyzed for correct syntax and to make sure that the links function properly.

W

Web browser: (*see* Browser)

Web directory: Sites that have organized lists of links to other Web sites classified hierarchically into categories and subcategories.

Web index: (*see* Search engine)

Webmaster: The person in charge of managing a Web site.

Web verification: (*see* Validation service)

Word processor: A program that is specifically designed for word processing, or for dealing with text-based documents.

World Wide Web (WWW): The term used to describe the distribution Web of hypertext based information developed at CERN, the European Laboratory for Particle Physics, in Geneva, Switzerland. It is the "world" of network-accessible information that uses hypertext Web pages and multimedia to make the network of resources easy to navigate and information easy to acquire.

World Wide Web Consortium: The group of representatives that decide upon acceptable HTML standards whose aim is to promote the stable development of the World Wide Web.

HTML Style Sheet

HTML Tag	Definition	Attributes	Example
Basic HTML Tags			
<BASE>	Used to denote the complete URL of the open HTML document.	HREF=	
<BODY></BODY>*	Indicates the body section of the HTML document, which contains all text and markup tags, essentially the bulk of a web page.	ALINK= BACKGROUND="..." BGCOLOR= LINK= TEXT= VLINK=	
<HEAD></HEAD>*	Head section of HTML document, contains descriptive information about the contents of the page, such as the title and keywords.		
<HTML></HTML>*	Indicates the type of document the web browser is viewing, these tags enclose the entire HTML document.	PROMPT="..."	
<ISINDEX>	Searchable document tag. Indicates to the server that the open document can be searched.		
<META></META>	Used to include identifying keywords that are referenced during a search conducted by search engines.	NAME= CONTENTS=	
<TITLE></TITLE>*	Used to specify the title area of the document and must be enclosed within the <HEAD></HEAD> tags.		
Hypertext Link Tags			
<A></A>	When combined with the HREF attribute, inserts a link into the HTML document. When combined with the NAME attribute, inserts an anchor into the document.	HREF= NAME=	
<AREA>	Determines the clickable region boundaries within a client-side imagemap.	COORDS=x,y,x,y HREF= NOHREF SHAPE=	
<MAP></MAP>	Designates a client-side imagemap.	NAME=	
Text Formatting Tags			
<ABBREV> </ABBREV>	Denotes that the enclosed text is an abbreviation.		
<ACRONYM> </ACRONYM>	Denotes that the enclosed text is an acronym.		
<ADDRESS> </ADDRESS>	Denotes the enclosed text as specific address information, such as authorship, e-mail address, etc. It is usually displayed in italics, and is separated by a paragraph break before and after the address.		This is *ADDRESS*

*Denotes Required Tag

HTML Tag	Definition	Attributes	Example
Text Formatting Tags *(continued)*			
<B></B>	Displays the enclosed text in boldface.		This is **BOLD**
<BASEFONT>	When combined with the SIZE attribute, overrides the default font size for the HTML document. The value of the SIZE attribute can be any number between 1 and 7, with 3 as the standard default size.	SIZE=	
<BIG></BIG>	Displays enclosed text in a larger font than the standard default size.		This is **BIG**
<BLINK></BLINK>	This tag causes the enclosed text to blink repeatedly. Perhaps the HTML tag held most in contempt by web users.		
<CITE></CITE>	Displays enclosed text in logical citation style, which is shown in italics by most browsers. Used most often when quoting material from other works.		This is *CITE*
<CODE></CODE>	Displays enclosed text as computer code, which through most browsers is a mono-spaced font. Often used when referring to computer programming languages or code.		This is CODE
<DEL></DEL>	Displays enclosed text having been marked as deleted, used mainly in legal documents, where it is necessary to refer to documents from which text has been removed from newer versions.		
<DFN></DFN>	Not widely supported yet, these tags display the enclosed text as a defined element of a term or phrase.		
<EM></EM>	Displays the enclosed text in italics.		This is *EMPHASIS*
<FONT></FONT>	Allows the HTML author to specify individual or combined text attributes. The SIZE attribute ranges from 1 to 7, with 3 as default. The FACE attribute determines the font style, which may not be supported by all browsers. The COLOR attribute incorporates hexadecimal color values.	COLOR="#******" FACE="..." SIZE= ******=Hexadecimal color number	
<H?></H?>	Creates a header with the enclosed text. The number following the H, represented here by a question mark (?) can have a value from 1 to 6 with 1 being the largest. Headers are usually followed by a paragraph break, setting them apart from the following text.	ALIGN= This can have any one of the following values: LEFT RIGHT CENTER	This is H1 This is H2 This is H3 This is H4 This is H5 This is H6
<I></I>	Displays the enclosed text in italics. This is the explicit style tag version of Emphasis.		This is *Italics*
<INS></INS>	Characterizes the enclosed text as inserted. Like the <DEL> tag, this is used often in legal documents where it is necessary to denote which text has been added to revised versions of documents.		
<KBD></KBD>	Denotes that the enclosed text should be typed in by reader exactly as displayed.		This is KBD

HTML Tag	Definition	Attributes	Example
Text Formatting Tags *(continued)*			
<MARQUEE> </MARQUEE>	Inserts scrolling text into the document. The different attributes are used to control the values of the marquee.	BEHAVIOR= BGCOLOR= DIRECTION= HEIGHT= LOOP= SCROLLAMOUNT= SCROLLDELAY= WIDTH=	
<PERSON> </PERSON>	Marks the names of people found within the text and highlights them. It is also used by indexing programs to extract names from the text.		
<Q></Q>	Formatted by the browser, based upon the semantics of the language used, it displays enclosed text as a quotation.		This is "Q"
<S></S>	Not widely supported, displays the enclosed text in strike-through appearance, introduced in HTML3.		This is S Example
<SAMP></SAMP>	Displays enclosed text as sample, which is generally shown as a monospaced font.		This is SAMP
<SMALL></SMALL>	Displays enclosed text in a smaller font than default.		This is small
<STRIKE> </STRIKE>	Strike-through text style, displays text with horizontal line through the middle of the text.		This is STRIKE
<STRONG> </STRONG>	Displays text in a boldface. This is the logical markup tag version of the bold tag.		This is **STRONG**
	Displays the enclosed text in a subscript style, which is smaller and offset lower than the rest of the text.		This is SUBSCRIPT
	Displays the enclosed text in a superscript style, which is smaller and offset higher than the rest of the text.		This is SUPERSCRIPT
<TT></TT>	Displays the enclosed text in a typewriter style font, generally a monospaced font.		This is TT
<U></U>	Displays the enclosed text as underlined, note widely supported by most browsers yet.		This is UNDER-LINED
<VAR></VAR>	The logical style tag used to indicate variables, items that are to be supplied by the viewer of the document.		
Alignment Tags			
<BLOCKQUOTE> </BLOCKQUOTE>	Denotes a block of text as a quote from another source and displays the quote as indented and set apart from the surrounding paragraph, usualy with a paragraph break width.		
 </BR>	Inserts a line break where indicated. The closing tag </BR> is not required.		
<CENTER> </CENTER>	Centers all elements of the HTML document enclosed within these tags.		EXAMPLE

HTML Tag	Definition	Attributes	Example

HTML Tag	Definition	Attributes	Example
<DIV></DIV>	Creates a division in the text formatting. The ALIGN attribute can have any of the following values: LEFT, RIGHT, CENTER, or JUSTIFY.	ALIGN=	
<HR></HR>	Places a horizontal rule or line across the document where indicated. The ALIGN attribute can have one of the following values: LEFT, RIGHT, or CENTER.	ALIGN= NOSHADE SIZE= WIDTH=	
<NOBR></NOBR>	Prevents line breaks in the formatting.		
<P></P>	Inserts a paragraph inside the document. A single <P> without the closing tag is used as a double return, whereas the <P> with the closing tag </P> is considered a container tag, defining a section of information as separate or set apart from the preceding and following text.	ALIGN=* ID="..." *can have any one of the following values: LEFT RIGHT CENTER	
<PRE></PRE>	The enclosed preformatted text is displayed in a monospaced font. It is displayed with the formatting as is in the HTML source.		
<WBR>	HTML tag that instructs the browser where to break a line if needed.		

List Tags

HTML Tag	Definition	Attributes	Example
<DD></DD>	Inserts a definition description into a definition list. Used in conjunction with definition term <DT></DT> tags.		
<DIR></DIR>	Inserts an indented directory list. Commonly the <LI> tag is used before each list item.		
<DL></DL>	Inserts a definition list into the HTML document, which is used in conjunction with the <DT> and <DD> tags to insert list items.		
<LI></LI>	Used with several different kinds of lists, the list item tag often has a bullet preceding the list item content. The closing tag is optional. The TYPE atrribute is sequential and can start with any one of the following: A, a, I, i, l	SKIP=* TYPE= (*This applies to ordered lists only)	
<MENU></MENU>	Inserts a menu list. The <LI> tag is commonly used in conjunction with menu lists.		
<OL></OL>	Inserts a list where the list items are presented in consecutive order. The TYPE attribute can have any one of the following values: A, a, I, i, l	SEQNUM= TYPE= CONTINUE	
<UL></UL>	Creates a bulleted list of items in no specific order (unordered list). The TYPE attribute can have any one of the following values: DISC, CIRCLE, SQUARE	TYPE=	

HTML Tag	Definition	Attributes	Example
Table Tags			
<CAPTION> </CAPTION>	Inserts a table caption. The ALIGN attribute can have the value of TOP or BOTTOM, being either above or below the table.	ALIGN=	
<TABLE></TABLE>	Inserts a table into the HTML document. BGCOLOR sets the background color of the table cells. The BORDER size is number in pixels set by the author. CELLSPACING and CELLPADDING are set in pixels and WIDTH is set in either pixels or percentage of page. The BORDERCOLOR (LIGHT&DARK) is fairly new to HTML and is not supported yet by all browsers.	BGCOLOR= BORDER= BORDERCOLOR= BORDERCOLORDARK= BORDERCOLORLIGHT= CELLSPACING= CELLPADDING= WIDTH=	
<TD></TD>	Inserts a table cell. Must be enclosed within the <TR></TR> tags. The ALIGN attribute has the optional values of LEFT, RIGHT, or CENTER. The VALIGN attribute has the optional values of TOP, MIDDLE, or BOTTOM. BGCOLOR is determined by a hexadecimal color value and COLSPAN and ROWSPAN are determined in either pixels or percentage.	ALIGN= BGCOLOR= COLSPAN= ROWSPAN= VALIGN=	
<TH></TH>	Inserts a table header cell, where the text within the tags is usually displayed in boldface and centered. The ALIGN attribute has the optional values of LEFT, RIGHT, or CENTER. The VALIGN attribute has the optional values of TOP, MIDDLE, or BOTTOM. COLSPAN and ROWSPAN are determined in either pixels or percentage.	ALIGN= BGCOLOR= COLSPAN= ROWSPAN= VALIGN=	
<TR></TR>	Defines a table row within the table. The ALIGN attribute has the optional values of LEFT, RIGHT, or CENTER. The VALIGN attribute has the optional values of TOP, MIDDLE, or BOTTOM. BGCOLOR is determined by a hexadecimal color value.	ALIGN= BGCOLOR= VALIGN=	
Form Tags			
<FORM></FORM>	Inserts a form that is used in obtaining user feedback into an HTML document. This generally requires a script on the server in order to process the acquired information. The ACTION and METHOD attributes are required. The two values for the METHOD attribute are GET and POST.	ACTION= METHOD=	
<INPUT>	Inserts an input field. The various TYPE attributes are as follows: CHECKBOX, HIDDEN, IMAGE, PASSWORD, RADIO, RESET, SUBMIT, and TEXT. The MAXLENGTH attribute determines the maximum number of characters the input field can contain. The SIZE is set in characters. CHECKED applies to checkboxes and radio buttons.	CHECKED MAXLENGTH= NAME= SIZE= TYPE= VALUE=	

HTML Tag	Definition	Attributes	Example
Form Tags *(continued)*			
<OPTION> </OPTION>	Distinguishes an item for a SELECT input object. <OPTION SELECTED> is the default option.	SELECTED	
<SELECT> </SELECT>	Inserts a selection list or pop-up menu. The SIZE is determined by the number of options. <SELECT MULTIPLE> is for multiple choice options.	MULTIPLE NAME= SIZE=	
<TEXTAREA> </TEXTAREA>	Inserts a multiple line text input field. The WRAP attribute (wordwrap) has the optional values of OFF, VIRTUAL, or PHYSICAL.	COLS= NAME= ROWS= WRAP=	
Graphics Tags			
<EMBED SRC>	Inserts an object or image into an HTML document.		
<FIG>	Not widely supported yet, gives the user greater control over image formatting, as well as the option of alternative text that appears in non-image supporting browsers.	SRC="..."	
<IMG>	Inserts an image into the document. The ALIGN attribute has the following options: LEFT, RIGHT, CENTER. The ALT attribute is used for browsers that do not support images. ISMAP requires a script; MAP NAME describes the imagemap, BORDER is set in pixels; WIDTH and HEIGHT are set in pixels; USEMAP defines an imagemap.	ALIGN= ALT="..." BORDER= CONTROLS DYNSRC="..." HEIGHT= HSPACE= ISMAP LOOP= MAP NAME="..." SRC="..." START= USEMAP="..." VSPACE= WIDTH=	
Sound Tags			
<BGSOUND>	Instructs the browser to play a background sound or music file. (Usually a .WAV or MIDI format)	LOOP= SRC="..."	
<EMBED SRC>	Inserts a sound or music file into an HTML document.		
Frame Tags			
<FRAME> </FRAME>	Distinguishes individual frames within a frame page.		
<FRAMESET> </FRAMESET>	Instructs the browser that the document is a frame layout page, not widely supported.		
Alternative Characters			
&amp;	Ampersand		&
&copy or ©	Copyright		©
&gt;	Greater-than symbol		>
&lt;	Less-than symbol		<
	Non-breaking space		
&quot;	Quotation mark		"

HTML Tag	Definition	Attributes	Example
Alternative Characters *(continued)*			
&reg or ®	Registered TM		®
&#35;	Number sign		#
&#37;	Percent sign		%
&#43;	Plus sign		+
&#61;	Equal sign		=
&#64;	Commercial at		@
&#153;	Trademark symbol		™
Miscellaneous			
<!–Comment–>	Surrounds text to be ignored.		

Index